ANDREW SULLIVAN

SAME-SEX MARRIAGE: PRO AND CON

Andrew Sullivan is a senior editor at The New Republic, *where he was editor from 1991 to 1996; a columnist for* Time *magazine; and daily writer for www.andrewsullivan.com, one of the most influential political weblogs. He is the author of* Virtually Normal: An Argument About Homosexuality *and* Love Undetectable: Notes on Friendship, Sex, and Survival. *He holds a B.A. in modern history and modern languages from Oxford University and a Ph.D. in political science from Harvard University. He lives in Washington, D.C., and Provincetown, Massachusetts.*

ALSO BY ANDREW SULLIVAN

Love Undetectable:
Notes on Friendship, Sex, and Survival

Virtually Normal:
An Argument About Homosexuality

SAME-SEX MARRIAGE: PRO AND CON

A READER

SAME-SEX

MARRIAGE:

PRO AND CON

A READER

EDITED AND WITH A PREFACE AND AN INTRODUCTION BY

ANDREW SULLIVAN

REVISED AND UPDATED

WITH RESEARCH ASSISTANCE BY JOSEPH LANDAU

VINTAGE BOOKS / A DIVISION OF RANDOM HOUSE, INC. / NEW YORK

A VINTAGE ORIGINAL, MAY 2004

Library of Congress has cataloged the
first Vintage edition as follows:
Same-Sex Marriage: Pro and Con : a reader /
edited and with an introduction by Andrew Sullivan.
— 1st ed.
p.   cm.
"A Vintage original."
ISBN 0-679-77637-0
1. Gay marriage.   2. Homosexuality—Religious aspects.
3. Gay couples—Legal status, laws, etc.
I. Sullivan, Andrew, 1963–   .

HQ76.25.F677   1997
306.84'8—dc21   96-51881

Updated edition ISBN 1-4000-7866-0

Pages 373–380 constitute an extension of this copyright page.

www.vintagebooks.com

Printed in the United States of America
10   9   8   7   6   5   4   3

FOR ALL THOSE, GAY AND STRAIGHT,
WHO HAVE FOUND THE STRENGTH
AND THE LOVE TO SUSTAIN THE
INSTITUTION OF MARRIAGE.

ACKNOWLEDGMENTS

This book would not have been possible without Joseph Landau, my research assistant. In many ways, this book is as much his work as it is mine. He is an adventurous researcher, a tireless administrator, a constant source of ideas and arguments, and also a good friend. I cannot thank him enough.

I would also like to thank professor Bill Eskridge of Georgetown University, whose pioneering research in the history of same-sex marriage gave us many of the leads we followed; *The New Republic* for generously giving me a base from which to work; Evan Wolfson for his courage, advice, and companionship; and the following people, who, in small ways and large, helped bring this together: professors Marcel Tetel, Dale Martin, and Robert Wintemute, Rabbi Margaret Moers Wenig, Chloe Tribich, Brian Jacobson, Steve Glass, Debra Durocher, Charlotte Patterson, Jordan Sable, Beatrice Dohrn, Gillian Chi, Pepper Schwartz, Mark Spengler, Stuart Spencer, Daniel McGlinchey, Robert Raben, Roy Tsao, and Guy Wilson. I am also indebted to Jane Garrett and Marty Asher for their faith in the project from the beginning and their patience in bringing it to fruition. The errors, of course, remain my own.

CONTENTS

Contents

Contents

Chapter Four: Why Marry? The Debate on the Left 121

Chapter Five: How Conservative a Project? The Debate on the Right 146

Contents

Contents

Contents

Chapter Ten: A Federal Marriage Amendment? The Future of the Legal and Political Battle 325

In the annals of publishing, there is always something called good timing. In the case of this anthology, the original timing was perhaps too good. The first edition of *Same-Sex Marriage* came out in 1997. It followed several years of litigation around equal marriage rights for gay citizens, litigation that came to a head in 1993 in Hawaii and then subsequently in Vermont. The Defense of Marriage Act had already been passed—barring any federal recognition of state marriages for same-sex couples and entrenching the constitutional tradition that no state need recognize a marriage from another state. For years after 1993, every legal or political breakthrough seemed to presage a national convulsion. And yet each time, the issue subsided as courts and legislatures balked at the final step. Civil unions proliferated across America—from California to Vermont. But civil marriage never quite arrived.

Until 2003—when Massachusetts' Supreme Judicial Court ruled that the ban on marriage licenses to gay couples violated the Commonwealth's guarantee of equal protection of the laws. When the court subsequently ruled in 2004 that no separate-but-equal institution of "civil unions" would suffice to meet constitutional requirements, civil marriage for gays came to America. The first time civil marriage licenses will be given to same-sex couples will be May 17, 2004. It also happens to be the fiftieth anniversary of the Supreme Court's ruling in *Brown v. Board of Education,* which abolished educational racial segregation in America.

In response, president George W. Bush and some of his supporters in the religious right endorsed an amendment to the U.S. Constitution barring civil marriage rights to gays, and, in its initial language, casting grave doubt on the legal validity of even civil unions and domestic partnerships. Meanwhile, in events no one foresaw, mayors in San Francisco, New Mexico, and New York State began spontaneously granting civil marriage licenses to gay couples in defiance of the law. Thousands of couples began lining up outside San Francisco City Hall on Valentine's Day weekend 2004 to celebrate their relationships in an act of civil disobedience. The debate once again took off, with opponents claiming that anarchy was now afoot and supporters citing the San Francisco demonstrations as another Rosa Parks moment in today's civil rights movement. Another ferocious culture war battle began—just in time for the election of 2004.

So we decided to update and revise this anthology. The new edition contains all the critical legal decisions on same-sex marriage that have emerged in the seven years since the original version. Some dated or superfluous material has been removed. The second edition also adds critical new polemical material, from writers as diverse as Maggie Gallagher, David Brooks, Stanley Kurtz, and Anthony Kennedy, as well as updates from Canada, Holland, and Belgium, where civil marriage is now available for all couples, gay and straight. The bulk of the new material is actually against marriage rights—but that only reflects the fact that the social conservative argument against gay marriage has been playing catch-up with the pioneering proponents of the case. We have also added President Bush's endorsement of a federal amendment to ban gay marriage, as well as Senator John Kerry's impassioned speech against the Defense of Marriage Act in 1996.

Preface

What has always been a matter of theological, legal, and civil debate is now also a central issue in the presidential election, with one candidate supporting an amendment to the Constitution and one opposed.

This isn't an exhaustive anthology on the issue; but it is, I think, the widest and fairest collection of views and data on the matter currently in print. If your mind is not made up, you will find arguments in this volume to tilt you in both directions, pro and con. I'm an advocate of marriage rights, of course, but I have tried hard to include the most cogent arguments against the proposition. How we conduct this debate is almost as important as its conclusion. And in many culture war debates, there is little time on one side for the arguments of the other. This collection stands against that tradition. I hope it provokes debate, and discussion and thought. Use it to marshal your own arguments or to question your own beliefs, whichever side you're on.

And may the most cogent and reasonable arguments win.

Andrew Sullivan
March 2004

"We deal with a right to privacy older than the Bill of Rights—
older than our political parties, older than our school system.
Marriage is a coming together for better or for worse, hopefully enduring, and intimate to the degree of being sacred. It
is an association that promotes a way of life, not causes; a harmony in living, not political faiths; a bilateral loyalty, not
commercial or social projects. Yet it is an association for as
noble a purpose as any involved in our prior decisions . . ."

—From Justice Douglas's ruling for the majority,
U.S. Supreme Court,
Griswold v. *Connecticut,* June 1965

Perhaps I should begin by telling a story.

A good friend of mine grew up in a small town on the pan-
handle of Florida. It's a classically Southern town with conservative politics and a solidly Democratic tradition, and during the
course of the last few years, I came to visit a few times and got to
know my friend's family a little. The town, like many in the region, is racially divided, with one part almost entirely black and
the other almost entirely white. You literally cross railroad tracks
from one neighborhood to the other, and the black section is still

colloquially known as "the quarters." Nevertheless, since the 1960s the public schools have been integrated, and race relations today seem relatively civil.

The process of integration, however, had been anything but easy. One night, on a visit with my friend's family, the conversation turned toward those years, and, after a few drinks, I asked my friend's father about them—and why they had been so traumatic. And what he told me was not something I had expected. "Well," he said, "it was a mixture of things. Politics—and worrying about your children's education and so on. But the thing people were most worried about was not integrating the schools as such—or the quality of the education they would get. They were worried that once they started integrating the schools, the kids would get to know one another better; and then maybe some of them would fall in love—and then maybe some of them would get married. That's what they were really worried about."

Marriage, it seems, has always been at the heart and center of political trauma. As a civil institution, it was instituted many centuries ago to solve political problems—to annex one family to another, to settle dynastic disputes, to distribute property. But since then it has also been the occasion for dramatic and sometimes violent political conflict. Churches have been created, monarchs deposed, civil wars initiated, and civil rights movements ignited by the struggle to control one of the most central institutions in most people's lives. From Romeo and Juliet to *Loving v. Virginia*, marriage has been a place where broader social divides and quarrels have been fought over and settled. So it is, perhaps, no accident that, in the last decade of the twentieth century and the first decade of the twenty-first, the institution of marriage has intersected with yet another major social convulsion. The same-sex marriage debate, indeed, is perhaps best seen not as some modern aberration in our peculiar culture wars but as yet another instance of how a particularly divisive social issue—

this time the place of homosexuals in society—has collided once again with the social institution that defines for many people the most meaningful part of their lives.

So two histories and two meanings interact in these pages: the history and meaning of marriage and the history and meaning of homosexuality. In the passages that follow, you will see all of these histories and meanings fought over. Marriage is alternately praised and derided as a lynchpin of procreation, love, power, economics, convenience, morality, civil rights. And homosexuality similarly evokes opposing judgments: it is seen as a perversion; a source of identity, love, and desire; a freely chosen lifestyle, a fabricated personality, a revolution against the status quo. And when these two contested areas are brought together, this matrix of interpretation is multiplied even more, so that, at times, it may seem as if no one is even speaking about the same thing.

Yet certain fundamental issues are discernible. Because marriage is such a central institution in so many people's lives, because it forms such an integral part of our own self-understanding, any change in it opens up a host of questions about what the union of two people means, what it has become, and what it could stand for—for everybody. And that is partly what is at stake here. When homosexuals seek the right to marry, heterosexuals who oppose same-sex marriage have to ask themselves what exactly it is that they're so eager to retain. And this questioning process can be disconcerting. It is at moments like this that we realize that marriage itself has changed. From being an institution governed by men, it has been placed on a radically more egalitarian footing. From being a contract for life, it has developed into a bond that is celebrated twice in many an American's lifetime. From being a means to bringing up children, it has become primarily a way in which two adults affirm their emotional commitment to one another. From being an institution that buttresses certain previous bonds—family, race, religion, class—it has become, for many, a deep expression of the modern individual's ability to transcend all of those ties in an exercise of radical autonomy. When we talk about the same-sex marriage debate, then, we are also talking about the marriage debate. Which is why the issue has so captured the broader public imagination, and why it will resonate for many years to come.

And yet it is also true that as well as being a debate about all of us, the same-sex marriage debate is also about a small minority of us. And because marriage is an institution so close to people's hearts, this debate has been particularly fraught. Including homosexuals within marriage, after all, would be a means of conferring the highest form of social approval imaginable. Bestowing or accepting such approval is not easy for any of the parties involved, given the human temptation, and often the need, to define oneself in contradistinction to others. Even now, across America and the world, young men and women still brace themselves before bringing home to their parents a girlfriend or boyfriend of another race or religion or class. Parents whose tolerance of other traditions and communities is unquestioned in general often find themselves balking when the meaning of their own family—particularly in the form of a wedding ceremony—is brought into the equation. If the issue is still contentious within a heterosexual context, it is no surprise that it should be explosive when homosexuality is involved.

And in a broader political setting, where the meaning of culture and nation are at stake, the tensions can be even greater. So in the history of race relations in the United States, approval of citizenship for African Americans was one thing, but equal economic opportunity was very much another. And it took decades for the full integration of the military and public schools and public accommodations to take place—areas, again, where the symbolism of the national identity was at stake. The fact that the constitutionality of interracial marriage was the last of these civil milestones to be established is therefore far from remarkable. The symbolic power of marriage, it turns out, is even deeper than that of citizenship, even starker than that of military glory, even clearer than that of public space. It is the institution where public citizenship most dramatically intersects with private self-definition. It is where people have historically drawn the line.

So in racial matters it was the last citadel of white supremacy to fall. But even then, it did not collapse entirely. Legality—and constitutionality—did not mean approval. The polls tell an interesting story. In 1968, the year that interracial marriage became legal across the United States, a Gallup poll found that some 72 percent of Americans still disapproved of such marriages, even if they were prepared to tolerate them. It wasn't until 1991 that a majority existed to approve them—by a narrow margin of 48 to 42 percent. Since then, there has been a standstill in American opinion on the issue. (Among blacks, on the same Gallup poll, there has even been a decline in approval rates from 70 to 63 percent.) To this day a significant minority of Americans—around 30 percent—disapprove of interracial marriage, even though they are prepared to see it legal. And the number of white and black Americans who would disapprove of such a marriage in their own family is undoubtedly a larger number still.

And so the notion that same-sex marriage is a simple matter of public debate, or is somehow inevitable, was never likely to be borne out. Like interracial marriage and the national debate over race, same-sex marriage stands at the very heart of the issue of accepting homosexuality in America yet remains the most elusive prize of all. So Americans are far more comfortable with workplace protections for homosexuals than they are with same-sex marriage; and far more comfortable with housing protection. In 1996, according to a *Newsweek* poll, some 84 percent of Americans favored protecting homosexuals from discrimination in employment, and 80 percent supported such protection in housing.

(The momentum in favor of those changes is considerable: only 56 percent of Americans favored such protections in 1976.) A large majority supports inheritance rights for gay spouses—61 to 29 percent—and a narrow majority even supports Social Security benefits for gay spouses—48 to 43 percent. And yet a clear majority—around 60 percent in most polls—still opposes legalizing same-sex marriage. Why? Perhaps because Americans rightly intuit, as they intuited with interracial marriage, that granting homosexuals entrance into this institution is tantamount to complete acceptance of homosexuality by American society. No other measure would signal approval in such a stark and unambiguous way. And many heterosexual Americans are not yet ready to go quite that far. They are prepared to tolerate, yes, even, in some ways, approve. But they are not yet ready to say that their heterosexual relationships are equivalent to homosexual ones; that their loves and gay loves are worth the same respect. That, it seems to me, is the issue that same-sex marriage starkly presents and that Americans are now furiously and anxiously trying to resolve.

But that doesn't mean that America will never legalize same-sex marriage—or that the issue is always going to be anathema to the center of American politics and culture. A glance at the interracial marriage analogy is revealing again. The polls show that hostility to same-sex marriage in 2004 is markedly less profound than hostility to interracial marriage was in 1968. And this despite the fact that, in terms of legal status, same-sex marriage is far more tenuous today than interracial marriage was in 1968. How to account for this extraordinary discrepancy? Growing levels of tolerance and liberalism in all facets of American life, perhaps. American popular culture embraces gay themes and personalities more openly than ever before in history. But one feature of American society today is more telling than any other. In 1985 a *Newsweek* poll found that only 22 percent of Americans had a friend or acquaintance whom they knew to be homosexual. Today the statistic is triple that. It is surely this new, and dramatic, integration of homosexuals into heterosexual society that accounts for the current levels of tolerance and approval—especially within families. And this, I think, is significant, because it is within families that fundamental issues, such as marriage, are clearly most contentious; and within families that such issues are ultimately resolved.

These family arguments were never as common with interracial marriage in the 1960s, since blacks and whites were more estranged from each other then than gays and straights are today. And this is especially true when you think of how many black families had white family members, and vice versa in 1968, compared with how many straight families knowingly have gay members today. The effects of this degree of integration on the acceptance of homosexuals in American society could be dramatic.

But, of course, volatility can work both ways. The Defense of Marriage Act of 1996 revealed how politically dangerous it is for most politicians to endorse anything as contentious an issue as same-sex marriage. And hefty majorities remain opposed to legalization. In many ways, although on the surface the issue of homosexuality may appear to be more flexible than race is, it is, at a deeper level, far more intractable. With race, after all, there is a broad public consensus that the inherent distinction at stake is not a matter of morals. Very few people argue that because a person is black, he or she is for that reason incapable of the moral and civil responsibilities of marriage. With homosexuality, of course, that is precisely the issue. Morals matter deeply in this debate, and religion matters, perhaps, more deeply than anything else.

So the objection to same-sex marriage cannot be dismissed out of hand as equivalent to the objection to interracial marriage, since it begs a different argument about the nature of homosexuality itself. And that argument, in turn, makes the resolution of this civic discussion that much more emotional and difficult to resolve, because it inevitably involves religious convictions that cannot, by their very nature, be subjected to reason. Faith is not equivalent to a prejudice; neither, unfortunately, is it equivalent to an argument. And although religion can legitimately be excluded in a strict sense from our civic discourse (there is, after all, a separation of Church and State in America), it cannot be excluded from the culture that informs and shapes politics. Religious belief is easily the most common objection cited for opposing the legalization of same-sex marriage. That is an issue that cannot be ignored.

So this debate has to operate on a whole variety of levels. The issue of same-sex marriage is a civil rights matter and a religious matter. It is a question of politics and a question of culture. It interacts with people as citizens and as parents, as lovers and as relatives, as people of faith and as people of reason. It requires from each of us the most patient of dialogues and the most exacting of distinctions. Hence the structure of this book. The motivating thought behind the selection of passages is to serve the purpose of helping us make those distinctions, to be surprised by the evidence, to be alert to the possibilities of argument, to be open to debate at every level. To get to the bottom of this debate, we have to talk theology as well as politics; we have to talk about life as well as law. So the book is framed around a variety of discrete questions—historical and religious, legal and political, cultural and sociological—and a variety of separate discourses. Every now and again, the same issue—polygamy, say, or child rearing—will crop up in a different context, but that only goes to show that each of these discourses is another way of addressing the same fascinating, if elusive, questions.

And in this diverse debate, the very methodologies are equally diverse. You will find here a celebrity interview, a political treatise, a book review, and a social science survey. There are anthropological reports and historical monographs, doctrinal statements and magazine editorials, parliamentary debates and op-ed articles. There are even poems and advice columns. Each of these, I am trying to say, has its place in the discussion that is going on. And each may show us a truth, or a shard of a truth, that can help deepen our understanding of what is at stake, or how people feel, or where the crux of an argument may lie. With any luck, these separate ways of looking at the issue can inform or deepen one another. That, at least, is my hope.

I cannot pretend, of course, that I am a neutral observer to this debate, as any reader will soon discover. I have been as engaged as anyone in this argument for the last fifteen years or so. But I hope that I have been able to put that partisanship aside in assembling the selections that follow. There are plenty of sentiments here with which I vigorously disagree. Nevertheless in each chapter, I have attempted to establish some semblance of balance. Including anti–same-sex marriage material was in some ways the most difficult part of the project—not because I have an aversion to it, but because, for a long time, the opposition didn't even feel the need to articulate itself. Recently, that has changed dramatically, especially as the Vermont and Massachusetts court decisions and their possible consequences have sunk in.

One final note: It seems to me that this debate represents something deeper than the mere questions revolving around marriage and homosexuality. In this culture war, profound and powerful arguments about human equality and integrity have clashed with deep convictions about an ancient institution. That's why this debate is ultimately about more than marriage and more than homosexuality. As a discussion, it is a crucible for the future shape of democratic liberalism. On the one hand, there is the unanswerable demand of a group of citizens to be treated equally by the government to which they pay taxes and bear allegiance. On the other, there is the common belief that to grant this right to the homosexual population would be to fatally undermine the meaning of the society to which those citizens belong. How to reconcile such irreconcilable demands? That, essentially, is the challenge of modern politics. Meeting that challenge is, in part, the aspiration of this book.

SAME-SEX MARRIAGE: PRO AND CON

A READER

CHAPTER ONE

For the First Time Ever?
SAME-SEX MARRIAGE IN HISTORY

One of the recurring clichés of the same-sex marriage debate is that the very notion of such a thing is a radical departure from anything entertained before in human history. Nothing, however, could be further from the truth. In many cultures and in many eras, the issue has emerged—and the themes of the arguments are quirkily similar. Same-sex love, as Plato's Symposium *shows, is as ancient as human love, and the question of how it is recognized and understood has bedeviled every human civilization. In most, it has never taken the form of the modern institution of marriage, but in some, surprisingly, it has. In seventeenth-century China and nineteenth-century Africa, for example, the institution seems identical to opposite-sex marriage. In other cultures (see the debate between Brent Shaw and Ralph Hexter) the meaning of same-sex unions remains opaque and complex. In Native American society, marriage between two men was commonplace, but its similarity to contemporary lesbian and gay marriages is far from evident. And today in a number of foreign countries, laws extending civil marriage to gay and lesbian couples have been or will soon be enacted.*

Judge for yourself what this might mean for our current con-vulsion. One thing emerges clearly: this issue is not a modern inven-tion. The need to balance human dignity and social norms is as old as civilization itself. Although much of the past history of this debate has been buried until recently, it has begun to emerge again with all the passion that now crackles through modern Western culture.

The Speech of Aristophanes
PLATO

From the Symposium, *by Plato, translated by Alexander Nehamas and Paul Woodruff, 1989*

In a dialogue on the meaning of love, Plato writes a master-piece for his sometime sparring partner, the playwright Aris-tophanes, to explain the mystery of our desire for one other person. This passage follows Aristophanes's myth about the origins of human beings. In the beginning, Aristophanes con-jectures, humans were essentially two people combined, each with two heads, four feet and four arms. There were three sexes: those with two male halves, those with two female halves, and those with one of each (the "androgynous" sort). At one point, however, Zeus, to punish humans for misbehav-ing, cut each human in two. Since then, each half wanders the earth in search of its lost other half, creating homosexual men, lesbians, and heterosexuals. Notice how same-sex love is put on the same plane as opposite-sex love, but also see how marriage is not identified with it.

Each of us, then, is a "matching half" of a human whole, because each was sliced like a flatfish, two out of one, and each of us is always seeking the half that matches him. That's why a man who is split from the double sort (which used to be called "androgynous") runs after women. Many lecherous men have come from this class, and so do the lecherous women who run after men. Women who are split from a woman, however, pay no attention at all to men; they are oriented more towards women, and lesbians come from this class. People who are split from a male are male-oriented. While they are boys, because they are chips off the male block, they love men and enjoy lying with men and being embraced by men; those are the best of boys and lads, because they are the most manly in their nature. Of course, some say such boys are shameless, but they're lying. It's not because they have no shame that such boys do this, you see, but because they are bold and brave and masculine, and they tend to cherish what is like themselves. Do you want me to prove it? Look, these are the only kind of boys who grow up to be politicians. When they're grown men, they are lovers of young men, and they naturally pay no attention to marriage or to making babies, except insofar as they are required by local custom. They, however, are quite satisfied to live their lives with one another unmarried. In every way, then, this sort of man grows up as a lover of young men and a lover of Love, always rejoicing in his own kind.

And so, when a person meets the half that is his very own, whatever his orientation, whether it's to young men or not, then something wonderful happens: the two are struck from their senses by love, by a sense of belonging to one another, and by desire, and they don't want to be separated from one another, not even for a moment.

These are the people who finish out their lives together and still cannot say what it is they want from one another. No one would think it is the intimacy of sex—that mere sex is the reason each lover takes so great and deep a joy in being with the other. It's obvious that the soul of every lover longs for something else; his soul cannot say what it is, but like an oracle it has a sense of what it wants, and like an oracle it hides behind a riddle. Suppose two lovers are lying together and Hephaestus stands over them with his mending tools, asking, "What is it you human beings really want from each other?" And suppose they're perplexed, and he asks them again: "Is this your heart's desire, then—for the two of you to become parts of the same whole, as near as can be, and never to separate, day or night? Because if that's your desire, I'd like to weld you together and join you into something that is naturally whole, so that the two of you are made into one. Then the two of you would share one life, as long as you lived, because you would be one being, and by the same token, when you died, you would be one and not two in Hades, having died a single death. Look at your love, and see if this is what you desire: wouldn't this be all the good fortune you could want?"

Surely you can see that no one who received such an offer would turn it down; no one would find anything else that he wanted. . . .

A Groom of One's Own?
BRENT D. SHAW

Same-Sex Unions in Pre-Modern Europe: A Response
RALPH HEXTER

From The New Republic, *July 18 and 24, 1994; and October 3, 1994*

The publication of Yale historian John Boswell's book Same-Sex Unions in Pre-Modern Europe *created a furor in 1994. The media hyped the notion that Boswell had discovered same-sex marriage rites from the ancient world, although his own work made far more sophisticated claims. Instead of extracting from the book itself, I've reprinted here a penetrating review that outlines the book's main arguments and attempts to refute them. It is followed by Ralph Hexter's response to the review, which shows that an accurate reading of the past can often be a complex undertaking. Boswell, alas, was too ill at that point to respond to the review of his work.*

A GROOM OF ONE'S OWN?

We find ourselves, all of us, in a historical crisis of gender. It has produced highly charged arguments over "Amendment 2" to the constitution of Colorado, and over the various legal actions that have stemmed from that controversial initiative. In Ontario, Canada, it has produced acerbic debate and the defeat of a legislative bill that would have recognized same-sex unions as "marital" in nature, and would have granted them comparable rights and duties. No small part of the disputation is about definitions—What is a family? What is a marriage?—and about the social and political consequences of these definitions.

The relationship of historians and their work to this crisis is fraught and dangerous. The stakes are high. And so the appearance of a large book by a well-known historian from Yale University on what are, he says, historical precedents for homosexual marriages in Christian society and their official recognition by the Christian church, is bound to find a large readership and to stoke a vigorous debate. The publisher's announcement excitedly warns that the work is "bound to be as controversial as the publication of the Dead Sea Scrolls." For John Boswell claims to have discovered a series of medieval manuscripts that record Christian church ceremonials for creating and blessing "same-sex unions"—for what were, in effect, marriages between men.

Apart from a foray into the problem of abandoned infants in ancient and early-modern European society, Boswell is best known for his investigation of the problematic relations between male homosexuals and the Christian church. His *Christianity, Social Tolerance and Homosexuality: Gay People in Western Europe from the Beginning of the Christian Era to the Fourteenth Century,* which appeared in 1980, was a learned and groundbreaking investigation of a subject that the author rightly categorized as "taboo." More than twelve years in the researching and writing, his new book on same-sex unions is similarly intended to reshape our interpretations of the past and our practices in the present.

Boswell attempts to demonstrate that "gay marriage ceremonies" were an accepted part of the early Christian church, and that the rituals that formalized such marriages were only later deliberately and consciously effaced by the church. He laudably provides the reader with transcriptions of the documents in the original Greek, along with his own English translations of them. No less laudably, he guides the reader through interpretations of his material that differ from his own.

Since the material that Boswell has uncovered is unfamiliar and impressive and controversial, it is perhaps best to give the reader some sense of it—his own English version of the text of one of these ceremonies. What follows is from an eleventh-century Greek manuscript labeled Grottaferrata Γ.Β.Π, and I have inserted some of the significant original Greek words in transcription.

Office for Same-Sex Union
[*Akolouthia eis adelphopoiesin*]

I.

The priest shall place the holy Gospel on the Gospel stand and they that are to be joined together place their right hands on it, holding lighted candles in their left hands. Then shall the priest cense them and say the following:

II.

In peace we beseech Thee, O Lord.

For heavenly peace, we beseech Thee, O Lord.

For the peace of the entire world, we beseech Thee, O Lord.

For this holy place, we beseech Thee, O Lord.

That these thy servants, N. and N., be sanctified with thy spiritual benediction, we beseech Thee, O Lord.

That their love [*agape*] abide without offense or scandal all the days of their lives, we beseech Thee, O Lord.

That they be granted all things needed for salvation and godly enjoyment of life everlasting, we beseech Thee, O Lord.

That the Lord God grant unto them unashamed faithfulness [*pistis*] and sincere love [*agape anhypokritos*], we beseech Thee, O Lord. . . .

Have mercy on us, O God.

"Lord, have mercy" shall be said three times.

III.

The priest shall say:

Forasmuch as Thou, O Lord and Ruler, art merciful and loving, who didst establish humankind after thine image and likeness, who didst deem it meet that thy holy apostles Philip and Bartholomew be united, bound one unto the other not by nature but by faith and the spirit. As Thou didst find thy holy martyrs Serge and Bacchus worthy to be united together [*adelphoi genesthai*], bless also these thy servants, N. and N., joined together not by the bond of nature but by faith and in the mode of the spirit [*ou desmoumenous desmi physeis alla pisteis kai pneumatikos tropi*], granting unto them peace [*eirene*] and love [*agape*] and oneness of mind. Cleanse from their hearts every stain and impurity and vouchsafe unto them to love one another [*to agapan allelous*] without hatred and without scandal all the days of their lives, with the aid of the Mother of God and all thy saints, forasmuch as all glory is thine.

IV.

Another Prayer for Same-Sex Union

O Lord Our God, who didst grant unto us all those things necessary for salvation and didst bid us to love one another and to forgive each other our failings, bless and consecrate, kind Lord and lover of good, these thy servants who love each other with a love of the spirit [*tous pneumatike agape heautous agapesantas*] and have come into this thy holy church to be blessed and consecrated. Grant unto them unashamed fidelity [*pistis*] and sincere love [*agape anhy-*

pokritos], and as Thou didst vouchsafe unto thy holy disciples and apostles thy peace and love, bestow them also on these, O Christ our God, affording to them all those things needed for salvation and life eternal. For Thou art the light and the truth and thine is the glory.

v.

Then shall they kiss the holy Gospel and the priest and one another, and conclude.

It is this ceremonial, and blessings like these, that Boswell claims to be part of a lost, or deliberately suppressed, tradition of church-legitimized same-sex marriages between men.

Boswell's argument stands or falls on his interpretation of a series of documents relating to a singular ritual practiced in the Christian church during antiquity and the high middle ages, principally in the lands of the eastern Mediterranean. The bonds between men that are confirmed in these church rituals are cautiously (and a little coyly) labeled by him as "same-sex unions." For his arguments to have the force that he wishes them to have, however, the words "same-sex" and "union" must be construed to mean "male homosexual" and "marriage." If they signify other sorts of associations that happened to be same-sex in gender, or unions that were meant for purposes other than marriage or a permanent affective union, then his claims fail.

For this reason, the narrative chapters of his book are ancillary, in that they digress on other aspects of the general problems of marriage and family formation in a way that is designed to support Boswell's claims about the supposed same-sex marriage rituals. His larger investigation of the nature of "heterosexual" marriage and love, and their attendant vocabulary in the Greco-Roman world, is undertaken to demonstrate that his interpretation of the "same-sex union" rituals is the most probable one.

Given the centrality of Boswell's "new" evidence, therefore, it is best to begin by describing his documents and their import. These documents are liturgies for an ecclesiastical ritual called *adelphopoiesis* or, in simple English, the "creation of a brother." Whatever these texts are, they are not texts for marriage ceremonies. Boswell's translation of their titles (*akolouthia eis adelphopoiesin* and parallels) as "The Order of Celebrating the Union of Two Men" or "Office for Same-Sex Union" is inaccurate. In the original, the titles say no such thing. And this sort of tendentious translation of the documents is found, alas, throughout the book. Thus the Greek words that Boswell translates as "be united together" in the third section of the document quoted above are, in fact, rather ordinary words that mean "become brothers" (*adelphoi genesthai*); and when they are translated in this more straightforward manner, they impart a quite different sense to the reader.

Whatever effect these liturgical ceremonials were intended to achieve, it is clear that they used ecclesiastical formalities to make two men "brothers," and employed various rituals and symbolic claims to confirm this relationship within the confines of the church. All of Boswell's documents relate to practices rooted in the societies of Greece, the Balkans and the eastern Mediterranean between the twelfth and sixteenth centuries— though, as he rightly argues, they surely reflect practices that were current from periods dating back to the end of the Roman empire, and probably earlier. The original documents that he cites are therefore in Greek, the ecclesiastical lingua franca of the eastern Mediterranean. The only Western versions of them are translations made into Latin from the original Greek prayer and liturgical books—wherein, notably, it seems that the Latin translators did not understand the purpose of the originals very well.

The ecclesiastical rituals that bless *adelphopoiesis,* or the making of a brother, include prayers and invocations of Christian virtues, particularly *agape,* or the Christian concept of love. They note that conditions of peace, not conditions of hate or vituperation, should exist between the two parties. Appeal is also made to pairs of men in the Christian tradition who were thought to exemplify these virtues: Philip and Bartholomew, among the disciples of Christ, and Serge and Bacchus, among the martyrs of the early church. Other elements of the ceremonial include, most significantly, the shaking or "juncture" of right hands; the exchanging of tokens; the mutual bestowing of a ritualistic kiss; and the holding of a celebratory feast or banquet to mark the occasion.

S uch agreements and rituals are "same-sex" in the sense that it is two men who are involved; and they are "unions" in the sense that the two men involved are co-joined as "brothers." But that is it. There is no indication in the texts themselves that these are marriages in any sense that the word would mean to readers now, nor in any sense that the word would have meant to persons then: the formation of a common household, the sharing of everything in a permanent co-residential unit, the formation of a family unit wherein the two partners were committed, ideally, to each other, with the intent to raise children, and so on.

Although it is difficult to state precisely what these ritualized relationships were, most historians who have studied them are fairly certain that they deal with a species of "ritualized kinship" that is covered by the term "brotherhood." (This type of "brotherhood" is similar to the ritualized agreements struck between members of the Mafia or other "men of honor" in our own society.) That explains why the texts on *adelphopoiesis* in the prayer-books are embedded within sections dealing with other kinship-forming rituals, such as marriage and adoption.

Giovanni Tomassia in the 1880s and Paul Koschaker in the 1930s, whose works Boswell knows and cites, had already reached this conclusion.

This likely interpretation is made more likely by an extensive modern study of which Boswell appears to be unaware. In 1987 Gabriel Herman, a professor of history at the Hebrew University in Jerusalem, published *Ritualized Friendship and the Greek City*. In that book, and in several papers and articles on the subject published in leading journals of history and literature, Herman has analyzed the phenomenon of fictive "brotherhood" and "friendship" in the context of the world of the Greek city-state, and also in the cultures of the ancient Near East and in the regions that would later become parts of Slavonic Europe. In Herman's studies one finds all the phenomena regarded as indicative of "same-sex marriage" by Boswell: the ritual of the handshake, the exchange of tokens and right hands (*dexiai*), the declaration of love and friendship and of "no hostility or animosity" between the two parties, the exchange of a ritualistic kiss and the celebration of a common feast or banquet at the time of the formation of the compact.

Such ceremonials created ritualized friends who often spoke of each other as "brothers" and forged a close bond of brotherhood between themselves. They were "made brothers" rather than "brothers by nature." Hence the terminology, in Boswell's documents, of *adelphopoiesis,* or the ritual connected with "the making of a brother," and the phrases in his liturgical documents that specify that the two men "are not joined by the bond of nature, but rather by means of faith / trust and spirit," or similar words. This is why the documents contain references to the right of "protective asylum" (*asylon anepereastos*) and "safe conduct" (*asphaleia*) as divine attributes.

The kinds of words used to express the new relationship of "brothers" (words that are also found in Boswell's ecclesiastical rituals) were employed precisely because the men often entered into these relationships not out of love, but out of fear and suspicion. Hence the effusive emphasis on safety and trust. These relationships form as close a parallel in social institutions and practices as one could wish to have as background to the church ceremonials described in the texts cited by Boswell. Although such rituals did create fictive kinship links between the parties to them, these links were never mistaken or confused with the union of marriage. They were not undertaken primarily for erotic or affective reasons, for household formation, nor, even theoretically, for the procreation of children and the continuation of household lines.

There is only one segment of one document in Boswell's book that contains part of a liturgical service designed for a marriage ceremony: the fifth and sixth sections of the Grottaferrata manuscript of the eleventh century. Its words, which do refer to a wedding (*gamos*) and to the ceremonial use of crowns (*stephanoi*) in the ritual "crowning" of the bride and groom, give Boswell grounds to expatiate on the significance of these terms and the ceremonials involved. But there is no mention here of a same-sex union. From even a cursory reading of all of the documents, it is apparent that the original text of the "making of a brother" ceremony terminates at the end of section four of the manuscript in question. What Boswell prints as section five and section six of this document, as if they were a seamless continuation of the ritual of *adelphopoiesis,* belong in fact to an entirely different and separate document, which was indeed connected with a ceremony of marriage. The questionable joining of the two documents as if they were one enables Boswell to appeal throughout his main text to the totality of the documents as if they are all variant types of a marriage ceremonial, which they are not. . . .

*   *   *

The practices and the rituals performed by the men in Boswell's documents, and also the emotional and erotic connections that are so richly described by him, may seem unusual or frightening to us, given our codes of civility, morality and masculinity. There is a nice irony here: the ancient and medieval world about which Boswell writes was not riven by the same anxieties and repressions that mark our own. In that world, public and affective bonds between men were typical, even banal. But this is not the same thing as the legitimization, or the sacralization, of homosexuality. The "new" documents that Boswell has unearthed are nothing more than a few additional texts that shed more light on a primitive and basic power linkage between men in the ancient Mediterranean, and the rituals attendant on its formation.

By the time Boswell's ecclesiastical documents celebrated or blessed this type of personal arrangement, it had been brought at least partially under the aegis of the Christian church. As the structures of the law and the civil institutions of the state became more dominant, particularly in Western Europe, the church wished to divest itself of a ceremonial that was intended to substantiate a type of personal power that, in synchrony with the state, it now excoriated. Ritualized friendship naturally survived much longer in parts of the eastern Mediterranean, and especially in the mountainous regions of the Balkans, where more primitive forms of personal power have tended to subsist. There might well have been homoerotic elements to some of these "brotherhood" relationships, and a rather alien Greek ritual may have been misunderstood by some of its Latin translators; both of those possibilities deserve more attention than they have received by historians. But same-sex marriages forged with the approval of the Christian church, and with its rituals? No. Such a reading is very misleading.

The data of the past may not be all that happy for the liberationist movement of our time. Why else would those movements come into being? But what the sources record is, for better or for worse, what the sources record. A good part of what they record, certainly, is made up of systematic and successful repressions; but tinkering with the moral balance of the past is a disservice to the study of history and to the reform of society. The past is dead. We cannot change it. What we can change is the future; but the way to a better future requires an unsentimental and accurate understanding of what happened in the past, and why. A more civil and humane modernity will not be achieved by tendentious misreadings of antiquity.

SAME-SEX UNIONS IN PRE-MODERN EUROPE: A RESPONSE

I am responding to Brent D. Shaw's recent review of John Boswell's book, *Same-Sex Unions in Premodern Europe*. I write as a professor of Classics, a medievalist and a longtime friend and associate of John Boswell. The best refutations of Shaw's criticisms, of course, are to be found in the book itself. But Shaw gives so distorted an account of the book that many readers may be disinclined to make that discovery themselves.

Shaw's first (mis)step is to describe *Same-Sex Unions* as a book about "male homosexual marriages," as if he were reviewing recent popular accounts, even comic strips, rather than a scholarly work. Shaw seems to abandon criticism for mind-reading when he asserts that "the bonds between men that are confirmed in these church rituals are cautiously (and a little coyly) labeled by him as 'same-sex unions.'" It is distinctly odd to accuse the author of *Christianity, Social Tolerance, and Homosexuality: Gay People in Western Europe from the Beginning of the Christian Era to the Fourteenth Century* (1980) of coyness. Boswell has never pulled punches. If he thought that the best, most inclusive description of what he was writing about were "gay marriage," he would have used it. It is precisely that label that he wishes to test, with a completely open mind, and he wishes to give readers the information, and the context, with which to come to their own conclusions.

Boswell's use of the broader term "union" is in part heuristic; to stimulate his readers to follow his discussion of the changing habits and ideals of hetero- and homosexual "partnerships" across centuries and thus be prepared to appreciate the full range of possibilities in other societies in their own terms. The answer to the question he expected readers to focus on—"Was it a marriage?"—"depends," he says, "to a considerable extent on one's conception of marriage. . . . It was unequivocally a marriage" if one believes marriage to be "a permanent emotional union acknowledged in some way by the community," his characterization of the common current conception. What it was for members of earlier societies is trickier to ascertain, and while Boswell tries to give a sense of the range of the possibilities, even ambiguities, in different times and places, he is clear that "same-sex unions were . . . neither a threat to nor a replacement of heterosexual marriage."

Shaw's strategy is to adopt a tone of authoritative dismissal, as if Boswell were either too stupid or too politically engaged to realize what errors he was making. Readers should not be misled by this tone: Shaw is not an authority on Christian doctrine or liturgy, nor is he in any sense a medievalist. Moreover, his knowledge of Greek, like that of so many Classicists, is rooted in Classical, not patristic and medieval, usage; and he gives no evidence of any familiarity with other languages Boswell has and uses (inter alia Hebrew, Arabic, and above all for this study, Old Church Slavonic).

What strikes the reader familiar with *Same-Sex Unions* is that virtually all of Shaw's caveats and criticisms derive from Boswell's own argumentation. Shaw presents as if it were a revelation that *adelphopoiesis* "in simple English" is "creation of a brother," and concludes that Boswell's title for the ceremony, "Office of Same-Sex Union," "is inaccurate." As if Boswell didn't spend dozens of pages discussing the problems of translation, and this problem in particular. Any reader of *Same-Sex Unions* would learn what the "literal" meaning of the term is, and would be able to weigh whether this would be the best rendering or not. Indeed, so sensitive is Boswell to the issues surrounding this translation that he takes the term as an exemplary case in his appendix of translations (No. 5), and in a note experiments with both literal and more tendentious language.

Shaw's view that *adelphopoiesis* must mean "the making of brothers" is about as absurd as if I were to argue that "husband" couldn't mean "male partner in a heterosexual marriage" because its etyma would force it to mean "householder." Or more suggestively (though such analogies are always difficult), a French Shaw of the thirty-fifth century might well argue that, based on his Cassell's, a late-twentieth-century English text with the phrase "gay man" should be translated *homme joyeux*. Indeed, if one were to be absolutely literal, only your parents could "make" you a "brother." Obviously, the term is being used figuratively. The question is, in what way? And Boswell, not Shaw, gives his reader abundant evidence and sophisticated linguistic guidelines to draw his or her own conclusions.

Early on Shaw pontificates: "From even a cursory reading of all the documents, it is apparent that the original text of the 'making of a brother' ceremony [in a certain eleventh-century Grottaferrata manuscript] terminates at the end of section four. . . ." Boswell discusses the problematics of this text and compares it, for both commonality and singularity, with many other manuscript versions of the ceremony. Without going into the issue of putative originality (a typically Classicist concern that is particularly inappropriate to the study of evolving medieval reality), there is no doubt that this manuscript has what Boswell presents. He made two trips to Grottaferrata to see this manuscript, and took the precaution of photographing it. Shaw clearly knows nothing about this original material other than what he can derive from Boswell's own notes, which should be praised, not criticized, for pointing out problems and exploring the limits of certainty. This is, obviously, an unusual manuscript, but despite what Shaw implies, even the strongest version of Boswell's argument doesn't rise or fall on the inclusion of its final prayers. Here Shaw simply fails to mention such things as the organization of ceremonies within liturgical manuscripts, iconography and, above all, historical data.

But Shaw already dismissed "the narrative chapters . . . [as] ancillary," so he doesn't need to consider the actual descriptions of real historical people joined in union across the centuries. In the words of Montaigne, who witnessed the *adelphopoiesis* ceremony performed in Rome in 1581, *"ils s'espousoint masle à masle à la messe"* ("they married, one man to another, at mass"). Apparently contemporary authorities didn't interpret the ceremony as the "ritualized" friendship Shaw would have us believe it is, unless we are also to believe that such friendships called for the burning that we know at least some of those who participated in the ceremony suffered in the sixteenth century.

It is this issue of "ritualized friendship" that brings us to a point that Shaw stage manages in such a way as to, he must hope, completely undermine any reader's confidence in Boswell as a scholar. Shaw adduces "an extensive modern study of which Boswell appears to be unaware. In 1987 Gabriel Herman . . . published *Ritualized Friendship and the Greek City.* . . . In Herman's studies one finds all the phenomena regarded as indicative of 'same-sex marriage' by Boswell." Whether Boswell knows this book or not, I cannot say. As a Classicist, I know it, and it is a fine study of "ritualized friendship" from Homeric society through the city states and into the Hellenistic states Alexander left behind. It ends, however, several hundred years before Boswell's major focus begins. Herman never addresses the particular ceremony that Boswell examines.

If Boswell had presented Herman's findings to his reader, the only value would have been to show up the differences between the institution that Herman describes and the medieval Christian ceremony. The essential point of the institution described by Herman is that the participating parties belong to different groups: *xenia* is an alliance between two men who are foreigners (or in some sense members of politically or socially opposed groups). This is not the hallmark of the medieval ceremony of union that Boswell describes. Shaw does not know it, but there is another ceremony in many of these same liturgical manuscripts that is intended to cement peace between two parties who have been enemies. It is completely distinct from *adelphopoiesis.* . . .

Readers should consider Shaw's views in light of Boswell's book, not in place of it.

A Strange Brotherhood

MICHEL DE MONTAIGNE

From his Travel Journal, *March 18, 1581*

In his journal of 1580–1581 (not published until two centuries later) the French skeptic and essayist Montaigne records a remarkable incident, as Ralph Hexter noted in the previous excerpt. Montaigne learned of same-sex marriages celebrated in a nuptial mass in Rome, but the participants had been subjected to vicious persecution.

On the 18th the ambassador of Portugal made obeisance to the Pope for the kingdom of Portugal on behalf of King Philip—the same ambassador who was here to represent the deceased king and the Cortes opposed to King Philip.

On my return from Saint Peter's I met a man who informed me humorously of two things: that the Portuguese made their obeisance in Passion week; and then, that on this same day the station was at San Giovanni Porta Latina, in which church a few years before certain Portuguese had entered into a strange brotherhood. They married one another, male to male, at Mass, with the same ceremonies with which we perform our marriages, read the same marriage gospel service, and then went to bed and lived together. The Roman wits said that because in the other conjunction, of male and female, this circumstance of marriage alone makes it legitimate, it had seemed to these sharp folk that this other action would become equally legitimate if they authorized it with ceremonies and mysteries of the Church. Eight or nine Portuguese of this fine sect were burned. . . .

Deviant Marriage Patterns in Chinese Society

JAMES MCGOUGH

From Normal and Abnormal Behavior in Chinese Culture, *edited by Arthur Kleinman and Tsung-Yi Lin, 1981*

Husbands, Boys, Servants

BRET HINSCH

From Passions of the Cut Sleeve, *by Bret Hinsch, 1990*

Historian James McGough here details how the growing economic power of women in nineteenth- and early twentieth-century southern China enabled many to form relationships outside of conventional marriage—and some to set up same-sex marriages. In Fukien Province in seventeenth-century China, same-sex marriages between gay men seem to have been common, if not fully accepted, as well. Bret Hinsch supplies the details of one of the actual ceremonies in Fukien.

DEVIANT MARRIAGE PATTERNS
IN CHINESE SOCIETY

There were few alternative life-styles for women in traditional Chinese Society. Apart from the officially endorsed role of wife and mother, there were few ways a woman could make a living. . . .

One alternative was domestic service in another family. Women who worked as domestic servants sometimes renounced "normal" marriage and family life, and instead banded together for moral and other kinds of support.

Another alternative was made possible by other forms of wage labor; something that became much more prevalent with increased foreign investments in China in the last century. Once factory jobs were available in any numbers, women had greatly increased sources of income, and could be much more independent of the family system.

This happened, for instance, [according to scholar Hu P'u-an,] in the silk producing areas around Canton:

In P'an-yu the land is fertile, and the people mainly make their living from silk production. Whether rich or poor, the daughters of the families there all know how to pick mulberry leaves and how to reel off silk from cocoons. In one day they can earn as much as eight or nine *chiao*, but at the least three or four *chiao*. The standard of living in rural areas is of course not as high as in the cities, and this amount is enough for self-sufficiency, and even for a bit of surplus. Such girls, then, have a means of support, and regard marriage as the most shameful of human affairs. Thus they form pacts not to marry. If they are forced to marry by their parents, they do not move to reside with the husband. These latter, after marriage, do not have intercourse with the husband, and the next day return to their natal family, to be companions to their sisters and female cousins. This means that they are lost to the husband's family.

It is in this context that we find transactional social forms that are similar to, or are, marriage. The nonmarrying pacts were in the form of groups, or associations, of girls. They all entered into a kind of sworn sisterhood, called a "golden orchid society," "mutual admiration society," or "workmates' society."

In some cases two individuals would establish such a bond, [Hu writes,] and unite as a pair:

> In the drawing up of the contract, both sides must agree, much as in the legal form of contracts. If both parties are interested, then one will prepare . . . gifts of respect, to symbolize her sentiments. If the other side accepts them, this constitutes consent. If not then it is refusal. When the contract is written up and put into effect, and if they have any savings, they invite friends for a night's feast, and the friends all congratulate them. After this they are inseparable, day and night, and happier than any married couple. After the contract has been established, if there is any difference of opinion, and one of them wishes to go back on the agreement, then they must submit to the judgment of one of their sisterhood leaders. Usually the punishment is some kind of beating or disgrace. Thus it has become a kind of customary law.
>
> As far as their cohabitation is concerned, though they cannot completely live as man and wife, yet they can actually have the pleasure that men and women do, either through massage and caresses, or through using mechanical aids. This is not a refined account, and it is difficult for a gentleman to speak of it. These women even select descendants, instituting a daughter to succeed to their estate, and later their adopted

daughter will also enter into one of these compacts, as though there were a daughter-in-law, and it is really just as in blood relationships. This is really strange.

Ch'en Tung-yuan attributed the custom to the unsettled economic situation: "To refrain from marrying because of lesbianism is really unnatural, and very harmful to the woman's health, but after the great changes in the circumstances of earning a livelihood, women not getting married at the proper time, and falling into lesbianism, has become much more widespread, and is truly a big problem."

Institutionalized same-sex unions for men were evidently much less widespread, though these are precisely the kinds of unions that one would expect to be least talked about and written about. This is a general problem in the study of many aspects of social life in traditional China. Only a small portion of the people were literate, and the use and contents of literary works were heavily influenced by socio-political factors. It is no accident that the standard histories and other works tend to ignore non-standard social forms and processes, and have very little that is reliable to say about non-elite social life.

This has been acknowledged by historians as a great pity, but not something about which anything could be done. More recently, however, more attention has been paid to the use of such things as short stories and plays as sources of historical material for the study of the "other side" of the traditional society. What little I have found on male-male marriages comes in part from a short story by Li Yu (1611–1679). For our purposes an important aspect of Li's literary philosophy is that he advocated a sort of "literature for the masses." Essays and other standard works were to be kept apart from stories and drama. The former were expected to be profound and even difficult; they were for the literate. The latter, on the contrary, were expected to be clear and simple, since they were intended for the illiterate as well as the literate. Furthermore, Li advocated a kind of realism; an author of plays and stories should stick to colloquial language and to realistic details, avoiding the fantastic and things outside of one's own experience and observation.

One of the stories of Li's collection titled *The Silent Play* (*Wu-sheng Hsi*) is about a young, brilliant, and handsome scholar in P'u-t'ien Hsien, Hsing-hua Prefecture, Fukien, during the late Ming period, named Wei Chi-fang, who married a young boy. Wei had earlier married a woman, who died after giving him a son. Having fulfilled his Confucian duty to provide offspring, he decided to remarry, this time to a young homosexual. The term for "remarriage" used here is *hsu-hsuan*, "to replace the string on one's lute," a common if somewhat literary term for remarriage. After a number of false starts, Wei finally managed to pay a brideprice of 500 taels, the two went through a marriage ceremony, and took up residence as man and "wife."

The background information provided by the author is very interesting. Fukien was said to be a center of homosexuality in China, and such marriages were said to be fairly common, with payment of brideprice:

> In Fukien it happens that homosexuals pay a brideprice, but usually it's no more than symbolic; several tens of taels at most, but sometimes as little as several taels. It is a symbol of entreaty.
>
> One must understand that with Fukien homosexuals, as in marrying women, first marriages are distinguished from later ones. For a virgin, men are prepared to pay a much higher brideprice, and to carry out a complete and proper wedding ceremony. If, then, one is not strict in controlling young boys, and they are seduced by someone, then they are called "fallen flowers." They do not become completely

worthless, but a buyer will generally be interested only in a casual and temporary relationship, and will not enter into a permanent marriage relationship, and he will not select the boy to come to live with him.

What is of interest is the institutionalization and permanence of such relationships. There is some fragmentary information tending to support Li's claim that there were institutionalized, marriage-like, male homosexual unions in China. A much later writer, Yao Ling-hsi, says

> The term "little brothers" (*hsiung-ti erh*) is the same as the Fukienese "bond younger brother" (*ch'i-ti*). . . . Homosexuals raise them like younger brothers. . . . Fukienese homosexuals consider themselves as brothers.

This term *ch'i*, "contract," "bond," shows up in many "deviant" social transactions. It is used for a kind of adoption found in many areas of China; it was used in connection with the consensual union described above under the term *p'ing-t'ou*. It indicated a kind of consensual union in Taiwan, and Hsu K'o says that "bond brother," *ch'i-ti*, means male prostitute in Cantonese. Indeed, this term (*kai-dai* in Cantonese) is common invective in Hong Kong today, used as a derogatory term for homosexuals.

It seems fairly clear to me, then, that there were at least in late Ming and Ch'ing China institutionalized relationships between males in some areas, and that these relationships were often expressed in terms of marriage and carried out in some of the social forms connected with "regular" marriage. . . .

HUSBANDS, BOYS, SERVANTS

We have a description of an actual ceremony for swearing friendship from the works of the invaluable Li Yu. Two men sacrifice a carp, a rooster, and a duck. They then exchange their exact times of birth, smear each other's mouths with the blood of the victims, and swear eternal loyalty to each other. The ceremony concludes with feasting on the sacrificial victims. Afterward they address each other as older brother (*xiong*) and younger brother (*di*). The similarity of this practice to the Fujianese [Fukienese] custom of male marriage is obvious, with similar terminology and an important ritual component. Li Yu even suggests erotic overtones to the subsequent encounters of these sworn brothers. And yet the Fujianese marriage ceremony went beyond this earlier custom by abandoning the earlier ritual of brotherhood and adopting the language and ceremonies of heterosexual marriage.

According to the terms of the Fujianese male marriage, the younger *qidi* would move into the *qixiong*'s household. There he would be treated as a son-in-law by his husband's parents. Throughout the marriage, many of which lasted for twenty years, the *qixiong* was completely responsible for his younger husband's upkeep. Wealthy *qixiong* even adopted young boys, whom the couple raised as sons. Usually, these marriages would eventually have to be dissolved because of the familial responsibilities of procreation. As a character in the early-Qing-dynasty short story "Chronicle of Sacrificing Love" ("Qing lie ji") rhetorically asks, "In all history when has there ever been a precedent for two men to live out their lives together?" Similarly, in Langxian's short story "Pan Wenzi" from *Shi dian tou,* two young men who decide to live out their lives together go back on their decision just before their respective fiancées are about to pressure them into heterosexual marriage. To men of the late Ming and early Qing, emotional and sexual relationships with other men could be intense and even enduring, yet they could not exclude heterosexuality.

At the end of a male marriage in Fujian [Fukien], the older husband paid the necessary price to acquire a suitable bride for his beloved *qidi*. Shen Defu marveled at the heights of devotion reached by these couples. Star-crossed lovers who encountered difficulties even strode together into the sea to drown in each other's arms. . . .

A Curious Married Couple
THE EDITORS

From Fincher's Trades' Review, *July 25, 1863*

This Philadelphia-based journal, directed at emigrant workers from Britain, included this story of an Englishwoman, Mary East, and her wife of thirty-four years. The only catch was that Ms. East was living undercover as one James How. Notice the matter-of-fact tone of the reporting—wry, but certainly not shocked.

In 1731, a girl named Mary East was engaged to be married to a young man for whom she entertained the strongest affection; but upon his taking to evil courses, or, to tell the whole truth, being hanged for highway robbery, she determined to run no risk of any such disappointment from the opposite sex in future. A female friend of hers having suffered in some similar manner, and being of the like mind with herself, they agreed to pass for the rest of their days as man and wife, in some place where they were not known. The question of which should be the husband was decided by lot in favor of Mary East, who accordingly assumed the masculine habit, and under the name of James How, took a small public house at Epping for himself and consort. Here, and subsequently at other inns, they lived together in good repute with their neighbors for eighteen years—during which neither experienced the least pang of marital jealousy—and realized a considerable sum of money. The supposed James How served all the parish offices without discovery, and was several times a foreman of juries. While occupying the *White Horse* at Poplar, however, his secret was discovered by a woman who had known him in his youth; and from that time the happy couple became the victims of her extortion. First five, then ten, then one hundred pounds were demanded as the price of her silence, and even these bribes were found to be insufficient. At last, however, the persecutor pushed matters too far, and killed the goose that laid such golden eggs. James brought the whole matter before a magistrate, and attired, awkwardly enough, in the proper garments of her sex, herself witnessed against the offender, who was imprisoned for a considerable term. Exposure, however, of course followed upon the trial, and the *White Horse* had to be disposed of, and the landlord and landlady to retire from public life into retirement. After thirty-four years of pretended matrimony, Mrs. How died; the disconsolate widower survived long afterwards, but never again took to himself another spouse. Neither husband nor wife had ever been seen to dress a joint of meat; nor did they give entertainment to their friends like other couples; neither, although in excellent circumstances (having acquired between three and four thousand pounds) did they keep man-servant or maid-servant, but Mary East served the customers and went on errands, while her wife attended solely to the affairs of the house.

A Note on "Woman Marriage" in Dahomey

MELVILLE J. HERSKOVITS

From Africa, *1937, Vol. 10*

A short scholarly note on a widespread practice observed in parts of West Africa in the early part of this century: one wealthy, infertile woman marrying another woman to produce offspring via a surrogate father.

Reports of the occurrence of "woman marriage" in parts of Africa as far distant from one another as northern and southern Nigeria, the Anglo-Egyptian Sudan, and the Union of South Africa indicate the possibility that there may be other instances of this institution that have gone unrecorded. The purpose of this paper is therefore to call attention to this striking phase of social organization by describing the form which "woman marriage" takes in Dahomey, presenting data collected in the field in 1931. In doing this, attention will be paid to such aspects of the social setting in which this kind of marriage is lodged as may be needed to allow it best to be understood, while some of the attitudes which arise from it will also be indicated.

Before proceeding to give the details of Dahomean "marriages" between women, however, the prior accounts may be reproduced in some detail, so that comparisons by the reader may be facilitated. The first quotation to be given, from [anthropologist C. K.] Meek, describes the institution as it exists in northern Nigeria:

> There is a curious and ancient custom found among some of the Yoruba, Yagba, Akoko, Nupe, and Gana-Gana communities—that of a woman going through a regular form of matrimony with other women. In the Osi district a barren woman will formally marry a young girl and hand her over to her husband with a view to bearing children—as Hagar was given by Sarah to Abraham. But a more striking example of this type of marriage is where a wealthy woman, who may or may not be normally married to a man, contracts a marriage with a young girl to whom she subsequently allows a *cicisbeo* to have access, the resultant children belonging to the female "husband." This is a common practice among the Yoruba, Nupe, Akoko, and Gana-Gana, and the female "husband" will even pay men to have connection with her young "wife." In some cases she exacts gifts of farm-service from the *cicisbei*. All the ceremonial of marriage is observed in these marriages of women to women, and a bride-price is even paid to the young girl's father. The usual rules of divorce apply. The legal "husband" can divorce her "wife" and recover her dowry, and if the young girl runs off with a man she can claim the resultant children as her own. The marriage of women to women is not regarded with disfavour, and the chiefs will even consent to their daughters being married in this way. . . .

Dahomean marriages take thirteen different forms. They are divided into two general classes, one called *akwénŭsî,* "woman-with-money," comprising those forms where the marriage-dues are paid by the spouse to the bride's father; the other, termed *xadudó*, "friend-custody," where these payments are not made. Expressed in another way, the first class includes those forms of marriage whose resultant offspring are under the control of the father; the second category being composed of those matings where the mother retains control of her children. Interestingly enough, though a woman who "marries" another must make all the payments and perform all the duties required in any marriage of the first class, the spirit of such a marriage is so foreign to what is regarded as normal procedure that every Dahomean with whom the matter of marriage-types was discussed placed this form in the second category rather than the one in which strictly and legally speaking it should belong.

The name given this form of marriage is *gbɔsú dɔ̃ɔ̃ gbɔsî*, "giving the goat to the buck." It occurs but rarely among commoners, but is frequent in upper class families, particularly among royalty, with girls of commoner or slave status figuring most often as the female mates. It is based directly upon the fact that women sometimes become independently wealthy. . . .

As has been stated, when a woman of means asks and is given a girl from a family other than her own to be her "wife," she supports all the payments and gifts decreed for this form of marriage as though she were a man. She causes a house to be built near her own, and installs the young woman there. She is regarded by the inhabitant of this house as her husband, and is actually called "husband" by her "wife." From among her male acquaintances, or perhaps from among the men of her husband's family, she chooses one to whom she "gives" the young woman she has "married." He is told that the girl is his to live with, that he may come to her as often as he likes, but that he may not take her to his own compound. The man is under no obligations of any sort, either toward the parents of the girl or toward the woman who has given her to him. All the obligations entailed in marriage have been discharged by the "husband" of the girl, while, as for this woman, her recompense is had in the children to be born of her "wife."

It now becomes clear why this type of marriage is given the name it bears. It could not be explained more concisely than in the terms stated by the Dahomeans: "When a goat becomes large, one does not ask which buck has caused her to conceive." . . .

A Normal Man

WALTER L. WILLIAMS

From The Spirit and the Flesh,
by Walter L. Williams, 1986

Here is an account of the astonishingly common same-sex marriages in Native American culture. Notice, however, that some stigma still attached to them, if only in the kidding that often went along with the acquisition of a male "wife."

In 1542, one of the earliest Spanish explorers in Florida, Cabeza de Vaca, reported on his previous five years among the Timucua Indians: "During the time I was thus among these people I saw a devilish thing, and it is that I saw one man married to another." The sources are extremely unsatisfactory in describing these relationships, but the fact that these relationships exist is noted for several tribes, usually by a brief statement saying that the berdache "lived together with a man, as his wife." This was noted as the socially accepted practice for some berdaches among the Ojibwa, Winnebago, Lakota, and Yuma. It was said that the only male homosexual behavior among the Quinault Indians involved those who had relationships with the *keknat-sa'nxwix* ("part woman male").

In a massive survey of northern California Indian cultures conducted in the 1930s, all but one of the groups who recognized a berdache status also recognized his marriage to a "normal man." Next to doing women's work and acting androgynously, sexual behavior with a man is the most commonly noted characteristic of berdache status. This aspect is even more widespread among berdaches than a special ceremonial role.

An ethnographer of the Omahas wrote in the 1880s: "*Mingu-ga* [*mexoga*] took other men as their husbands. Frank La Fleche knew one such man, who had had several men as his husbands. . . . [They] are publicly known, and do not appear to be despised or to excite disgust." Among the Southern Maidus, a traditionalist informant in the 1920s explained in a respectful manner about *osa'pu:* "They just grew that way, being half-man and half-woman," and in a similar matter-of-fact way said "he lives with a man. . . . No contempt was shown them." The berdache's sexuality is accepted in the same way as his androgyny; both are seen as reflections of his spirit, his basic nature. . . .

Marriage between a berdache and a man existed in the context of the general position of marriage in aboriginal American Indian society. Although wide ranges of activities are open for both women and men, there is in most Native American societies a basic division of labor into two halves. This is usually referred to as a "division of labor by sex." By dividing the necessary tasks into "men's work" and "women's work," each person has to learn only half of the jobs available. This is important to small-scale societies that do not have much role specialization. It is, however, more accurate to call this pattern a division of labor by *gender*, because people can take on a gender role that is divergent from their genital sex.

Within a marriage in a gender-divided economy, there can be only two roles: husband and wife. The sex of the person who takes these roles may vary, but the roles generally do not. This is an additional reason that two berdaches would not marry, and two masculine men would not marry. Masculine men might have sex, which is their private business, but marriage is a public matter and an economic concern.

Each person has something to gain by entering a marriage. They gain the expertise of the other in tasks that are different from their own skills. Why should two hunters marry, if neither of them is good at gathering plants? The closest exception to this rule is among the Navajos. When *nadle* marry, they dress like men. A Navajo informant explains, "If they marry men, it is just like two men working together." Yet it must be remembered that *nadle* also do women's work, so such a marriage is still viable. Economically, the husband has both a wife and a husband, which partly explains the reputation these marriages have for economic success.

When people get married, they gain another advantage: the economic security that comes with a wider circle of relatives. Nothing is worse in a kin-based society than to be without kin. Marriage creates an alliance of families, whereby one has twice as many relatives on which to draw for support. In the context of a subsistence economy, with a division of labor by gender, it makes sense that such an economy would be family centered. Families provide extra productive labor and take care of the aged.

Marriages between men and berdaches fit into this pattern. In such a marriage, the man takes the husband role, and the berdache takes the wife role. Recognizing the fluidity of women's and men's roles and the mixed-gender status of the berdache means that there can be considerable variation from this simply stated dichotomy. The Navajo example just cited illustrates the variation in spousal relationships and the mixed-gender status of *nadle*.

In a marriage between a man and a berdache, the berdache supplies women's work and a network of kin, like any other wife. Lakota chief Crazy Horse, for example, had one or two *winktes* for wives, along with his female wives. A berdache wife offered the same economic advantages of any other polygynous marriage. While it is true that a berdache cannot reproduce, many of the reports of such marriages mention that the husband already had children, either through a previous marriage or by taking a berdache as a second or third wife. But with adoption being so commonly accepted, children may even be gained by the berdache. Thus, the same advantages of heterosexual marriage also accrue to the man who marries a berdache.

The two roles of husband and berdache are not to be confused. After I had been living in the household of a well-known *winkte* on a particular reservation for a while, a medicine man told me in private, "People say———is a 'he-she' and you must be his lover." They did not say I was a "he-she," because he was clearly the androgynous one. Personal character and gender role, not sexual behavior per se, distinguish the *winkte* role.

Sexual behavior of berdaches is often considered a serious reflection of their spiritual natures. But for other people, it can be an object of humor. . . .

Kidding is often directed more toward the husbands than toward berdaches themselves. According to a Crow berdache,

"If a Crow man moved in with me, other men would tease him. They wouldn't tease me, because they all know what I am." The joking toward the husband could also be due to the reputation that berdaches have for being highly productive workers. Since the berdaches are very good providers, a Crow traditionalist pointed out to me, and give many gifts to their boyfriends, the man could get a reputation for being lazy. One of the common taunts that Plains Indians might aim at the husband of the berdache is that he wants a wife who not only keeps house but hunts for him as well.

Why would a man go against all this teasing and marry a berdache anyway? Most of the early ethnographers who interviewed berdaches never asked this question. When I have asked Indians this, I get a mere shrug of the shoulders and a vague statement like "I don't know, he just wants to do it." Mohaves attribute the ability of an *alyha* to attract a man to their shamanistic powers of love magic. More concretely, they consider *alyha* to be lucky, and their luck extends to their husband. Such beliefs can predispose some men to marry berdaches.

This belief is realistic, in the sense that a husband benefits from the much-publicized prosperity of a berdache household. Among the Hidatsa, for example, berdaches did all the work that women did for their husbands. Yet beyond this, they were noted as being stronger than women, and never burdened with pregnancy or nursing an infant. Hidatsa statements from the 1930s tell of berdaches working harder than the average wife and exceeding the usual productivity of women in many activities. This was the reason given for chiefs and other prominent men among the California Mission Indians wanting to marry *cuit, uluqui,* or *coia.* A *lhamana* that Matilda Coxe Stevenson knew at Zuni was one of the richest persons of the pueblo. In the 1880s he "allied himself to a man" and until the time when Stevenson left the pueblo in 1897 "this couple were living together, and they were two of the hardest workers in the pueblo and among the most prosperous."

Another reason for a man to be attracted to marriage with a berdache has to do with marital stability. In contrast to Western notions of feminine "nest building" and masculine promiscuity, among the Mohaves the stereotypes are reversed. Young women are known for their licentious habits and their disinclination to stick with one man for long. Men, who more likely crave a stable home, will often turn to an older woman or an *alyha.* . . .

Traditionally, Lakota culture accepted the *winkte* only as a secondary spouse, to be married after a man already had a female wife and children. Since Lakotas no longer have plural marriages, if a man takes a *winkte* for a spouse that means there would be no heterosexual marriage and progeny. A way to discourage this exclusive homosexuality on the part of men is to make them an object of laughter. The berdache is exempt from the kidding because he is not seen as a man. The culture, after all, is not objecting to the homosexual behavior. If a man wishes to have sexual relations with a berdache, there is no objection among the Lakotas as long as he does not settle into a permanent relationship. What society objects to is behavior that might prevent reproduction. Still, despite this discouragement, some men will go against the norm and marry a berdache.

The laughter among the Mohaves is a case in point. Any kind of sexual matter is an occasion for humor among them, but the jokes about the husband of the *alyha* fly so thick around him that many of the men will eventually leave the berdache. Despite the fact that the berdache provides a stable home and is more likely to be faithful than a female wife, such marriages are not stable. Rather than see the laughter as a condemnation of homosexuality, we should understand it as a balancing mechanism. With all the advantages that marriage with an *alyha* offers for Mohave men (prosperity, stability, luck, sex), if there were not some disadvantages then too many men might marry berdaches and the population growth might be threatened. But by keeping the majority of male marriages short-term, the joking ensures that most men mate with women at some point and have children.

Other cultures accomplish this same goal by restricting male marriages to those men who have already had children. Thus, it is only acceptable for a berdache to become a second or third wife in a polygynous family where the female wife has already reproduced. Among the Hidatsas, berdaches usually marry older men who are beyond their childbearing years. None of these patterns of marriage threatens the reproduction of the population.

The Zapotecs are typical of a culture in which men customarily marry a berdache only after they have married women and produced children. While boys may participate in homosexual behavior before their marriage, by the time Zapotec men are thirty years old almost all of them (not including berdaches, of course) marry women and have children. Yet it is not uncommon for men to leave a heterosexual marriage after a time. According to ethnographer Beverly Chiñas, "A middle-aged man with a grown family may leave his wife and move in with a male lover and generally this scarcely raises an eyebrow. Over the nearly two decades since my fieldwork began several prominent citizens with grown children have left their heterosexual mates to live with same-sex lovers." One case involved a former mayor of the town. People might talk about this for a little while, but they soon adapt to the change in the same way they would to a new heterosexual pairing after a divorce. There is no ostracism of a same-sex couple.

In the case of a wife's death, berdaches will be praised for stepping in to rescue a family. Among the Zapotecs a famous case occurred when a man's wife died while their several children were still young. The man married a *muxe* who became a substitute mother. The berdache cooked, laundered clothes, and did the shopping for the family. Other Zapotecs admired the *muxe* greatly for the sacrifices he made, saying "every one of those children got an education and was sent to school clean and well-fed." He and the widower lived together as a respected couple, until the *muxe*'s death many years later. Zapotecs judged him by his sacrifices for the children, rather than by his sexual behavior. . . .

The Precedents Abroad

From the Harvard Law Review
Vol. 116, no. 7 (2003)

Outside the United States, the Netherlands and Belgium are the only two countries that recognize civil marriages for gays and lesbians. But two rulings in 2003 by Canadian appellate courts ending marriage discrimination will become effective in July and September 2004. Before that happens, the Canadian legislature is expected to pass legislation that would extend marriage to gays and lesbians throughout the nation. This excerpt from the Harvard Law Review *surveys the current state of gay partnership law across the world. Even though numerous European nations have surpassed the United States in recognizing gay partnerships, many of them trail the U.S. on the important issues of adoption and custody.*

W hen the *Harvard Law Review* last addressed the subject of same-sex marriage in Developments in the Law, in 1989 . . . same-sex marriage was not legal anywhere in the world. A great deal has changed in the last fourteen years.

Progress toward the legalization of same-sex marriage has occurred most rapidly in Northern and Western Europe. . . . The Netherlands legalized same-sex marriage in 2001, when the country "opened up" the official definition of marriage to include "two persons of different sex or of the same sex." This change established complete parity between same-sex and opposite-sex couples, extending to same-sex couples identical rights to sanctify their relationships publicly, to label those relationships "marriages," and thereby to assume all the benefits and burdens associated with marriage, including the right to adopt children. The Belgian Parliament approved similar legislation permitting same-sex marriages in early 2003, though without accompanying rights of adoption. "Registered partnerships"—involving most, but not all, of the same rights and responsibilities as those associated with opposite-sex marriage—were legalized for same-sex couples in Denmark in 1989, in Norway in 1993, in Sweden in 1995, in Iceland in 1996, and in Finland in 2002. Less expansive forms of same-sex unions were legalized in Hungary in 1998, in France in 1999, in Germany in 2000, and in Portugal in 2001.

The experience of some Western European nations demonstrates that the acceptance of same-sex marriage can occur relatively quickly. In the Netherlands, the legalization of same-sex marriage occurred just three years after the legalization of registered partnerships. Similarly, Finland enacted antidiscrimination legislation in 1995, equalized the age of consent three years later, and legalized registered partnerships four years after that. One reason for this speed may be that so much of the expansion of civil rights has come legislatively, rather than through the courts—itself a product of the countries' small sizes and cultural homogeneity. Changes have generally been achieved by legislative consensus, rather than through countermajoritarian court orders. Another factor may be what Robert Wintemute labels the "friendly human rights competition" of the Nordic countries, in which progress in one country helps spur progress among its neighbors.

Nevertheless, rapid change is far from the rule in Europe. To the contrary, the European experience provides considerable evidence that progress may stall, perpetuating the second-class status of same-sex couples. It is noteworthy that outside the Netherlands and Belgium, European recognition of same-sex unions has thus far ended with registered partnerships—and only in the Netherlands does same-sex marriage include full rights of adoption.

Only the Netherlands, Denmark, and Iceland allow same-sex registered partners to adopt each other's children—and only in the Netherlands can such partners adopt unrelated children. In Norway, Sweden, France, and Germany, adoptions by same-sex couples are prohibited outright. One justification frequently offered for these prohibitions is that adoption is far less frequent in Europe than in the United States, where the number of children up for adoption exceeds the number of available parents. Many European adoptions involve children from less developed countries, leading to the speculative fear that these nations might block adoptions to nations that allow children to be placed in same-sex households. The broader implication is that where there is a closer balance between supply and demand, the preference should be to place children with two opposite-sex parents. This justification relies on the assertion—unsupported by the vast bulk of empirical research—that opposite-sex parents are necessarily more qualified than same-sex parents. Moreover, the supply-demand imbalance fails to explain why even custody rights are denied to same-sex couples in Denmark, Norway, Sweden, and France, and why across Europe (with the exception of the Netherlands) lesbian women are barred from obtaining artificial insemination. Thus, a more convincing explanation may be that religious and cultural traditions cause Europeans to distinguish between offering limited official recognition to same-sex couples and allowing such couples to marry and form families of their own. This explanation, in turn, suggests that incrementalism has its limits, such that the process of "small change" will not automatically culminate in full marriage equality, as it has in the Netherlands . . .

[S]omewhat counterintuitively, same-sex couples in the United States have greater rights to form families—through such techniques as adoption and artificial insemination—than do such couples in Europe. If cultural, political, and constitutional factors have slowed official recognition of same-sex unions in this country, official sanction is being granted in piecemeal fashion, through legislative and court-ordered recognition of same-sex civil unions and domestic partnerships, as well as through the court-ordered extension to same-sex couples of many of the rights and privileges attendant to traditional marriage.

CHAPTER TWO

In God's Name?
THE RELIGIOUS WAR CONTINUES

Although much of the current debate about same-sex marriage concerns the civil and secular, it cannot help but invoke the religious and the sacred. By far the most powerful organization involved in the same-sex marriage fight is the Christian Coalition, which bases its opposition primarily on religious and scriptural grounds. Presented here are those very biblical injunctions—from Genesis, Leviticus, and Paul—and the Catholic bishops' defense of traditional notions of the meaning of marriage and family. Here, too, are modern, secular defenses of the Scriptures and the position of the church, from Dennis Prager's account of the Judeo-Christian prohibitions on homosexuality to Jean Bethke Elshtain's natural law–based concerns about same-sex marriage.

Much has now also been written from an explicitly Christian and Jewish perspective in defense of same-sex marriages: Bishop John Shelby Spong's and Rabbi Yoel Kahn's are among the most powerful arguments that now exist. And the refusal of many lesbian and gay people of faith to acquiesce in being excluded from their religious traditions is one of the more remarkable phenomena now driving the debate forward. This chapter can provide, alas, only a flavor of the thinking and praying that is now taking place in congregations across the West.

The Holy Bible
The King James Version

Translations, interpretations, and inferences disagree about the meanings of these passages. Note, for example, how the prohibition against homosexual intercourse in Leviticus is in the same chapter as prohibitions on incest and failing to keep kosher dietary laws. But here are the biblical texts at the center of the controversy, in the most gripping English translation ever printed. Judge for yourself.

GENESIS 2: 18–24

And the LORD God said, *It is* not good that the man should be alone; I will make him an help meet for him.

And out of the ground the LORD God formed every beast of the field, and every fowl of the air; and brought *them* unto Adam to see what he would call them: and whatsoever Adam called every living creature, that *was* the name thereof.

And Adam gave names to all cattle, and to the fowl of the air, and to every beast of the field; but for Adam there was not found an help meet for him.

And the LORD God caused a deep sleep to fall upon Adam, and he slept: and he took one of his ribs, and closed up the flesh instead thereof;

And the rib, which the LORD God had taken from man, made he a woman, and brought her unto the man.

And Adam said, This *is* now bone of my bones, and flesh of my flesh: she shall be called Woman, because she was taken out of Man.

Therefore shall a man leave his father and his mother, and shall cleave unto his wife: and they shall be one flesh.

LEVITICUS 20: 7–16; 22–27

Sanctify yourselves therefore, and be ye holy: for I *am* the LORD your God.

And ye shall keep my statutes, and do them: I *am* the LORD which sanctify you.

For every one that curseth his father or his mother shall be surely put to death: he hath cursed his father or his mother; his blood *shall be* upon him.

And the man that committeth adultery with *another* man's wife, *even he* that committeth adultery with his neighbour's wife, the adulterer and the adulteress shall surely be put to death.

And the man that lieth with his father's wife hath uncovered his father's nakedness: both of them shall surely be put to death; their blood *shall be* upon them.

And if a man lie with his daughter in law, both of them shall surely be put to death: they have wrought confusion; their blood *shall be* upon them.

If a man also lie with mankind, as he lieth with a woman, both of them have committed an abomination: they shall surely be put to death; their blood *shall be* upon them.

And if a man take a wife and her mother, it *is* wickedness: they shall be burnt with fire, both he and they; that there be no wickedness among you.

And if a man lie with a beast, he shall surely be put to death: and ye shall slay the beast.

And if a woman approach unto any beast, and lie down thereto, thou shalt kill the woman, and the beast: they shall surely be put to death; their blood *shall be* upon them. . . .

Ye shall therefore keep all my statutes, and all my judgments, and do them: that the land, whither I bring you to dwell therein, spue you not out.

And ye shall not walk in the manners of the nation, which I cast out before you: for they committed all these things, and therefore I abhorred them.

But I have said unto you, Ye shall inherit their land, and I will give it unto you to possess it, a land that floweth with milk and honey: I *am* the LORD your God, which have separated you from *other* people.

Ye shall therefore put difference between clean beasts and unclean, and between unclean fowls and clean: and ye shall not make your souls abominable by beast, or by fowl, or by any manner of living thing that creepeth on the ground, which I have separated from you as unclean.

And ye shall be holy unto me: for I the LORD *am* holy, and have severed you from *other* people, that ye should be mine.

A man also or woman that hath a familiar spirit, or that is a wizard, shall surely be put to death: they shall stone them with stones: their blood *shall be* upon them.

SAME-SEX MARRIAGE: PRO AND CON

THE EPISTLE OF PAUL THE APOSTLE
TO THE ROMANS 1: 18–19; 22–32

For the wrath of God is revealed from heaven against all ungodliness and unrighteousness of men, who hold the truth in unrighteousness;

Because that which may be known of God is manifest in them; for Goth hath shewed *it* unto them. . . .

Professing themselves to be wise, they became fools,

And changed the glory of the uncorruptible God into an image made like to corruptible man, and to birds, and to fourfooted beasts, and creeping things.

Wherefore God also gave them up to uncleanness through the lusts of their own hearts, to dishonour their own bodies between themselves:

Who changed the truth of God into a lie, and worshipped and served the creature more than the Creator, who is blessed for ever. Ă-mĕn.

For this cause God gave them up unto vile affections: for even their women did change the natural use into that which is against nature:

And likewise also the men, leaving the natural use of the woman, burned in their lust one toward another; men with men working that which is unseemly, and receiving in themselves that recompence of their error which was meet.

And even as they did not like to retain God in *their* knowledge, God gave them over to a reprobate mind, to do those things which are not convenient;

Being filled with all unrighteousness, fornication, wickedness, covetousness, maliciousness; full of envy, murder, debate, deceit, malignity; whisperers,

Backbiters, haters of God, despiteful, proud, boasters, inventors of evil things, disobedient to parents,

Without understanding, convenantbreakers, without natural affection, implacable, unmerciful;

Who knowing the judgment of God, that they which commit such things are worthy of death, not only do the same, but have pleasure in them that do them.

1 CORINTHIANS 6: 1–3; 7–11

Dare any of you, having a matter against another, go to law before the unjust, and not before the saints?

Do ye not know that the saints shall judge the world? and if the world shall be judged by you, are ye unworthy to judge the smallest matters?

Know ye not that we shall judge angels? how much more things that pertain to this life? . . .

Now therefore there is utterly a fault among you, because ye go to law one with another. Why do ye not rather take wrong? why do ye not rather *suffer yourselves to* be defrauded?

Nay, ye do wrong, and defraud, and that *your* brethren.

Know ye not that the unrighteousness shall not inherit the kingdom of God? Be not deceived neither fornicators, nor idolators, nor adulterers, nor effeminate, nor abusers of themselves with mankind,

Nor thieves, nor covetous, nor drunkards, nor revilers, nor extortioners, shall inherit the kingdom of God.

And such were some of you: but ye are washed, but ye are

sanctified, but ye are justified in the name of the Lord Jesus, and by the Spirit of our God. . . .

Statement on Same-Sex Marriage

REV. JOSEPH L. CHARRON AND
REV. WILLIAM S. SKYLSTAD

for the National Conference of Catholic Bishops,
July 19, 1996

The essential Roman Catholic position.

The Roman Catholic Church believes that marriage is a faithful, exclusive, and lifelong union between one man and one woman, joined as husband and wife in an intimate partnership of life and love. This union was established by God with its own proper laws. By reason of its very nature, therefore, marriage exists for the mutual love and support of the spouses and for the procreation and education of children. These two purposes, the unitive and the procreative, are equal and inseparable. The institution of marriage has a very important relationship to the continuation of the human race, to the total development of the human person, and to the dignity, stability, peace, and prosperity of the family and of society.

Furthermore, we believe the natural institution of marriage has been blessed and elevated by Christ to the dignity of a sacrament. This means that Christian marriage is more than a contract. Because they are married in the Lord, the spouses acquire a special relationship to each other and to society. Their love becomes a living image of the manner in which the Lord personally loves his people and is united with them. Living a Christian sacramental marriage becomes their fundamental way of attaining salvation.

Because the marital relationship offers benefits, unlike any other, to persons, to society, and to the church, we wish to make it clear that the institution of marriage, as the union of one man and one woman, must be preserved, protected, and promoted in both private and public realms. At a time when family life is under significant stress, the principled defense of marriage is an urgent necessity for the wellbeing of children and families, and for the common good of society.

Thus, we oppose attempts to grant the legal status of marriage to a relationship between persons of the same sex. No same-sex union can realize the unique and full potential which the marital relationship expresses. For this reason, our opposition to "same-sex marriage" is not an instance of unjust discrimination or animosity toward homosexual persons. In fact, the Catholic Church teaches emphatically that individuals and society must respect the basic human dignity of all persons, including those with a homosexual orientation. Homosexual persons have a right to and deserve our respect, compassion, understanding, and defense against bigotry, attacks, and abuse.

We therefore urge Catholics and all our fellow citizens to commit themselves both to upholding the human dignity of every person and to upholding the distinct and irreplaceable community of marriage.

Marriage's True Ends

THE EDITORS

From Commonweal, *May 17, 1996*

Against Gay Marriage

JEAN BETHKE ELSHTAIN

From Commonweal, *October 22, 1991*

Why, for Catholics, procreation cannot be completely divorced from the true meaning of marriage—and why same-sex marriage is therefore unacceptable. Two complementary pieces from the generally liberal American Catholic magazine Commonweal.

MARRIAGE'S TRUE ENDS

Should marriage be essentially a contractual arrangement between two individuals to be defined as they see fit? Or does marriage recognize and embody larger shared meanings that cannot be lightly divorced from history, society, and nature—shared meanings and social forms that create the conditions in which individuals can achieve their own fulfillment? Popular acceptance of premarital sex and cohabitation gives us some sense of the moral and social trajectory involved. Both developments were welcomed as expressions of greater honesty and even better preparations for marriage. Yet considerable evidence now suggests that these newfound "freedoms" have contributed to the instability and trivialization of marriage itself, and have not borne the promises once made for them of happier lives. Similarly, elevating same-sex unions to the same moral and legal status as marriage will further throw into doubt marriage's fundamental purposes and put at risk a social practice and moral ideal vital to all.

The heterosexual exclusivity of marriage can be defended in the same way social policy rightly shows a preference for the formation of intact two-parent families. In both cases, a normative definition of family life is indispensable to any coherent and effective public action. Certainly mutual love and care are to be encouraged wherever possible. But the justification and rationale for marriage as a social institution cannot rest on the goods of companionship alone. Resisting such a reductionist understanding is not merely in the interests of heterosexuals. There are profound social goods at stake in holding together the biological, relational, and procreative dimensions of human love.

"There are countless ways to 'have' a child," writes theologian Gilbert Meilaender of the social consequences and human meaning of procreation (*Body, Soul, & Bioethics*, University of Notre Dame Press, 1996). "Not all of them amount to doing the same thing. Not all of them will teach us to discern the equal humanity of the child as one who is not our product but, rather, the natural development of shared love, like to us in dignity. . . . To conceive, bear, give birth to, and rear a child ought to be an affirmation and a recognition: affirmation of the good of life that we ourselves were given; recognition that this life bears its own creative power to which we should be faithful."

Is there really any doubt that in tying sexual attraction to love and love to children and the creation of families, marriage fundamentally shapes our ideas of human dignity and the nature of society? Same-sex marriage, whatever its virtues, would narrow that frame and foreshorten our perspective. Marriage, at its best, tutors us as no other experience can in the given nature of human life and the acceptance of responsibilities we have not willed or chosen. Indeed, it should tutor us in respect for the given nature of homosexuality and the dignity of homosexual persons. With this respect comes a recognition of difference—a difference with real consequences.

Still, it is frequently objected that if the state does not deny sterile or older heterosexual couples the right to marry, how can it deny that right to homosexual couples, many of whom are already rearing children?

Exceptions do not invalidate a norm or the necessity of norms. How some individuals make use of marriage, either volitionally or as the result of some incapacity, does not determine the purpose of that institution. In that context, heterosexual sterility does not contradict the meaning of marriage in the way same-sex unions would. If marriage as a social form is first a procreative bond in the sense that Meilaender outlines, then marriage necessarily presupposes sexual differentiation, for human procreation itself presupposes sexual differentiation. We are all the offspring of a man and a woman, and marriage is the necessary moral and social response to that natural human condition. Consequently, sexual differentiation, even in the absence of the capacity to procreate, conforms to marriage's larger design in a way same-sex unions cannot. For this reason sexual differentiation is marriage's defining boundary, for it is the precondition of marriage's true ends.

AGAINST GAY MARRIAGE

Every society embraces an image of a body politic. This complex symbolism incorporates visions and reflections on who is inside and who is outside; on what counts as order and disorder; on what is cherished and what is despised. This imagery is fluid but not, I will argue, entirely up for grabs. For without some continuity in our imagery and concern, we confront a deepening nihilism. In a world of ever-more transgressive enthusiasms, the individual—the self—is more, not less, in thrall to whatever may be the reigning ethos. Ours is a culture whose reigning ethic is surely individualism and freedom. Great and good things have come from this stress on freedom and from the insistence that there are things that cannot and must not be done for me and to me in the name of some overarching collective. It is, therefore, unsurprising that anything that comes before us in the name of "rights" and "freedom" enjoys a *prima facie* power, something akin to political grace.

But perhaps we have reached the breaking point. When Madonna proclaims, in all sincerity, that mock masturbation before tens of thousands is "freedom of expression" on a par, presumably, with the right to petition, assemble, and protest, something seems a bit out of whack—distorted, quirky, not-quite-right. I thought about this sort of thing a lot when I listened to the stories of the "Mothers of the Disappeared" in Argentina and to their invocation of the language of "human rights" as a fundamental immunity—the right not to be tortured and "disappeared." I don't believe there is a slippery slope from queasiness at, if not repudiation of, public sexual acts for profit, orchestrated masturbation, say, and putting free speech as a fundamental right of free citizens in peril. I don't think the body politic has to be nude and sexually voracious—getting, consuming, demanding pleasure. That is a symbolism that courts nihilism and privatism (however publicly it may be trumpeted) because it repudiates intergenerational, familial, and communal contexts and believes history and tradition are useful only to be trashed. Our culture panders to what social critic John O'Neill calls the "libidinal body," the body that titillates and ravishes and is best embodied as young, thin, antimaternal, calculating, and disconnected. Make no mistake about it: much of the move to imagery of the entitled self and the aspirations to which it gives rise are specifically, deeply, and troubingly antinatal—hostile to the regenerative female body and to the symbolism of social regeneration to which this body is necessarily linked and has, historically, given rise.

Don't get me wrong: not every female body must be a regenerative body. At stake here is not mandating and coercing the lives of individuals but pondering the fate of a society that, more and more, repudiates generativity as an animating image in favor of aspiration without limit of the contractual and "wanting" self. One symbol and reality of the latter is the search for intrusive intervention in human reproducing coming from those able to command the resources of genetic engineers and medical reproduction experts, also, therefore, those who have more clout over what gets lifted up as our culture's dominant sense of itself. One finds more and more the demand that babies can and must be made whenever the want is there. This demandingness, this transformation of human procreation into a technical operation, promotes a project Oliver O'Donovan calls "scientific self-transcendence." The technologizing of birth is antiregenerative, linked as it is to a refusal to accept any natural limits. What technology "can do," and the law permits, we seem ready to embrace. Our ethics rushes to catch up with the rampant rush of our forged and incited desires.

These brief reflections are needed to frame my equally brief comments on the legality, or not, of homosexual marriage. I have long favored domestic partnership possibilities—ways to regularize and stabilize commitments and relationships. But marriage is not, and never has been, primarily about two people—it is and always has been about the possibility of generativity. Although in any given instance, a marriage might not have led to the raising of a family, whether through choice or often unhappy recognition of, and final reconciliation to, the infertility of one or another spouse, the symbolism of marriage-family as social regenesis is fused in our centuries-old experience with marriage ritual, regulation, and persistence.

The point of criticism and contentions runs: in defending the family as framed within a horizon of intergenerationality, one privileges a restrictive ideal of sexual and intimate relations. There are within our society, as I already noted, those who believe this society can and should stay equally open to all alternative arrangements, treating "life-styles" as so many identical peas in a pod. To be sure, families in modernity coexist with those who live another way, whether heterosexual and homosexual unions that are by choice or by definition childless; communalists who diminish individual parental authority in favor of the preeminence of the group; and so on.

But the recognition and acceptance of plural possibilities does not mean each alternative is equal to every other with reference to specific social goods. No social order has ever existed that did not endorse certain activities and practices as preferable to others. Ethically responsible challenges to our terms of exclusion and inclusion push toward a loosening but not a wholesale negation in our normative endorsement of intergenerational family life. Those excluded by, or who exclude themselves from, the familial intergenerational ideal, should not be denied social space for their own practices. And it is possible that if what were at stake were, say, seeking out and identifying those creations of self that enhance an aesthetic construction of life and sensibility, the romantic bohemian or rebel would get higher marks than the Smith family of Remont, Nebraska. Nevertheless, we should be cautious about going too far in the direction of a wholly untrammeled pluralism lest we become so vapid that we are no longer capable of distinguishing between the moral weightiness of, say, polishing one's Porsche and sitting up all night with an ill child. The intergenerational family, as symbolism of social regenesis, as tough and compelling reality, as defining moral norm, remains central and critical in nurturing recognitions of human frailty, mortality, and finitude and in inculcating moral limits and constraints. To resolve the untidiness of our public and private relations by either reaffirming and unambiguously a set of unitary, authoritative norms or eliminating all such norms as arbitrary is to jeopardize the social goods that democratic and familial authority, paradoxical in relation to one another, promise—to men and women as parents and citizens and to their children.

Homosexuality, the Bible, and Us— A Jewish Perspective
DENNIS PRAGER

From Volume 6, no. 2 of Ultimate Issues
April–June, 1990

*A conservative talk-show host and popular Jewish intellectual
wrestles with why modern Jews should not dispense with ancient injunctions—in a leading neoconservative journal.*

. . . The Hebrew Bible, in particular the Torah (the first five
books of the Bible), has done more to civilize the world than any
other book or idea in history. It is the Hebrew Bible that gave
humanity such ideas as a universal, moral, loving God; ethical
obligations to this God; the need for history to move forward to
moral and spiritual redemption; the belief that history has meaning; and the notion that human freedom and social justice are
the divinely desired states for all people. It gave the world the
Ten Commandments and ethical monotheism.

Therefore, when this Bible makes strong moral procla-
mations, I listen with great respect. And regarding male homosexuality—female homosexuality is not mentioned—this Bible
speaks in such clear and direct language that one does not have
to be a religious fundamentalist in order to be influenced by its
views. All that is necessary is to consider oneself a serious Jew or
Christian.

Jews or Christians who take the Bible's views on homosexuality seriously are not obligated to prove that they are not funda-
mentalists or literalists, let alone bigots (though people have

used the Bible to defend bigotry). The onus is on those who view homosexuality as compatible with Judaism or Christianity to reconcile this view with their Bible.

Given the unambiguous nature of the biblical attitude toward homosexuality, however, such a reconciliation is not possible. All that is possible is to declare: "I am aware that the Bible condemns homosexuality, and I consider the Bible wrong." That would be an intellectually honest approach.

But this approach leads to another problem. If one chooses which of the Bible's moral values to take seriously (and the Bible states its prohibition of homosexuality not only as a law, but as a value—"it is an abomination"), of what moral use is the Bible?

Advocates of religious acceptance of homosexuality respond that while the Bible is morally advanced in some areas, it is morally regressive in others. Its condemnation of homosexuality is cited as one example, and the Torah's acceptance of slavery as another.

Far from being immoral, however, the Torah's prohibition of homosexuality was a major part of its liberation of the human being from the bonds of unrestrained sexuality and of women from being peripheral to men's lives.

As for slavery, while the Bible declares homosexuality wrong, it never declares slavery good. If it did, I would have to reject the Bible as a document with moral relevance to our times. With its notion of every human being created in God's image and with its central event being liberation from slavery, it was the Torah which first taught humanity that slavery is wrong. The Torah's laws regarding slavery exist not to perpetuate it, but to humanize it. And within Jewish life, these laws worked. Furthermore, the slavery that is discussed in the Torah bears no resemblance to black slavery or other instances with which we are familiar. Such slavery, which includes the kidnapping of utterly innocent people, was prohibited by the Torah.

Another argument advanced by advocates of religious acceptance of homosexuality is that the Bible prescribes the death penalty for a multitude of sins, including such seemingly inconsequential acts as gathering wood on the Sabbath. Since we no longer condemn people who violate the Sabbath, why continue to condemn people who engage in homosexual acts?

The answer is that we do not derive our approach toward homosexuality only from the fact that the Torah made it a capital offense. We learn it from the fact that the Bible *makes a moral statement* about homosexuality. It makes no such statement about gathering wood on the Sabbath. The Torah uses its strongest term of disapprobation, "abomination," to describe homosexuality. It is the Bible's moral evaluation of homosexuality that distinguishes homosexuality from other offenses, capital or otherwise. As Professor Greenberg, who betrays no inclination toward religious belief, writes, "When the word *toevah* ("abomination") does appear in the Hebrew Bible, it is sometimes applied to idolatry, cult prostitution, magic, or divination, and is sometimes used more generally. *It always conveys great repugnance*" [emphasis added].

Moreover, it lists homosexuality together with child sacrifice among the "abominations" practiced by the peoples living in the land about to be conquered by the Jews. The two are certainly not morally equatable, but they both characterized the morally primitive world that Judaism opposed. They both characterized a way of life opposite to the one that God demanded of Jews (and even of non-Jews—homosexuality is among the sexual offenses that is covered by one of the "seven laws of the children of Noah" which Judaism holds all people must observe).

Finally, the Bible adds a unique threat to the Jews if they engage in homosexuality and the other offenses of the Canaanites: "You will be vomited out of the land" just as the non-Jews who practice these things were vomited out of the land. Again, as

Greenberg notes, this threat "suggests that the offenses were considered serious indeed."

It is impossible for Judaism to make peace with homosexuality, because homosexuality denies many of Judaism's most fundamental values. It denies life; it denies God's expressed desire that men and women cohabit; and it denies the root structure that the Bible prescribes for all mankind, the family.

If one can speak of Judaism's essence, it is contained in the Torah statement, "I have set before you life and death, the blessing and the curse, and you shall choose life." Judaism affirms whatever enhances life, and it opposes or separates whatever represents death. Thus, meat (death) is separated from milk (life); menstruation (death) is separated from sexual intercourse (life); carnivorous animals (death) are separated from vegetarian, kosher animals (life). This is probably why the Torah juxtaposes child sacrifice with male homosexuality. Though they are not morally analogous, both represent death: One deprives children of life, the other prevents their having life.

God's first declaration about man (the human being generally, and the male specifically) is, "It is not good for man to be alone." Now, presumably, in order to solve the problem of man's aloneness, God could have made another man, or even a community of men. However, God solved man's aloneness by creating one other person, a woman—not a man, not a few women, not a community of men and women. Man's solitude was not a function of his not being with other people; it was a function of his being without a woman.

Of course, Judaism also holds that women need men. But both the Torah statement and Jewish law have been more adamant about men marrying than about women marrying. Judaism is worried about what happens to men and to society when men do not channel their drives into marriage. In this regard, the Torah and Judaism were highly prescient: The overwhelming majority of violent crimes are committed by unmarried men.

In order to become fully human, male and female must join. In the words of Genesis, "God created the human . . . male and female He created them." The union of male and female is not merely some lovely ideal; it is the essence of the biblical outlook on becoming human. To deny it is tantamount to denying a primary purpose of life. . . .

Judaism has a sexual ideal—marital sex. All other forms of sexual behavior, though not equally wrong, deviate from that ideal. The further they deviate, the stronger Judaism's antipathy. Thus there are varying degrees of sexual wrongs. There is, one could say, a continuum of wrong which goes from premarital sex, to adultery, and on to homosexuality, incest, and bestiality.

We can better understand why Judaism rejects homosexuality by understanding its attitudes toward these other unacceptable practices. For example, if a Jew were to argue that never marrying is as equally valid a lifestyle as marrying, normative Judaism would forcefully reject this claim. Judaism states that a life without marrying is a less holy, less complete, and a less Jewish life. Thus, only married men were allowed to be high priests, and only men who had children could sit as judges on the Jewish supreme court, the Sanhedrin.

To put it in modern terms, while an unmarried rabbi can be the spiritual leader of a congregation, he would be dismissed by almost any congregation if he publicly argued that remaining single is as Jewishly valid a way of life as married life.

Despite all this, no Jew could argue that single Jews must be ostracized from Jewish communal life. Single Jews are to be loved and included in Jewish family, social, and religious life.

These attitudes toward not marrying should help clarify Judaism's attitude toward homosexuality. First, it contradicts the Jewish ideal. Second, it cannot be held to be equally valid.

Third, those publicly committed to it may not serve as public Jewish role models. But fourth, homosexuals must be included in Jewish communal life and loved as fellow human beings and as Jews. . . .

Accepting homosexuality as the social, moral, or religious equivalent of heterosexuality would constitute the first modern assault on the extremely hard-won, millenia-old battle for a family-based, sexually monogamous society. While it is labeled as progress, the acceptance of homosexuality would not be new at all. . . .

Gay activists and some liberal groups such as the ACLU argue for the right of homosexuals to marry. Generally, two arguments are advanced—that society should not deny anyone the right to marry, and that if male homosexuals were given the right to marry, they would be considerably less likely to cruise.

The first argument is specious because there is no "right to marry." There is no right to marry more than one partner at a time, or to marry an immediate member of one's family. Society does not allow either practice. Though the ACLU and others believe that society has no rights, only individuals do, most Americans feel otherwise. Whether this will continue to be so, as Judaism and Christianity lose their influence, remains to be seen.

The second argument may have some merit, and insofar as homosexual marriages would decrease promiscuity among gay men, it would be a very positive development for both gays and society. But homosexual marriage would be unlikely to have such an effect. The male propensity to promiscuity would simply overwhelm most homosexual males' marriage vows. It is women who keep most heterosexual men monogamous, or at least far less likely to cruise, but gay men have no such brake on their cruising natures. Male nature, not the inability to marry, compels gay men to wander from man to man. This is proven by the behavior of lesbians, who, though also prevented from marrying each other, are not promiscuous. . . .

Blessing Gay and Lesbian Commitments
BISHOP   JOHN   SHELBY   SPONG

From Living in Sin?, *1990*

An Episcopalian bishop details his own coming to terms with the reality of homosexual partnerships—and why he believes gay men and women deserve the church's blessing.

Everything I now know about homosexuality, through conversations with gay and lesbian people, the books I have read, and the experts with whom I have talked, has led me to the conclusion that a homosexual orientation is a minority but perfectly natural characteristic on the human spectrum of sexuality. It is not something one chooses, it is something one is. . . .

Gays and lesbians, like all people, have unique gifts and contributions to offer the human family, some of which might well be present in them because of, not in spite of, their sexual orientation. But it is hard to discover gifts that celebrate one's being when the atmosphere in which one lives is laced with a murderous, oppressive hostility toward who one is. . . .

If my conclusions about gay and lesbian people are valid, then the whole of society must be seen as guilty of a cruel oppression of this courageous minority. The time has surely come not just to tolerate, or even to accept, but to celebrate and welcome the presence among us of our gay and lesbian fellow human beings.

One way to do that is for the church to admit publicly its own complicity in their oppression, based on its vast ignorance and prejudice. It is time to overcome that dark chapter of church history by living new chapters with an attitude that embraces yesterday's exile, practices the inclusiveness of God's love, and celebrates the unique gifts of all of God's diverse children. The one act that above all others will best show a serious intention to change the church's attitude will be for the church to state its willingness and eager desire to bless and affirm the love that binds two persons of the same gender into a life-giving relationship of mutual commitment. That ritual act alone will announce to the homosexual world and to ourselves a shift that will be believed. No matter how that liturgy is discussed or defined, the media, the critics, and the world at large will hear it and talk about it as the marriage of homosexuals. But before we decide what to call this service, we need to understand what it is and what it is not. The central clue to this is to discover what the church does and does not do in marriage.

The church does not, in fact, marry anyone. People marry each other. The state, not the church, defines the nature of legal marriage. It does so by giving to married couples the right of joint property ownership. It is not within the power of the church to change this legal fact, though its implications need to be addressed. What the church does in holy matrimony is hear people's public vows to love each other, to live in a faithful relationship, and to be mutually supportive and caring in all of life's vicissitudes. Then the church adds to that vow of commitment its blessing. That blessing is really the church's only contribution. The church blesses the commitment to be a couple that issues from the vows of the two people who stand before "God and this company." That blessing conveys ecclesiastical sanction on the relationship and the official willingness of the church and, through the church, of society to support, undergird, and stabilize in every way possible the life of the newly formed couple. The hope of the church is that this sanction and the resultant public support might enable the vows exchanged in good faith before the altar to have an increased chance of being kept.

If the conveying of blessing and official approval is the church's gift to give, then surely that can be given to any relationship of love, fidelity, commitment, and trust that issues in life for the two people involved. We have not in the past as a church withheld blessing from many things. We have blessed fields when crops were planted, houses when newly occupied, pets in honor of Saint Francis, and even the hounds at a Virginia fox hunt. We have blessed MX missiles called "Peacemakers" and warships whose sole purpose was to kill and destroy, calling them, in at least one instance, *Corpus Christi*—the Body of Christ. Why would it occur to us to withhold our blessing from a human relationship that produces a more complete person in each of the partners, because of their life together? Surely the only possible answer to that question is that the church has shared in the habitual prejudice of the ages. Now I call on the church to step out of this prejudice and bless relationships between human beings that are marked by love, fidelity, and the hope of a lifetime of mutual responsibility. What this service is called can then be left to the people involved, and they can then urge the state to accord such relationships the legal benefits of marriage. . . .

The heterosexual community needs to see and experience homosexual unions that are marked by integrity and caring and are filled with grace and beauty. The heterosexual majority seems to assume that the only form homosexual lovemaking takes is the promiscuous life of gay bars, pornography, and one-night stands. They are ever ready to condemn that behavior pattern as morally unacceptable—and so it is. But two things seem to have been overlooked by those who make these judgments. First, promiscuity, pick-up bars, pornography, and one-night stands are not unknown in the heterosexual world. That kind of behavior is destructive no matter what the sexual orientation of those who live out that style of life. Second, heterosexual people have the publicly accepted, blessed, and affirmed alternative of marriage that has as yet not been available to the homosexual population. If there is no such positive alternative for homosexual persons, then what is the church's expectation for them? If the church or society refuses to recognize or promote any positive alternative in which love and intimacy can sustain a gay or lesbian couple, then those institutions are guilty of contributing to the very promiscuity that they condemn. . . .

The fact is that the homosexual population has recognized and supported committed couples, long ahead of the church. In numbers far greater than the "straight" majority suspects, gay people have forged this alternative for themselves with no official help or sanction from anyone. Though those homosexual persons alienated from the church might not welcome the church's Johnny-come-lately arrival on this scene, I believe that the vast majority who crave a sign of society's acceptance of their existence would, if not for themselves then for others. But whether welcomed or not, this is a step the church must take *for the church's sake*. We need to be cleansed from our sin. . . .

People do change, and the knowledge explosion continues each day. I am a living example of these facts. Ten years ago I would have been shocked and aghast at the things I am writing at this moment. Five years ago I still had to be pushed to take an inclusive position. However, scientific data that made me aware that my prejudice grew out of ignorance combined with the witness of gay and lesbian people, some of whom were clergy, to educate me. When I became open to new possibilities, then the humanity of representatives of the homosexual world was able to touch my humanity. They loved me and they invited me into the integrity and life-giving power present in their relationships. It was my recognition of the meaning and validity at work in their mutually committed lives that enabled me to accept the new data and to walk slowly but surely away from the prejudice of a lifetime. . . .

The *Kedushah* of Homosexual Relationships

RABBI YOEL H. KAHN

From the Central Conference of American Rabbis Yearbook, *XCIV, 1989*

If God made some people homosexual, a rabbi at the Congregation Sha'ar Zahav in San Francisco argues, why would He not want them brought fully into the Jewish community of faith and custom?

If the goal of Jewish life is to live in *kedushah* (sanctity), can we sanctify and bless homosexual relationships without compromising the integrity of our tradition? If we do wish to bless these relationships, can we reconcile this new stand with the historical

Jewish teaching in favor of heterosexual, procreative marriage as the normative and ideal form of Jewish family life? . . . We will examine this question in relation to God, Torah, and Israel.

I begin with the most fundamental yet unanswerable question: What does God want of us? As a liberal Jew, I am usually reluctant to assert that I know precisely what "God wants." For me to begin by stating that "God calls us to affirm the sanctity of homosexual relationships" (a statement I believe to be true) would be to assert a privileged claim as little open to dispute as the counter-assertion by Rabbi David Bleich that these relationships today remain *"to'evah"* (an abomination). How would one respond to such an argument?

Thus, although our assertion of what God wants properly begins our debate, in fact it cannot. Our conclusions about God's expectations of us in a particular matter develop against the background of our unfolding, wider understanding of what God summons us to do—rooted in what we know about God and God's nature. In the foreground is all that we have learned from the scientific disciplines, from universal ethics, from Jewish tradition, and from our own prayerful conscience. It is when they touch, where the background of what we have already learned of God's expectations of us and God's nature meets foreground of knowledge, prayer, and conscientious reflection about a subject, that we may discern God's will.

My teacher Eugene Borowitz writes that he does not hear a clear message from God about homosexuality, as he has in other areas. I differ from Rabbi Borowitz. I believe that we can hear and affirm what God expects of us in this matter. My understanding of what God wants emerges from the background of God's justice and compassion, and is shaped in the foreground by religious interpretation of the insights of modern science. It is this foreground which has changed in recent years and leads me to dissent from the teachings of our received tradition.

The overwhelming consensus of modern science—in every discipline—is that homosexual relations are as "natural" to us as heterosexuality is. Now, to call something "natural" is a descriptive act; what occurs in nature is not inherently good or bad. Assigning of meaning is a religious act. I, along with many others, have come to recognize sexual orientation as a primary, deep part of the human personality, inseparably bound up with the self. Science does not know what creates homosexual attraction in some people, heterosexual attraction in others; yet today we recognize that some people can only be fulfilled in relationships with people of the same sex. What do we say to them? What does God expect of them and of us?

I do not believe that God creates in vain. Deep, heartfelt yearning for companionship and intimacy is not an abomination before God. God does not want us to send the gays and lesbians among us into exile—either cut off from the Jewish community or into internal exile, living a lie for a lifetime. I believe that the time has come, I believe that God summons us to affirm the proper and rightful place of the homosexual Jew—and her or his family—in the synagogue and in the Jewish people. . . .

When we confront the text [of the Bible] honestly, we face a twofold challenge: first, we must dissent from an explicit Biblical injunction which has been in force until modern times. Now, dissenting from Leviticus has not been an obstacle for us before; Reform Judaism has long abandoned the Biblical and rabbinic proscriptions in the area of ritual purity in marriage. Robert Kirschner . . . argues convincingly that the Biblical and rabbinic injunctions forbidding male homosexual acts are no longer applicable to the situation of homosexuals today. It is important for us to realize that the Biblical authors proscribed particular sexual acts, the motivation for which they could only understand as sinful.

We begin from an entirely different perspective than our

ancestors did. If we grant that homosexual acts are not inherently sinful, then can a homosexual relationship be sanctified? When two Jews, graduates of our schools, alumni of our camps and youth movements, members of our synagogues, promise to establish a Jewish home, pledge to live together in faithfulness and integrity, and ask for God's blessing and our own on their union, is this *to'evah* or is it *kedushah?*

Do we look at this committed and loving couple from an I–It perspective, which sees a particular act and condemns it, or with I–Thou understanding, which affirms the propriety of sexual intimacy in the context of holistic and enduring relationship? Let me be clear: I do not propose merely that we politely overlook the historical Jewish teaching condemning homosexual behavior but that we explicitly affirm its opposite: the movement from *to'evah* to *kedushah.* This transformation in our Jewish standard, from a specific act to the evaluation of the context in which acts occur, seems to me entirely consistent with Reform Jewish thought and practice.

Many are prepared to affirm that for some Jews homosexuality is the proper expression of the human need for intimacy and fulfillment. Still, I know that some are reluctant to endorse *kiddushin* (sanctified covenantal union, usually translated "marriage") for same-sex couples because these relationships apparently disregard the historical and continuing Jewish preference for what Eugene Borowitz and others have called "the procreative family." How can we grant Jewish sanctity, they ask, to a form of family which by its essence precludes procreation, a primary purpose of *kiddushin?*

My reply has three parts. First, we cannot hold homosexual families to a higher standard than we do heterosexual ones. We do not require proof of fertility or even an intention to become parents before we are willing to marry a heterosexual couple. Is the homosexual couple who uses adoption, artificial insemination, or other means to fulfill the Jewish responsibility to parent so different from the heterosexual family who does the same?

Second, does *kiddushin* require procreation? While Judaism has always had a preference for procreative marriage, our tradition has also validated the possibility that some unions will not produce children. *Halachah* states that a woman who does not bear children after ten years can be divorced by her husband. But the evidence that this law was reluctantly or negligibly enforced is precisely the type of historical example Reform responsa often cite to support the explicit expansion of a value we find implicit in our historical tradition. The Jewish tradition has never insisted that the sole purpose of sexual expression is procreation, as evidenced by the numerous rabbinic discussions on the *mitzvah* of sexual intimacy and pleasure.

Third, the situation of the gay and lesbian Jews among us points out the need for new categories in our thinking. Reform Judaism is committed to affirming the responsibility of the individual. Can we not teach that a heterosexual relationship is the proper form of *kedushah* for many and a homosexual relationship may be a proper form for others? Can we not create a plurality of expressions of convenantal responsibility and fulfillment and teach that different Jews will properly fulfill their Jewish communal and religious responsibilities in different ways?

Finally, I would like to introduce into this discussion of Torah a different text than those which have shaped our debate so far. Mine is a classic Jewish text, the record of a uniquely Jewish form of revelation—the text of our history. The history of our people, writ large, has been a continuing source of revelation. For our own generation the recollection of events that we witnessed has assumed the force of Torah, and makes demands upon us as a people and as individual Jews. But our history is not only writ large—history is also written in the small, daily events of our lives. . . .

When I arrived to assume my pulpit in San Francisco four years ago, deep down I still believed that gay and lesbian relationships and families were, somehow, not as real, not as stable, not as committed as heterosexual marriages. I could tell many stories of what I have learned since. There are the two women who have lived together for many years without familial or communal support, who have endured long distances and job transfers, because employers thought them both single and admitting their homosexuality would have endangered their livelihoods, women who have cared for each other without benefit of insurance coverage or health benefits or any legal protection. They came to me one Friday night and simply asked: "Rabbi, this is our twenty-fifth anniversary, will you say a blessing?"

Mine is a synagogue living with AIDS. I have been humbled by the unquestioning devotion of the man who, for more than two years, went to work each morning, calling intermittently throughout the day to check in on his partner, and spent each night comforting, talking, preparing meals, and waking in the middle of the night to carry his loved one to the bathroom. Who would have imagined, when they first chatted twelve years before, that their life together would take this path? The loving caregiver stayed at his partner's side throughout the period of his illness and until his death.

These many lives have taught me about the possibility of enduring loyalty, the meaning of commitment, and the discovery of reservoirs of strength in the face of unimaginable pain and suffering. If the covenant people are summoned to be God-like, then these Jews live their lives *b'tzelem Elohim* and these relationships are surely of true covenantal worth. *Kiddushin* is, in Eugene Borowitz's words, "Judaism's preferred condition in which to work out one's destiny. . . . Because it is a unique fusion of love and demand, of understanding and judgment, of personal giving and receiving, nothing else can teach us so well the meaning of covenant." If "[i]t is the situation where we are most thoroughly challenged to be a Jew and where . . . we may personally exemplify what it means to be allied with God in holiness," then the Torah scroll of lived history records the *kedushah* of these relationships.

I would like to conclude with a word about *kiddushin* and the Jewish people. I have been repeatedly asked, If we elevate homosexual families to an equal status with heterosexual families, will we not undermine the already precarious place of the traditional family? I do not believe that encouraging commitment, stability, and openness undermines the institution of family—it enhances it. At present, many gay and lesbian Jews are estranged from the synagogue, the Jewish community, and their families of origin because of continued fear, stigma, and oppression. Welcoming gay and lesbian families into the synagogue will strengthen all our families by bringing the exiles home and by reuniting children, parents, and siblings who have been forced to keep their partners and innermost lives hidden. *K'lal yisrael* (the community and unity of the Jewish people) is strengthened when we affirm that there can be more than one way to participate in the Covenant.

Creation and Natural Law

JEFFREY JOHN

From Permanent, Faithful, Stable: Christian
Same-Sex Partnerships, *1993*

*John argues from an Anglican standpoint that fidelity should
be a more central issue for Christian marriage than procreation, and that homosexuals can pass that test, if they would
only be allowed to.*

Some will still argue that even a relationship of this quality
must be condemned on the ground of Paul's so-called natural
law objection that it is against the God-given pattern of creation.
In an article defending this position one writer sums up such an
argument with the comment that "to accept homosexual acts by
inverts would be to deny the doctrine of creation . . . the whole
biblical teaching on creation, sex, marriage, forgiveness and redemption will be fundamentally altered" (G. Wenham).

So let's consider the biblical argument from creation. What,
scripturally speaking, is the purpose of sex? What was God's will
in creating male and female? One might have assumed childbirth, but, surprisingly perhaps, in Genesis itself the primary
reason that God created a companion for Adam is not said to be
procreation, but because "God said, 'It is not good for man to be
alone'" (2:18). Complementarity and companionship are at least
as much a part of God's plan in creation as childbirth. Indeed it
is remarkable that in the Genesis account childbirth emerges
only as an afterthought, and in the rather negative context of

God's punishment of Eve (3:16). It is highly significant that Jesus and Paul, while both referring to the creation story, never once mention procreation or physical sexual difference in their teaching about marriage. On the contrary, their stress is entirely on the quality of the relationship, and in particular that it should be a covenant of total sexual fidelity and indissoluble union. Furthermore, the insistence on fidelity is never explained, as we might expect, with reference to practical reasons of childbearing or domestic stability, but always with reference to the personal and spiritual implications of sexual union.

For Paul, sexual union *always* has spiritual consequences, whether for good or ill. Promiscuous sexual activity involves desecration of the body, which is a temple of the Spirit and itself a member of the Body of Christ (1 Corinthians 6: 15–20). But where sexual union expresses mutual love and commitment, that relationship becomes a μυστήριον (Ephesians 5: 32), a holy mystery or sacrament which reflects the covenant union of the faithful love between Christ and the Church, and which itself becomes a channel of love and grace in the world. For each human being to make such a covenant is for him or her to realize an important part of what it means to be made in God's image. It means to further his primary and ultimate purpose in creation by reproducing the kind of creative (but not necessarily procreative) self-giving love that is basic to God's own nature. Accepting homosexual relationships does not mean jettisoning this fundamental biblical teaching about the sacramental character of human sexuality.

Those who continue to cling to a natural law argument against homosexuality on the basis of Romans 1 should also be reminded that Paul appeals more frequently and clearly to natural law and the creation story in order to justify his now abandoned teachings about the veiling and silencing of women. Paul said that women must be veiled because man was created first and it is primarily man who is the image of God (1 Corinthians 11: 7–8). It is shameful for a man to wear long hair and a woman to wear short hair because "nature itself teaches us so" (1 Corinthians 11: 14; a much clearer expression of "natural law" than anything in Romans 1). No woman is permitted to teach or to hold authority over men, and women are commanded to be silent "because Adam was formed first, then Eve; and Adam was not deceived, but the woman was deceived and became a transgressor" (1 Timothy 2: 12–14). These are theological arguments which appeal to God's plan in creation no less than Romans 1: 18ff., and indeed Paul is much clearer about their authoritative status and the practical rules he intends to deduce from them, even to the point of saying the silencing of women is a command of the Lord, and if anyone disputes it he is to be rejected (1 Corinthians 14: 33–38). It is obvious that Paul lays far more weight of doctrine and authority on this teaching about women than on his passing references to homosexuality. Yet the fact that today it is consistently ignored, even in the most traditional churches, is not felt to "deny the doctrine of creation" or "to alter fundamentally the whole biblical teaching on creation, sex, marriage, forgiveness and redemption."

I remarked that the original biblical prohibition of homosexuality was probably written in the situation of the Babylonian exile, as a mark of Jewish separateness from the surrounding culture. Babylon remains a powerful symbol for modern secular society, and in one sense it might fairly be argued that the situation of Christians has *not* changed. As "aliens and exiles" Christians still understand themselves to be called, no less than the Jews in Babylon, to a distinctive morality and a distinctive holiness which will challenge the world in sexual matters as in all else (1 Peter 2: 3). This is not to be denied. The point is that the most

distinctive and constructive witness that homosexual Christians
can offer, both to "Babylon" in the shape of the secular gay scene
and to the Church itself, is the witness of relationships marked
by the same quality of holy and faithful love to which heterosexual Christians are called in marriage. . . .

What You Do
ANDREW   SULLIVAN

From The New Republic, *March 3, 1996*

*If procreation is essential to marriage, then why doesn't
Patrick Buchanan have any children?*

A ndrew, it's not who you are. It is what you do!" Buchanan
yelled across the table. We were engaged in a typically subtle
"Crossfire" debate on same-gender marriage. I'd expected the
explosion, but it nevertheless surprised me. Only minutes before, off the air, Buchanan had been cooing over my new hair-
cut. But at least he could distinguish, like any good Jesuit,
between the sin and the sinner. It was when his mind drifted to
thoughts of homosexual copulation that his mood violently
swung.

Okay, Pat, let's talk copulation. It isn't only me that has a
problem here.

Buchanan's fundamental issue with "what homosexuals do"

is that it's what he calls a "vice." (I'll leave aside the demeaning reduction of "what homosexuals do" to a sexual act.) Now, there's a clear meaning for a vice: it's something bad that a person freely chooses to do, like, say, steal. But Buchanan concedes that gay relations aren't quite like that; they are related to a deeper, "very powerful impulse," (his words) to commit them. So a homosexual is like a kleptomaniac who decides to steal. Kleptomania is itself an involuntary, blameless condition, hard to resist, but still repressible. Kleptomaniacs, in Buchanan's words, "have the capacity not to engage in those acts. They have free will."

So far, so persuasive. The question begged, of course, is why same-gender sexual acts are wrong in the first place. In the case of kleptomania it's a no-brainer: someone else is injured directly by your actions; they're robbed. But, in the case of homosexual acts, where two consenting adults are engaged in a private activity, it's not at all clear who the injured party is. Buchanan's concern with homosexual acts derives, of course, from the Roman Catholic Church. And the Church's teaching about homosexual sex is closely related to its teaching about the sinfulness of all sexual activity outside a loving, procreative Church marriage.

The sexual act, the Church affirms, must have two core elements: a "procreative" element, the willingness to be open to the creation of new life; and a "unitive" element, the intent to affirm a loving, faithful union. In this, the Church doesn't single out homosexuals for condemnation. The sin of gay sex is no more and no less sinful on these grounds than masturbation, extramarital sex, marital sex with contraception, heterosexual oral sex or, indeed, marital sex without love.

In some ways, of course, homosexual sex is *less* sinful. The heterosexual who chooses in marriage to use contraception, or who masturbates, is turning away from a viable alternative: a unitive, procreative sexual life. The homosexual has no such option; she is denied, because of something she cannot change, a sexual act which is both unitive and procreative. If a lesbian had sexual relations with a man, she could be procreative but not unitive, because she couldn't fully love him. And if she had sex with another woman, she could be unitive in her emotions but, because of biology, not procreative. So the lesbian is trapped by the Church's teaching, excluded from a loving relationship for no fault of her own; and doomed to a loveless life as a result.

The Church urges compassion for such people (a teaching which, somewhere along the way, seems to have escaped Buchanan). But the Church's real compassion is reserved for another group of people who, like homosexuals, are unable, through no fault of their own, to have unitive and procreative sex: infertile heterosexuals. The Church expresses its compassion not by excluding these couples from the sacrament of marriage, but by including them. Sterile couples are allowed to marry in church and to have sex; so are couples in which the wife is post-menopausal. It's understood that such people have no choice in the matter; they may indeed long to have unitive and procreative sex; and to have children. They are just tragically unable, as the Church sees it, to experience the joy of a procreative married life.

The question, of course, is Why doesn't this apply to homosexuals? In official teaching, the Church has conceded (Buchanan hedges on this point) that some homosexuals "are definitively such because of some kind of innate instinct or a pathological constitution judged to be incurable." They may want, with all the will in the world, to have a unitive and procreative relationship; they can even intend to be straight. But they can't and they aren't. So why aren't they allowed to express their love as humanely as they possibly can, along with the infertile and the elderly?

The theologians' best answer to this is simply circular. Marriage, they assert, is by definition between a man and a woman. When pressed further, they venture: well, sexual relations between two infertile heterosexuals could, by a miracle, yield a child. But, if it's a miracle you're counting on, why couldn't it happen to two gay people? Who is to put a limit on the power of God? Well, the Church counters, homosexuality isn't natural, it's an "objective disorder." But what is infertility if it isn't a disorder? The truth is, as the current doctrine now stands, the infertile are defined by love and compassion, while homosexuals are defined by loneliness and sin. The Church has no good case why this should be so.

I harp on this issue of the infertile for one delicate reason: Patrick and Shelley Buchanan do not have kids. Why not? Generally, I wouldn't dream of bringing up such a question, but I am merely adhering to the same rules Buchanan has laid out for me. From the public absence of his children, as from the public statement of my homosexuality, I can infer certain things about Buchanan's "lifestyle." Either Buchanan is using contraception, in which case he is a hypocrite; or he or his wife is infertile, and he is, one assumes, engaging in non-procreative sex. Either way, I can see no good reason why his sexual life is any more sinful than mine.

Of course, by merely bringing up Buchanan's childlessness, I will be judged to have exceeded the bounds of legitimate debate. But why doesn't the same outrage attach to Buchanan for his fulminations against others whose inability to lead a procreative married life is equally involuntary? Of course, Buchanan goes even further: because of what he infers about my private sexual life, he would celebrate discrimination against me and use the bully pulpit of a campaign to defame me. Why is it unthinkable that someone should apply the same standards to him?

I'll tell you why it's unthinkable. No one should be singled out and stigmatized for something he cannot change, especially if that something is already a source of pain and struggle. Indeed, I would regard anyone's inability to have children, if he wanted to, to be a sadness I should privately sympathize with and publicly say nothing about. Why, I wonder, cannot Buchanan express the same compassion and fairness for me?

CHAPTER THREE

It Is So Ordered?
THE PATH OF THE COURTS

Until recently, no court anywhere in the United States extended civil marriage rights to lesbians and gay men. Within the past decade, however, state courts in Hawaii, Alaska, Vermont, and Massachusetts have interpreted their own constitutions—which are often more protective of civil rights than the federal Constitution—to recognize the rights of gays and lesbians to enter the institution of civil marriage. Both the Hawaii and Alaska rulings were invalidated by legislative initiatives amending their respective constitutions, defining marriage as heterosexual in nature. In Vermont, the state's highest court gave the legislature an opportunity to create a parallel institution—"civil unions"—that bestows on gays and lesbians all of the state (but not federal) rights and obligations of marriage, without actually opening up the institution of marriage itself.

Although the United States Supreme Court has not ruled on the issue of civil marriage for gays and lesbians, it has issued a number of important rulings on the distinct issues of marriage and homosex-

uality. For instance, in 2003 the High Court upheld sexual privacy rights for gays and lesbians, a ruling some criticized as paving the way for recognition of civil marriage. Shortly afterward, the highest court in Massachusetts ordered civil marriage for all citizens, gay and straight alike, and rejected proposals for a civil-union measure proposed by the state legislature. The Massachusetts legislature is considering amending its constitution to invalidate the court decision, but the amendment process would not be completed until long after the court ruling takes effect, on May 17, 2004.

In the wake of the Massachusetts ruling, members of the U.S. Congress began to introduce proposals to amend the U.S. Constitution that would define, for federal purposes, marriage as between one man and one woman, as well as prohibit state courts from interpreting their own constitutions to require any formal recognition of same-sex relationships and preclude state legislatures from passing legislation extending marriage to gays and lesbians. (The U.S. amendment would purportedly allow legislatures to enact civil union bills, though the actual wording of the amendment is ambiguous at best.) The debate over the amendment rages as this book goes to print.

The extracts that follow present a chronology of the major state and federal rulings on marriage and homosexuality. Taken together, these diverse rulings show the wrestling of the legal mind with the issues raised by marriage equality. Should an institution that bestows such important legal safeguards be denied law-abiding lesbians and gay men? What about gay families, and the situation befalling children of gay parents who exist in a state of legal limbo? The implications of these legal arguments for the broader political debate are discussed further in Chapters 6 and 10.

Race and the Right to Marry
LOVING V. VIRGINIA

From Justice Warren's ruling for the
U.S. Supreme Court, June 1967

*This is the finding of the famous interracial marriage case that
struck down antimiscegenation laws on the grounds that they
violated equal protection. Notice how strongly the Court defends the freedom to marry: "one of the vital personal rights
essential to the orderly pursuit of happiness by free men."*

The two statutes under which appellants were convicted and
sentenced are part of a comprehensive statutory scheme aimed
at prohibiting and punishing interracial marriages. The Lovings
were convicted of violating § 20–58 of the Virginia Code:

"Leaving State to evade law.—If any white person and colored person shall go out of this State, for the purpose of being
married, and with the intention of returning, and be married out
of it, and afterwards return to and reside in it, cohabiting as man
and wife, they shall be punished as provided in § 20–59, and the
marriage shall be governed by the same law as if it had been solemnized in this State. The fact of their cohabitation here as man
and wife shall be evidence of their marriage.". . .

There can be no question but that Virginia's miscegenation
statutes rest solely upon distinctions drawn according to race.
The statutes proscribe generally accepted conduct if engaged
in by members of different races. Over the years, this Court has
consistently repudiated "[d]istinctions between citizens solely

because of their ancestry" as being "odious to a free people whose institutions are founded upon the doctrine of equality.". . .

At the very least, the Equal Protection Clause demands that racial classifications, especially suspect in criminal statutes, be subjected to the "most rigid scrutiny,". . . and if they are ever to be upheld, they must be shown to be necessary to the accomplishment of some permissible state objective, independent of the racial discrimination which it was the object of the Fourteenth Amendment to eliminate. Indeed, two members of this Court have already stated that they "cannot conceive of a valid legislative purpose . . . which makes the color of a person's skin the test of whether his conduct is a criminal offense.". . .

There is patently no legitimate overriding purpose independent of invidious racial discrimination which justifies this classification. The fact that Virginia prohibits only interracial marriages involving white persons demonstrates that the racial classifications must stand on their own justification, as measures designed to maintain White Supremacy. We have consistently denied the constitutionality of measures which restrict the rights of citizens on account of race. There can be no doubt that restricting the freedom to marry solely because of racial classifications violates the central meaning of the Equal Protection Clause. . . .

These statutes also deprive the Lovings of liberty without due process of law in violation of the Due Process Clause of the Fourteenth Amendment. The freedom to marry has long been recognized as one of the vital personal rights essential to the orderly pursuit of happiness by free men. . . .

Marriage is one of the "basic civil rights of man," fundamental to our very existence and survival. . . .

To deny this fundamental freedom on so unsupportable a basis as the racial classifications embodied in these statutes, classifications so directly subversive of the principle of equality at the heart of the Fourteenth Amendment, is surely to deprive all the State's citizens of liberty without due process of law. The Fourteenth Amendment requires that the freedom of choice to marry not be restricted by invidious racial discriminations. Under our Constitution, the freedom to marry, or not marry, a person of another race resides with the individual and cannot be infringed by the State. . . .

These convictions must be reversed.

It is so ordered.

The Definitional Argument
JONES V. HALLAHAN

From the ruling of the Court of Appeals of Kentucky, November 1973

The Court of Appeals of Kentucky sets out the classic legal argument: marriage by definition involves a man and a woman. End of discussion.

The sections of Kentucky statutes relating to marriage do not include a definition of that term. It must therefore be defined according to common usage.

Webster's New International Dictionary, second edition, defines marriage as follows:

A state of being married, or being united to a person or persons of the opposite sex as husband or wife; also, the mutual relation of husband and wife; wedlock; abstractly, the institution whereby men and women are joined in a special kind of social and legal dependence, for the purpose of founding and maintaining a family.

The *Century Dictionary and Encyclopedia* defines marriage as:

The legal union of a man with a woman for life; the state or condition of being married; the legal relation of spouses to each other; wedlock; the formal declaration or contract by which a man and a woman join in wedlock.

Black's Law Dictionary, fourth edition, defines marriage as:

The civil status, condition or relation of one man and one woman united in law for life, for the discharge to each other and the community of the duties legally incumbent upon those whose association is founded on the distinction of sex.

Kentucky statutes do not specifically prohibit marriage between persons of the same sex nor do they authorize the issuance of a marriage license to such persons.

Marriage was a custom long before the state commenced to issue licenses for that purpose. For a time the records of marriage were kept by the church. Some states even now recognize a common-law marriage which has neither the benefit of license nor clergy. In all cases, however, marriage has always been considered as the union of a man and a woman and we have been presented with no authority to the contrary.

It appears to us that appellants are prevented from marrying, not by the statutes of Kentucky or the refusal of the County Court Clerk of Jefferson County to issue them a license, but rather by their own incapability of entering into a marriage as that term is defined.

A license to enter into a status or a relationship which the parties are incapable of achieving is a nullity. If the appellants had concealed from the clerk the fact that they were of the same sex and he had issued a license to them and a ceremony had been performed, the resulting relationship would not constitute a marriage . . .

No Right to Sodomy
BOWERS V. HARDWICK

From Justice White's and Justice Blackmun's opinions for the U.S. Supreme Court, June 1986

Here's the now-famous (and overruled) decision upholding Georgia's ban on sodomy. The Court ruled that popular sentiment regarding the immorality of homosexuality was a valid basis for the legislation. However, twenty years later, in Lawrence v. Texas, *the Court ruled that such morals-based legislation no longer satisfied the dictates of the Court's minimal rational-basis test.*

The Path of the Courts

Justice White

. . . After being charged with violating the Georgia statute criminalizing sodomy by committing that act with another adult male in the bedroom of his home, respondent Hardwick (respondent) brought suit in Federal District Court, challenging the constitutionality of the statute insofar as it criminalized consensual sodomy. The court granted the defendants' motion to dismiss for failure to state a claim. The Court of Appeals reversed and remanded, holding that the Georgia statute violated respondent's fundamental rights.

Held: The Georgia statute is constitutional. . . .

The Constitution does not confer a fundamental right upon homosexuals to engage in sodomy. None of the fundamental rights announced in this Court's prior cases involving family relationships, marriage, or procreation bear any resemblance to the right asserted in this case. And any claim that those cases stand for the proposition that any kind of private sexual conduct between consenting adults is constitutionally insulated from state proscription is unsupportable. . . .

Against a background in which many States have criminalized sodomy and still do, to claim that a right to engage in such conduct is "deeply rooted in this Nation's history and tradition" or "implicit in the concept of ordered liberty" is, at best, facetious. . . .

There should be great resistance to expand the reach of the Due Process Clauses to cover new fundamental rights. Otherwise, the Judiciary necessarily would take upon itself further authority to govern the country without constitutional authority. The claimed right in this case falls far short of overcoming this resistance. . . .

The fact that homosexual conduct occurs in the privacy of the home does not affect the result. . . .

Sodomy laws should not be invalidated on the asserted basis that majority belief that sodomy is immoral is an inadequate rationale to support the laws. . . .

Justice Blackmun

. . . This case is no more about "a fundamental right to engage in homosexual sodomy," as the Court purports to declare . . . than *Stanley v. Georgia* . . . was about a fundamental right to watch obscene movies, or *Katz v. United States* . . . was about a fundamental right to place interstate bets from a telephone booth. Rather, this case is about "the most comprehensive of rights and the right most valued by civilized men," namely "the right to be let alone" *Olmstead v. United States.*

Like Justice Holmes, I believe that "[i]t is revolting to have no better reason for a rule of law than that so it was laid down in the time of Henry IV. It is still more revolting if the grounds upon which it was laid down have vanished long since, and the rule simply persists from blind imitation of the past.". . . A State can no more punish private behavior because of religious intolerance than it can punish such behavior because of racial animus. "The Constitution cannot control such prejudices, but neither can it tolerate them. Private biases may be outside the reach of the law, but the law cannot, directly or indirectly, give them effect" *Palmore v. Sidoti.*

Even Prisoners Can Marry
TURNER V. SAFELY

*From Justice O'Connor's ruling for the majority,
U.S. Supreme Court, June 1987*

*Justice Sandra Day O'Connor explains why many aspects of
marriage can apply even to prison inmates. The right of convicted murderers to marry is inviolable, yet the right of homosexuals is not.*

It is settled that a prison inmate "retains those [constitutional]
rights that are not inconsistent with his status as a prisoner or
with the legitimate penological objectives of the corrections
system." . . .

The right to marry, like many other rights, is subject to substantial restrictions as a result of incarceration. Many important
attributes of marriage remain, however, after taking into account
the limitations imposed by prison life. First, inmate marriages,
like others, are expressions of emotional support and public
commitment. These elements are an important and significant
aspect of the marital relationship. In addition, many religions
recognize marriage as having spiritual significance; for some inmates and their spouses, therefore, the commitment of marriage
may be an exercise of religious faith as well as an expression of
personal dedication. Third, most inmates eventually will be released by parole or commutation, and therefore most inmate
marriages are formed in the expectation that they ultimately will
be fully consummated. Finally, marital status often is a precondition to the receipt of government benefits (e.g., Social Security

benefits), property rights (e.g., tenancy by the entirety, inheritance rights), and other, less tangible benefits (e.g., legitimation of children born out of wedlock). These incidents of marriage, like the religious and personal aspects of the marriage commitment, are unaffected by the fact of confinement or the pursuit of legitimate corrections goals. Taken together, we conclude that these remaining elements are sufficient to form a constitutionally protected marital relationship in the prison context. . . .

The Sex Discrimination Point: Upheld
BAEHR V. LEWIN

From the Supreme Court's ruling,
Supreme Court of Hawaii, May 1993

Here's the ruling that roiled America. The Hawaii court's decision that banning same-sex marriage violated the Hawaii Constitution's equal rights clause put the ruling on very firm legal ground. Notice how the Court dismisses civil marriage rights as an extension of a right to privacy. It is a ruling as dramatic in its implications as it is conservative in its methodology.

The precise question facing this court is whether we will extend the present boundaries of the fundamental right of marriage to include same-sex couples, or, put another way, whether we will hold that same-sex couples possess a fundamental right to marry. In effect, as the applicant couples frankly admit, we are being asked to recognize a new fundamental right. There is no doubt that "[a]s the ultimate judicial tribunal with final, unreviewable authority to interpret and enforce the Hawaii Constitution, we are free to give broader privacy protection . . . than that given by the federal constitution.". . . However, we have also held that the privacy right found in article I, section 6 is similar to the federal right and that no "purpose to lend talismanic effect" to abstract phrases such as "intimate decision" or "personal autonomy" can "be inferred from [article I, section 6], any more than . . . from the federal decisions.". . .

In the case that first recognized a fundamental right to privacy, *Griswold v. Connecticut,* . . . the Court declared that it was "deal[ing] with a right . . . older than the Bill of Rights[.]". . . And in a concurring opinion, Justice Goldberg observed that judges "determining which rights are fundamental" must look not to "personal and private notions," but

> to the "traditions and [collective] conscience of our people" to determine whether a principle is "so rooted [there] . . . as to be ranked as fundamental.". . . The inquiry is whether a right involved "is of such a character that it cannot be denied without violating those 'fundamental principles of liberty and justice which lie at the base of all our civil and political institutions.'". . .

Applying the foregoing standards to the present case, we do not believe that a right to same-sex marriage is so rooted in the traditions and collective conscience of our people that failure to recognize it would violate the fundamental principles of liberty and justice that lie at the base of all our civil and political institutions. Neither do we believe that a right to same-sex marriage is implicit in the concept of ordered liberty, such that neither liberty nor justice would exist if it were sacrificed. Accordingly, we hold that the applicant couples do not have a fundamental constitutional right to same-sex marriage arising out of the right to privacy or otherwise. . . .

Marriage is a state-conferred legal status, the existence of which gives rise to rights and benefits reserved exclusively to that particular relationship. This court construes marriage as "'a partnership to which both partners bring their financial resources as well as their individual energies and efforts.'". . . So zealously has this court guarded the state's role as the exclusive progenitor of the marital partnership that it declared, over seventy years ago, that "common law" marriages—*i.e.,* "marital" unions existing in the absence of a state-issued license and not performed by a person or society possessing governmental authority to solemnize marriages—would no longer be recognized in the Territory of Hawaii. . . .

The applicant couples correctly contend that the [Department of Health's] refusal to allow them to marry on the basis that they are members of the same sex deprives them of access to a multiplicity of rights and benefits that are contingent upon that status. Although it is unnecessary in this opinion to engage in an encyclopedic recitation of all of them, a number of the most salient marital rights and benefits are worthy of note. They include: (1) a variety of state income tax advantages, including deductions, credits, rates, exemptions, and estimates . . . (2) public assistance from and exemptions relating to the Department of Human Services . . . (3) control, division, acquisition, and disposition of community property . . . (4) rights relating to dower, curtesy, and inheritance . . . (5) rights to notice, protection, benefits, and inheritance . . . (6) award of child custody and support payments in divorce proceedings . . . (7) the right to spousal support . . . (8) the right to enter into premarital agreements . . . (9) the right to change of name . . . (10) the right to file a nonsupport action . . . (11) post-divorce rights relating to support and property division . . . (12) the benefit of the spousal privilege and confidential marital communications . . . (13) the benefit of the exemption or real property from attachment or execution . . . and (14) the right to bring a wrongful death action. . . .

The equal protection clauses of the United States and Hawaii Constitutions are not mirror images of one another. The fourteenth amendment to the United States Constitution somewhat concisely provides, in relevant part, that a state may not "deny to any person within its jurisdiction the equal protection of the laws." Hawaii's counterpart is more elaborate. Article I, section 5 of the Hawaii Constitution provides in relevant part that "[n]o person shall . . . be denied the equal protection of the laws, *nor be denied the enjoyment of the person's civil rights or be discriminated against in the exercise thereof because of* race, religion, *sex,* or ancestry" (emphasis added). Thus, by its plain language, the Hawaii Constitution prohibits state-sanctioned discrimination against any person in the exercise of his or her civil rights on the basis of sex. . . . Rudimentary principles of statutory construction render manifest the fact that, by its plain language, HRS § 572-1 restricts the marital relation to a male and a female. . . . Accordingly, on its face and (as Lewin admits) as applied, HRS § 572-1 denies same-sex couples access to the marital status and its concomitant rights and benefits. . . .

Relying primarily on four decisions construing the law of other jurisdictions, Lewin contends that "the fact that homosexual [sic—actually, same-sex] partners cannot form a state-licensed marriage is not the product of impermissible discrimination" implicating equal protection considerations, but rather "a function of their biologic inability as a couple to satisfy the definition of the status to which they aspire.". . . Put differently, Lewin proposes that "the right of persons of the same sex to marry one another does not exist because marriage, by definition and usage, means a special relationship between a man and a woman.". . .

We believe Lewin's argument to be circular and unpersuasive. . . .

The facts in *Loving* and the respective reasoning of the Virginia courts, on the one hand, and the United States Supreme Court, on the other, both discredit the reasoning . . . and unmask the tautological and circular nature of Lewin's argument that HRS § 572-1 does not implicate article I, section 5 of the Hawaii Constitution because same-sex marriage is an innate impossibility. Analogously to Lewin's argument and the rationale of the *Jones* court, the Virginia courts declared that interracial marriage simply could not exist because the Deity had deemed such a union intrinsically unnatural . . . , and, in effect, because it had theretofore never been the "custom" of the state to recognize mixed marriages, marriage "always" having been construed to presuppose a different configuration. With all due respect to the Virginia courts of a bygone era, we do not believe that trial judges are the ultimate authorities on the subject of Divine Will, and, as *Loving* amply demonstrates, constitutional law may mandate, like it or not, that customs change with an evolving social order. . . .

"Whenever a denial of equal protection of the laws is alleged, as a rule our initial inquiry has been whether the legislation in question should be subjected to 'strict scrutiny' or to a 'rational basis' test.". . . [The Court then examined its own constitution's Equal Rights Amendment in light of Supreme Court case law, and concluded that any state legislation making distinctions based on sex would be subjected to the most rigorous "strict scrutiny" test.]

Accordingly, we hold that sex is a "suspect category" for purposes of equal protection analysis under article I, section 5 of the Hawaii Constitution and that HRS § 572-1 is subject to the "strict scrutiny" test. It therefore follows, and we so hold, that (1) HRS § 572-1 is presumed to be unconstitutional (2) unless Lewin, as an agent of the State of Hawaii, can show that (a) the statute's sex-based classification is justified by compelling state interests and (b) the statute is narrowly drawn to avoid unnecessary abridgements of the applicant couples' constitutional rights. . . .

As a final matter, we are compelled to respond to Judge Heen's suggestion that denying the appellants access to the multitude of statutory benefits "conferred upon spouses in a legal marriage . . . is a matter for the legislature, which can express the will of the populace in deciding whether such benefits should be extended to persons in [the applicant couples'] circumstances.". . . . In effect, we are being accused of engaging in judicial legislation. We are not. The result we reach today is in complete harmony with the *Loving* Court's observation that any state's powers to regulate marriage are subject to the constraints imposed by the constitutional right to the equal protection of the laws. . . .

If it should ultimately be determined that the marriage laws of Hawaii impermissibly discriminate against the appellants, based on the suspect category of sex, then that would be the result of the interrelation of existing legislation.

[W]hether the legislation under review is wise or unwise is a matter with which we have nothing to do. Whether it . . . work[s] well or work[s] ill presents a question entirely irrelevant to the issue. The only legitimate inquiry we can make is whether it is constitutional. If it is not, its virtues, if it have any, cannot save it; if it is, its faults cannot be invoked to accomplish its destruction. If the provisions of the Constitution be not upheld when they pinch as well as when they comfort, they may as well be abandoned. . . .

Homosexuals and Equal Protection

ROMER V. EVANS

From Justice Kennedy's majority ruling and Justice Scalia's dissent, U.S. Supreme Court, May 1996

In the middle of the marriage wars came this decision in the summer of 1996: that Colorado's Amendment 2 unconstitutionally singled out homosexuals as a class by deeming them ineligible for protective legislation. For several years constitutional scholars debated the significance of Justice Kennedy's majority opinion. And even though the Court did not rely on the Romer decision when, seven years later, in Lawrence v. Texas (see page 106), it invalidated thirteen state laws prohibiting consensual sodomy, Romer appears to signal the Court's growing solicitude for the concerns of lesbians and gay men.

Justice Kennedy

One century ago, the first Justice Harlan admonished this Court that the Constitution "neither knows nor tolerates classes among citizens" *Plessy v. Ferguson* (1896) (dissenting opinion). Unheeded then, those words now are understood to state a commitment to the law's neutrality where the rights of persons are at stake. The Equal Protection Clause enforces this principle and today requires us to hold invalid a provision of Colorado's Constitution.

The enactment challenged in this case is an amendment to the Constitution of the State of Colorado, adopted in a 1992 statewide referendum. The parties and the state courts refer to it as "Amendment 2," its designation when submitted to the voters. The impetus for the amendment and the contentious campaign that preceded its adoption came in large part from ordinances that had been passed in various Colorado municipalities. . . . What gave rise to that statewide controversy was the protection the ordinances afforded to persons discriminated against by reason of their sexual orientation. Amendment 2 repeals these ordinances to the extent they prohibit discrimination on the basis of "homosexual, lesbian or bisexual orientation, conduct, practices or relationships."

Yet Amendment 2, in explicit terms, does more than repeal or rescind these provisions. It prohibits all legislative, executive or judicial action at any level of state or local government designed to protect the named class. . . .

The state's principle argument in defense of Amendment 2 is that it puts gays and lesbians in the same position as all other persons. So, the state says, the measure does no more than deny homosexuals special rights. This reading of the amendment's language is implausible. . . .

Sweeping and comprehensive is the change in legal status effected by this law. So much is evident from the ordinances that the Colorado Supreme Court declared would be void by operation of Amendment 2. Homosexuals, by state decree, are put in a solitary class with respect to transactions and relations in both the private and governmental spheres. The amendment withdraws from homosexuals, but no others, specific legal protection from the injuries caused by discrimination, and it forbids reinstatement of these laws and policies. . . .

· We cannot accept the view that Amendment 2's prohibition on specific legal protections does no more than deprive homosexuals of special rights. To the contrary, the amendment imposes a special disability upon those persons alone. Homosexuals are forbidden the safeguards that others enjoy or may seek without constraint. . . . We find nothing special in the protections Amendment 2 withholds. These are protections taken for granted by most people either because they already have them or do not need them. . . .

Central to the idea of the rule of law and to our own Constitution's guarantee of equal protection is the principle that government and each of its parts remain open on impartial terms to all who seek its assistance. Respect for this principle explains why laws singling out a certain class of citizens for disfavored legal status or general hardships are rare. A law declaring that in general it shall be more difficult for one group of citizens than for all others to seek aid from the government is itself a denial of equal protection of the laws in the most literal sense. "The guaranty of 'equal protection of the laws is a pledge of the protection of equal laws.'". . .

The primary rationale the state offers for Amendment 2 is respect for other citizens' freedom of association, and in particular the liberties of landlords or employers who have personal or religious objections to homosexuality.

Colorado also cites its interest in conserving resources to fight discrimination against other groups. The breadth of the amendment is so far removed from these particular justifications that we find it impossible to credit them. . . .

We must conclude that Amendment 2 classifies homosexuals not to further a proper legislative end but to make them unequal to everyone else. This Colorado cannot do. A state cannot so deem a class of persons a stranger to its laws. . . .

Justice Scalia

The Court has mistaken a Kulturkampf for a fit of spite. . . . No principle set forth in the Constitution . . . prohibits what

Colorado has done here. But the case for Colorado is much stronger than that. What it has done is not only unprohibited, but eminently reasonable. . . .

The Court's opinion contains grim, disapproving hints that Coloradans have been guilty of "animus" or "animosity" toward homosexuality. . . . Of course it is our moral heritage that one should not hate any human being or class of human beings. But I had thought that one could consider certain conduct reprehensible—murder, for example, or polygamy, or cruelty to animals—and could exhibit even "animus" toward such conduct. . . . The Colorado amendment does not, to speak entirely precisely, prohibit giving favored status to people who are homosexuals; they can be favored for many reasons—for example, because they are senior citizens or members of racial minorities. But it prohibits giving them favored status because of their homosexual conduct. . . .

There is a problem, however, which arises when criminal sanction of homosexuality is eliminated but moral and social disapprobation of homosexuality is meant to be retained. . . . Because those who engage in homosexual conduct tend to reside in disproportionate numbers in certain communities, have high disposable income and of course care about homosexual-rights issues much more ardently than the public at large, they possess political power much greater than their numbers, both locally and statewide. Quite understandably, they devote this political power to achieving not merely a grudging social toleration, but full social acceptance, of homosexuality. . . .

Today's opinion has no foundation in American constitutional law, and barely pretends to. The people of Colorado have adopted an entirely reasonable provision which does not even disfavor homosexuals in any substantive sense, but merely denies them preferential treatment. Amendment 2 is designed to prevent piecemeal deterioration of the sexual morality favored by a majority of Coloradans, and is not only an appropriate means to that legitimate end, but a means that Americans have employed before. Striking it down is an act not of judicial judgment, but of political will.

The Right to Sodomy Upheld
LAWRENCE V. TEXAS

From Justice Kennedy's majority ruling and Justice Scalia's dissent, U.S. Supreme Court, June 2003

The single most serious barrier to recognizing the right to marry was a 1986 Supreme Court decision, Bowers v. Hardwick, *which upheld state laws criminalizing consensual sodomy. In 2003, the Supreme Court revisited the issue of sodomy laws, striking down the remaining thirteen state provisions (four of which targeted exclusively same-sex behavior) and overruling* Bowers. *The* Lawrence *majority opinion, penned by Justice Anthony Kennedy, made little if any reference to the marriage issue. But Justice Antonin Scalia, in an acerbic dissent, pulled language from the majority ruling suggesting that the Court might eventually extend marriage rights to gays and lesbians.*

The Path of the Courts

Justice Kennedy

The question before the Court is the validity of a Texas statute making it a crime for two persons of the same sex to engage in certain intimate sexual conduct.

In Houston, Texas, officers of the Harris County Police Department were dispatched to a private residence in response to a reported weapons disturbance. They entered an apartment where one of the petitioners, John Geddes Lawrence, resided. The right of the police to enter does not seem to have been questioned. The officers observed Lawrence and another man, Tyron Garner, engaging in a sexual act. The two petitioners were arrested, held in custody overnight, and charged and convicted before a Justice of the Peace.

The complaints described their crime as "deviate sexual intercourse, namely anal sex, with a member of the same sex (man)."

The petitioners were adults at the time of the alleged offense. Their conduct was in private and consensual.

The laws involved in *Bowers* and here are, to be sure, statutes that purport to do no more than prohibit a particular sexual act. Their penalties and purposes, though, have more far-reaching consequences, touching upon the most private human conduct, sexual behavior, and in the most private of places, the home. The statutes do seek to control a personal relationship that, whether or not entitled to formal recognition in the law, is within the liberty of persons to choose without being punished as criminals.

This, as a general rule, should counsel against attempts by the State, or a court, to define the meaning of the relationship or to set its boundaries absent injury to a person or abuse of an institution the law protects. It suffices for us to acknowledge that adults may choose to enter upon this relationship in the confines of their homes and their own private lives and still retain their dignity as free persons. When sexuality finds overt expression in intimate conduct with another person, the conduct can be but one element in a personal bond that is more enduring. The liberty protected by the Constitution allows homosexual persons the right to make this choice.

The central holding of *Bowers* has been brought in question by this case, and it should be addressed. Its continuance as precedent demeans the lives of homosexual persons.

Bowers was not correct when it was decided, and it is not correct today. It ought not to remain binding precedent. *Bowers v. Hardwick* should be and now is overruled.

The present case does not involve minors. It does not involve persons who might be injured or coerced or who are situated in relationships where consent might not easily be refused. It does not involve public conduct or prostitution. It does not involve whether the government must give formal recognition to any relationship that homosexual persons seek to enter. The case does involve two adults who, with full and mutual consent from each other, engaged in sexual practices common to a homosexual lifestyle. The petitioners are entitled to respect for their private lives. The State cannot demean their existence or control their destiny by making their private sexual conduct a crime. Their right to liberty under the Due Process Clause gives them the full right to engage in their conduct without intervention of the government.

Had those who drew and ratified the Due Process Clauses of the Fifth Amendment or the Fourteenth Amendment known the components of liberty in its manifold possibilities, they might have been more specific. They did not presume to have this insight. They knew times can blind us to certain truths and later generations can see that laws once thought necessary and proper in fact serve only to oppress. As the Constitution endures, persons in every generation can invoke its principles in their own search for greater freedom.

Justice Scalia

"Liberty finds no refuge in a jurisprudence of doubt." That was the Court's sententious response, barely more than a decade ago, to those seeking to overrule *Roe v. Wade*. The Court's response today, to those who have engaged in a seventeen-year crusade to overrule *Bowers v. Hardwick,* is very different. The need for stability and certainty presents no barrier.

The Texas statute undeniably seeks to further the belief of its citizens that certain forms of sexual behavior are "immoral and unacceptable"—the same interest furthered by criminal laws against fornication, bigamy, adultery, adult incest, bestiality, and obscenity. *Bowers* held that this was a legitimate state interest. The Court today reaches the opposite conclusion. The Texas statute, it says, "furthers no legitimate state interest which can justify its intrusion into the personal and private life of the individual." The Court embraces instead Justice Stevens' declaration in his *Bowers* dissent, that "the fact that the governing majority in a State has traditionally viewed a particular practice as immoral is not a sufficient reason for upholding a law prohibiting the practice." This effectively decrees the end of all morals legislation. If, as the Court asserts, the promotion of majoritarian sexual morality is not even a legitimate state interest, none of the above-mentioned laws can survive rational-basis review.

Today's opinion is the product of a Court, which is the product of a law-profession culture, that has largely signed on to the so-called homosexual agenda, by which I mean the agenda promoted by some homosexual activists directed at eliminating the moral opprobrium that has traditionally attached to homosexual conduct.

So imbued is the Court with the law profession's anti-anti-homosexual culture, that it is seemingly unaware that the attitudes of that culture are not obviously "mainstream"; that in most States what the Court calls "discrimination" against those who engage in homosexual acts is perfectly legal.

Let me be clear that I have nothing against homosexuals, or any other group, promoting their agenda through normal democratic means. Social perceptions of sexual and other morality change over time, and every group has the right to persuade its fellow citizens that its view of such matters is the best. That homosexuals have achieved some success in that enterprise is attested to by the fact that Texas is one of the few remaining States that criminalize private, consensual homosexual acts. But persuading one's fellow citizens is one thing, and imposing one's views in absence of democratic majority will is something else. I would no more *require* a State to criminalize homosexual acts—or, for that matter, display any moral disapprobation of them—than I would *forbid* it to do so. What Texas has chosen to do is well within the range of traditional democratic action, and its hand should not be stayed through the invention of a brand-new "constitutional right" by a Court that is impatient of democratic change. It is indeed true that "later generations can see that laws once thought necessary and proper in fact serve only to oppress," and when that happens, later generations can repeal those laws. But it is the premise of our system that those judgments are to be made by the people, and not imposed by a governing caste that knows best.

One of the benefits of leaving regulation of this matter to the people rather than to the courts is that the people, unlike judges, need not carry things to their logical conclusion. The people may feel that their disapprobation of homosexual conduct is strong enough to disallow homosexual marriage, but not strong enough to criminalize private homosexual acts—and may legislate accordingly. The Court today pretends that it possesses a similar freedom of action, so that we need not fear judicial imposition of homosexual marriage, as has recently occurred in Canada (in a decision that the Canadian Government has chosen not to appeal).

At the end of its opinion—after having laid waste the foundations of our rational-basis jurisprudence—the Court says that the present case "does not involve whether the government must give formal recognition to any relationship that homosexual persons seek to enter." Do not believe it. Today's opinion dismantles the structure of constitutional law that has permitted a distinction to be made between heterosexual and homosexual unions, insofar as formal recognition in marriage is concerned. If moral disapprobation of homosexual conduct is "no legitimate state interest" for purposes of proscribing that conduct; and if, as the Court coos (casting aside all pretense of neutrality), "when sexuality finds overt expression in intimate conduct with another person, the conduct can be but one element in a personal bond that is more enduring," what justification could there possibly be for denying the benefits of marriage to homosexual couples exercising "the liberty protected by the Constitution," ibid.? Surely not the encouragement of procreation, since the sterile and the elderly are allowed to marry. This case "does not involve" the issue of homosexual marriage only if one entertains the belief that principle and logic have nothing to do with the decisions of this Court. Many will hope that, as the Court comfortingly assures us, this is so.

I dissent.

No Second Class Citizenship

GOODRIDGE V. DEPARTMENT OF PUBLIC HEALTH

From the ruling of the Supreme Judicial Court of Massachusetts, November 2003

Opinions of the Justices to the Senate, Supreme Judicial Court of Massachusetts, February 2004

In 2003, the highest court in Massachusetts ruled that preventing gays and lesbians from entering civil marriage violated the state constitutional provisions of due process and equal protection. The court's opinion gave the legislature time to amend state law to comply with the ruling. Shortly afterward, the legislature, taking advantage of an unusual provision of Massachusetts law, requested the court's opinion on a Vermont-style civil union measure. The court responded that marriage, and only marriage, would satisfy the dictates of the state constitution.

From the Court's Ruling

The plaintiffs are fourteen individuals from five Massachusetts counties. As of April 11, 2001, the date they filed their complaint, the plaintiffs Gloria Bailey, sixty years old, and Linda Davies, fifty-five years old, had been in a committed relationship for thirty years; the plaintiffs Maureen Brodoff, forty-nine years old, and Ellen Wade, fifty-two years old, had been in a committed relationship for twenty years and lived with their twelve-year-old daughter; the plaintiffs Hillary Goodridge, forty-four years old, and Julie Goodridge, forty-three years old, had been in a committed relationship for thirteen years and lived with their five-year-old daughter; the plaintiffs Gary Chalmers, thirty-five years old, and Richard Linnell, thirty-seven years old, had been in a committed relationship for thirteen years and lived with their eight-year-old daughter and Richard's mother; the plaintiffs Heidi Norton, thirty-six years old, and Gina Smith, thirty-six years old, had been in a committed relationship for eleven years and lived with their two sons, ages five years and one year; the plaintiffs Michael Horgan, forty-one years old, and Edward Balmelli, forty-one years old, had been in a committed relationship for seven years; and the plaintiffs David Wilson, fifty-seven years old, and Robert Compton, fifty-one years old, had been in a committed relationship for four years and had cared for David's mother in their home after a serious illness until she died.

The plaintiffs include business executives, lawyers, an investment banker, educators, therapists, and a computer engineer. Many are active in church, community, and school groups. They have employed such legal means as are available to them—for example, joint adoption, powers of attorney, and joint ownership of real property—to secure aspects of their relationships. Each plaintiff attests a desire to marry his or her partner in order to affirm publicly their commitment to each other and to secure the legal protections and benefits afforded to married couples and their children.

In March and April, 2001, each of the plaintiff couples attempted to obtain a marriage license from a city or town clerk's office. In each case, the clerk either refused to accept the notice of intention to marry or denied a marriage license to the couple on the ground that Massachusetts does not recognize same-sex marriage.

The larger question is whether, as the department claims, government action that bars same-sex couples from civil marriage constitutes a legitimate exercise of the State's authority to regulate conduct, or whether, as the plaintiffs claim, this categorical marriage exclusion violates the Massachusetts Constitution. We have recognized the long-standing statutory understanding, derived from the common law, that "marriage" means the lawful union of a woman and a man. But that history cannot and does not foreclose the constitutional question.

We begin by considering the nature of civil marriage itself. Simply put, the government creates civil marriage. In Massachusetts, civil marriage is, and since pre-Colonial days has been, precisely what its name implies: a wholly secular institution.

Without question, civil marriage enhances the "welfare of the community." It is a "social institution of the highest importance." Civil marriage anchors an ordered society by encouraging stable relationships over transient ones. It is central to the way the Commonwealth identifies individuals, provides for the orderly distribution of property, ensures that children and adults are cared for and supported whenever possible from private rather than public funds, and tracks important epidemiological and demographic data.

Marriage also bestows enormous private and social advantages on those who choose to marry. Civil marriage is at once a deeply personal commitment to another human being and a highly public celebration of the ideals of mutuality, companionship, intimacy, fidelity, and family. "It is an association that promotes a way of life, not causes; a harmony in living, not political faiths; a bilateral loyalty, not commercial or social projects." Because it fulfills yearnings for security, safe haven, and connection that express our common humanity, civil marriage is an esteemed institution, and the decision whether and whom to marry is among life's momentous acts of self-definition.

The benefits accessible only by way of a marriage license are enormous, touching nearly every aspect of life and death. The department states that "hundreds of statutes" are related to marriage and to marital benefits. With no attempt to be comprehensive, we note that some of the statutory benefits conferred by the Legislature on those who enter into civil marriage include, as to property: joint Massachusetts income tax filing; tenancy by the entirety (a form of ownership that provides certain protections against creditors and allows for the automatic descent of property to the surviving spouse without probate); extension of the benefit of the homestead protection (securing up to $300,000 in equity from creditors) to one's spouse and children; automatic rights to inherit the property of a deceased spouse who does not leave a will; the rights of elective share and of dower (which allow surviving spouses certain property rights where the decedent spouse has not made adequate provision for the survivor in a will); entitlement to wages owed to a deceased employee; eligibility to continue certain businesses of a deceased spouse; the right to share the medical policy of one's spouse; thirty-nine week continuation of health coverage for the spouse of a person who is laid off or dies; preferential options under the Commonwealth's pension system; preferential benefits in the Commonwealth's medical program, MassHealth; access to veterans' spousal benefits and preferences; financial protections for spouses of certain Commonwealth employees (fire fighters, police officers, prosecutors, among others) killed in the performance of duty; the equitable division of marital property on divorce; temporary and permanent alimony rights; the right to separate support on separation of the parties that does not result in divorce; and the right to bring claims for wrongful death and loss of consortium, and for funeral and burial expenses and punitive damages resulting from tort actions.

Exclusive marital benefits that are not directly tied to property rights include the presumptions of legitimacy and parentage of children born to a married couple; and evidentiary rights, such as the prohibition against spouses testifying against one another about their private conversations, applicable in both civil and criminal cases. Other statutory benefits of a personal nature available only to married individuals include qualification for bereavement or medical leave to care for individuals related by blood or marriage; an automatic "family member" preference to make medical decisions for an incompetent or disabled spouse who does not have a contrary health care proxy; the application of predictable rules of child custody, visitation, support, and removal out-of-State when married parents divorce; priority rights to administer the estate of a deceased spouse who dies without a will, and requirement that surviving spouse must consent to the appointment of any other person as administrator; and the right to interment in the lot or tomb owned by one's deceased spouse.

Where a married couple has children, their children are also directly or indirectly, but no less auspiciously, the recipients of the special legal and economic protections obtained by civil marriage. Notwithstanding the Commonwealth's strong public policy to abolish legal distinctions between marital and nonmarital children in providing for the support and care of minors, the fact remains that marital children reap a measure of family stability and economic security based on their parents' legally privileged status that is largely inaccessible, or not as readily accessible, to nonmarital children. Some of these benefits are social, such as the enhanced approval that still attends the status of being a marital child. Others are material, such as the greater ease of access to family-based State and Federal benefits that attend the presumptions of one's parentage.

The Massachusetts Constitution protects matters of personal liberty against government incursion as zealously, and often more so, than does the Federal Constitution, even where both Constitutions employ essentially the same language.

Whether and whom to marry, how to express sexual intimacy, and whether and how to establish a family—these are among the most basic of every individual's liberty and due process rights. And central to personal freedom and security is the assurance that the laws will apply equally to persons in similar situations. The liberty interest in choosing whether and whom to marry would be hollow if the Commonwealth could, without sufficient justification, foreclose an individual from freely choosing the person with whom to share an exclusive commitment in the unique institution of civil marriage.

The department posits three legislative rationales for prohibiting same-sex couples from marrying: (1) providing a "favorable setting for procreation;" (2) ensuring the optimal setting for child rearing, which the department defines as "a two-parent family with one parent of each sex;" and (3) preserving scarce State and private financial resources.

Fertility is not a condition of marriage, nor is it grounds for divorce. People who have never consummated their marriage, and never plan to, may be and stay married. While it is certainly true that many, perhaps most, married couples have children together (assisted or unassisted), it is the exclusive and permanent commitment of the marriage partners to one another, not the begetting of children, that is the sine qua non of civil marriage.

Protecting the welfare of children is a paramount State policy. Restricting marriage to opposite-sex couples, however, cannot plausibly further this policy. Excluding same-sex couples from civil marriage will not make children of opposite-sex marriages more secure, but it does prevent children of same-sex couples from enjoying the immeasurable advantages that flow from the assurance of "a stable family structure in which children will be reared, educated, and socialized."

An absolute statutory ban on same-sex marriage bears no rational relationship to the goal of economy.

Here, the plaintiffs seek only to be married, not to undermine the institution of civil marriage. They do not want marriage abolished. They do not attack the binary nature of marriage, the consanguinity provisions, or any of the other gate-keeping provisions of the marriage licensing law. Recognizing the right of an individual to marry a person of the same sex will not diminish the validity or dignity of opposite-sex marriage, any more than recognizing the right of an individual to marry a person of a different race devalues the marriage of a person who marries someone of her own race. If anything, extending civil marriage to same-sex couples reinforces the importance of marriage to individuals and communities. That same-sex couples are willing to embrace marriage's solemn obligations of exclusivity, mutual support, and commitment to one another is a testament to the enduring place of marriage in our laws and in the human spirit.

We declare that barring an individual from the protections, benefits, and obligations of civil marriage solely because that person would marry a person of the same sex violates the Massachusetts Constitution. Entry of judgment shall be stayed for 180 days to permit the Legislature to take such action as it may deem appropriate in light of this opinion.

The Advisory Opinion

[I]n *Goodridge* the court was asked to consider the constitutional question "whether the Commonwealth may use its formidable regulatory authority to bar same-sex couples from civil marriage." The court has answered the question. We have now been asked to render an advisory opinion on Senate No. 2175, which creates a new legal status, "civil union," that is purportedly equal to "marriage," yet separate from it. The constitutional difficulty of the proposed civil union bill is evident in its stated purpose to "preserve the traditional, historic nature and meaning of the institution of civil marriage." Preserving the institution of civil marriage is of course a legislative priority of the highest order, and one to which the Justices accord the General Court the greatest deference. We recognize the efforts of the Senate to draft a bill in conformity with the *Goodridge* opinion. Yet the bill, as we read it, does nothing to "preserve" the civil marriage law, only its constitutional infirmity. This is not a matter of social policy but of constitutional interpretation. As the court concluded in *Goodridge*, the traditional, historic nature and meaning of civil marriage in Massachusetts is as a wholly secular and dynamic legal institution, the governmental aim of which is to encourage stable adult relationships for the good of the individual and of the community, especially its children. The very nature and purpose of civil marriage, the court concluded, renders unconstitutional any attempt to ban all same-sex couples, as same-sex couples, from entering into civil marriage.

The same defects of rationality evident in the marriage ban considered in *Goodridge* are evident in, if not exaggerated by, Senate No. 2175. Segregating same-sex unions from opposite-sex unions cannot possibly be held rationally to advance or "preserve" what we stated in *Goodridge* were the Commonwealth's legitimate interests in procreation, child rearing, and the conservation of resources. Because the proposed law by its express terms forbids same-sex couples entry into civil marriage, it continues to relegate same-sex couples to a different status. The holding in *Goodridge*, by which we are bound, is that group classifications based on unsupportable distinctions, such as that embodied in the proposed bill, are invalid under the Massachusetts Constitution. The history of our nation has demonstrated that separate is seldom, if ever, equal.

The bill's absolute prohibition of the use of the word "marriage" by "spouses" who are the same sex is more than semantic.

The dissimilitude between the terms "civil marriage" and "civil union" is not innocuous; it is a considered choice of language that reflects a demonstrable assigning of same-sex, largely homosexual, couples to second-class status. The denomination of this difference by the separate opinion of Justice Sosman (separate opinion) as merely a "squabble over the name to be used" so clearly misses the point that further discussion appears to be useless. If, as the separate opinion posits, the proponents of the bill believe that no message is conveyed by eschewing the word "marriage" and replacing it with "civil union" for same-sex "spouses," we doubt that the attempt to circumvent the court's decision in *Goodridge* would be so purposeful. For no rational reason the marriage laws of the Commonwealth discriminate against a defined class; no amount of tinkering with language will eradicate that stain. The bill would have the effect of maintaining and fostering a stigma of exclusion that the Constitution prohibits. It would deny to same-sex "spouses" only a status that is specially recognized in society and has significant social and other advantages. The Massachusetts Constitution, as was explained in the *Goodridge* opinion, does not permit such invidious discrimination, no matter how well intentioned.

We are of the opinion that Senate No. 2175 violates the equal protection and due process requirements of the Constitution of the Commonwealth and the Massachusetts Declaration of Rights. Further, the particular provisions that render the pending bill unconstitutional are not severable from the remainder. The bill maintains an unconstitutional, inferior, and discriminatory status for same-sex couples, and the bill's remaining provisions are too entwined with this purpose to stand independently.

The answer to the question is "No."

CHAPTER FOUR

Why Marry?

THE DEBATE ON THE LEFT

For decades, the issue of same-sex marriage has been anything but noncontroversial among gay men and lesbians. Although the idea of marriage rights goes back centuries, the American gay rights movement, in its post-1969 incarnation, eschewed it. Marriage, the argument ran, was an oppressive, sexist, and inherently heterosexual institution. The movement's goal was to weaken the institution as a whole, to subvert and undermine it, and to create alternative structures within which to explore homosexual desire, love, and family. Even now, many gay rights organizations devote almost no energy or resources to the issue, considering it unnecessarily emotive and irrelevant. And academic "queer theorists" remain deeply suspicious of marriage. But in the last twenty years advocates who see marriage as the linchpin of gay civil rights have grown in strength and numbers. Intellectuals and activists have generated a structure of support and arguments for the many lesbian and gay couples who have sought the right to marry. And recent court cases, together with the ensuing legislative debates, have raised the issue to a new level among gay men and lesbians.

What follows are among the most eloquent and cogent of the arguments that have emerged over the years—from Paula Ettelbrick's early worries to Evan Wolfson's confidence and conviction. Mary Dunlap's poem "Choosing" expresses the acute emotional conflicts many homosexuals feel about the institution as a whole. Lesbian writer E. J. Graff argues that equality in marriage is a deeply radicalizing move; Frank Browning laments its normalizing effect on gay life. Finally, Hannah Arendt—the only heterosexual writer in this chapter—asserts the centrality of marriage to any civil equality.

Since When Is Marriage a Path to Liberation?

PAULA ETTELBRICK

From OUT/LOOK National Gay and Lesbian Quarterly, *no. 6, Fall 1989*

A traditional leftist worries about what same-sex marriage would do to the radical agenda.

Marriage is a great institution . . . if you like living in institutions," according to a bit of T-shirt philosophy I saw recently. Certainly, marriage is an institution. It is one of the most venerable, impenetrable institutions in modern society. Marriage provides the ultimate form of acceptance for personal, intimate relationships in our society, and gives those who marry an insider status of the most powerful kind.

Steeped in a patriarchal system that looks to ownership, property, and dominance of men over women as its basis, the institution of marriage has long been the focus of radical-feminist revulsion. Marriage defines certain relationships as more valid than all others. Lesbian and gay relationships, being neither legally sanctioned nor commingled by blood, are always at the bottom of the heap of social acceptance and importance.

Given the imprimatur of social and personal approval that marriage provides, it is not surprising that some lesbians and gay men among us would look to legal marriage for self-affirmation. After all, those who marry can be instantaneously transformed from "outsiders" to "insiders," and we have a desperate need to become insiders.

It could make us feel okay about ourselves, perhaps even relieve some of the internalized homophobia that we all know so well. Society will then celebrate the birth of our children and mourn the death of our spouses. It would be easier to get health insurance for our spouses, family memberships to the local museum, and a right to inherit our spouse's cherished collection of lesbian mystery novels even if she failed to draft a will. Never again would we have to go to a family reunion and debate about the correct term for introducing our lover/partner/significant other to Aunt Flora. Everything would be quite easy and very nice.

So why does this unlikely event so deeply disturb me? For two major reasons. First, marriage will not liberate us as lesbians and gay men. In fact, it will constrain us, make us more invisible, force our assimilation into the mainstream, and undermine the goals of gay liberation. Second, attaining the right to marry will not transform our society from one that makes narrow, but dramatic, distinctions between those who are married and those who are not married to one that respects and encourages choice of relationships and family diversity. Marriage runs contrary to two of the primary goals of the lesbian and gay movement: the affirmation of gay identity and culture and the validation of many forms of relationships.

When analyzed from the standpoint of civil rights, certainly lesbians and gay men should have a right to marry. But obtaining a right does not always result in justice. White male firefighters in Birmingham, Alabama, have been fighting for their "rights" to retain their jobs by overturning the city's affirmative-action guidelines. If their "rights" prevail, the courts will have failed in rendering justice. The "right" fought for by the white male firefighters, as well as those who advocate strongly for the "rights" to legal marriage for gay people, will result, at best, in limited or narrowed "justice" for those closest to power at the expense of those who have been historically marginalized. . . .

Justice for gay men and lesbians will be achieved only when we are accepted and supported in this society despite our differences from the dominant culture and the choices we make regarding our relationships. Being queer is more than setting up house, sleeping with a person of the same gender, and seeking state approval for doing so. It is an identity, a culture with many variations. It is a way of dealing with the world by diminishing the constraints of gender roles that have for so long kept women and gay people oppressed and invisible. Being queer means pushing the parameters of sex, sexuality, and family, and in the process transforming the very fabric of society. Gay liberation is inexorably linked to women's liberation. Each is essential to the other.

The moment we argue, as some among us insist on doing, that we should be treated as equals because we are really just like married couples and hold the same values to be true, we undermine the very purpose of our movement and begin the dangerous process of silencing our different voices. As a lesbian, I am fundamentally different from nonlesbian women. That's the point. Marriage, as it exists today, is antithetical to my liberation as a lesbian and as a woman because it mainstreams my life and voice. I do not want to be known as "Mrs. Attached-To-Somebody-Else." Nor do I want to give the state the power to regulate my primary relationship. . . .

By looking to our sameness and de-emphasizing our differences, we do not even place ourselves in a position of power that would allow us to transform marriage from an institution that emphasizes property and state regulation of relationships to an institution that recognizes one of many types of valid and respected relationships. Until the Constitution is interpreted to respect and encourage differences, pursuing the legalization of same-sex marriage would be leading our movement into a trap; we would be demanding access to the very institution that, in its current form, would undermine our movement to recognize many different kinds of relationships. We would be perpetuating the elevation of married relationships and of "couples" in general, and further eclipsing other relationships of choice.

Ironically, gay marriage, instead of liberating gay sex and sexuality, would further outlaw all gay and lesbian sex that is not performed in a marital context. Just as sexually active nonmarried women face stigma and double standards around sex and sexual activity, so too would nonmarried gay people. The only legitimate gay sex would be that which is cloaked in and regulated by marriage. Its legitimacy would stem not from an acceptance of gay sexuality, but because the Supreme Court and society in general fiercely protect the privacy of marital relationships. Lesbians and gay men who do not seek the state's stamp of approval would clearly face increased sexual oppression.

Undoubtedly, whether we admit it or not, we all need to be

accepted by the broader society. That motivation fuels our work to eliminate discrimination in the workplace and elsewhere, fight for custody of our children, create our own families, and so on. The growing discussion about the right to marry may be explained in part by this need for acceptance. Those closer to the norm or to power in this country are more likely to see marriage as a principle of freedom and equality. Those who are acceptable to the mainstream because of race, gender, and economic status are more likely to want the right to marry. It is the final acceptance, the ultimate affirmation of identity.

On the other hand, more marginal members of the lesbian and gay community (women, people of color, working class, and poor) are less likely to see marriage as having relevance to our struggles for survival. After all, what good is the affirmation of our relationships (that is, marital relationships) if we are rejected as women, people of color, or working class?

The path to acceptance is much more complicated for many of us. For instance, if we choose legal marriage, we may enjoy the right to add our spouse to our health insurance policy at work, since most employment policies are defined by one's marital status, not family relationship. However, that choice assumes that we have a job and that our employer provides us with health benefits. For women, particularly women of color who tend to occupy the low-paying jobs that do not provide health-care benefits at all, it will not matter one bit if they are able to marry their women partners. The opportunity to marry will neither get them the health benefits nor transform them from outsider to insider.

Of course, a white man who marries another white man who has a full-time job with benefits will certainly be able to share in those benefits and overcome the only obstacle left to full societal assimilation—the goal of many in his class. In other words, gay marriage will not topple the system that allows only the privileged few to obtain decent health care. Nor will it close the privilege gap between those who are married and those who are not.

Marriage creates a two-tier system that allows the state to regulate relationships. It has become a facile mechanism for employers to dole out benefits, for businesses to provide special deals and incentives, and for the law to make distinctions in distributing meager public funds. None of these entities bothers to consider the relationship among people; the love, respect, and need to protect that exists among all kinds of family members. Rather, a simple certificate of the state, regardless of whether the spouses love, respect, or even see each other on a regular basis, dominates and is supported. None of this dynamic will change if gay men and lesbians are given the option of marriage. . . .

If the laws changed tomorrow and lesbians and gay men were allowed to marry, where would we find the incentive to continue the progressive movement we have started that is pushing for societal and legal recognition of all kinds of family relationships? To create other options and alternatives? To find a place in the law for the elderly couple who, for companionship and economic reasons, live together but do not marry? To recognize the right of a longtime, but unmarried, gay partner to stay in his rent-controlled apartment after the death of his lover, the only named tenant on the lease? To recognize the family relationship of the lesbian couple and the two gay men who are jointly sharing child-raising responsibilities? To get the law to acknowledge that we may have more than one relationship worthy of legal protection?

The lesbian and gay community has laid the groundwork for revolutionizing society's views of family. The domestic-partnership movement has been an important part of this progress insofar as it validates nonmarital relationships. Because it is not limited to sexual or romantic relationships, domestic partnership provides an important opportunity for many who are not related by blood or marriage to claim certain minimal protections.

It is crucial, though, that we avoid the pitfall of framing the push for legal recognition of domestic partners (those who share a primary residence and financial responsibilities for each other) as a stepping-stone to marriage. We must keep our eyes on the goals of providing true alternatives to marriage and of radically reordering society's view of family. . . . We must not fool ourselves into believing that marriage will make it acceptable to be gay or lesbian. We will be liberated only when we are respected and accepted for our differences and the diversity we provide to this society. Marriage is not a path to that liberation.

Choosing
MARY C. DUNLAP

From Law and Sexuality: A Review of Lesbian and Gay Legal Issues *1 (1991)*

In a poetic footnote to a legal article, Mary Dunlap confronts her own conflicts about marriage as an instrument of her op-pression—and liberation.

The girls I watched so closely and adoringly
in fifth grade, then young women in eighth,
eleventh, college, law school, life after
At first, they varied so, a bright rainbow
I cherished

But revolved more and more, faster and faster
Around a common, central myth
Of devastating, even deadly, force:

To marry
Would give life, value to the life,
Identity to each female
Lucky enough, attractive enough
To draw a man
To vows.

This myth, this centrifuge of sexist conformity,
Built on a vicious cycle of female inferiority
Tossed, cajoled and ultimately smashed these beings
into a sameness: increasingly fearful deference
To the male.

Meanwhile, my sister scolded me, "you'll never say, 'yes,'
in a wedding, the most you'd yield is
'Maybe.'"

"Or, maybe not," I answered.

Proud and hurt, and very deeply blessed
by my belief, defiant, resilient
That I am valuable in my self,
I escaped
The centrifuge of marriage.

And now I see
The vows they took have turned to blows
Too often, and jokes, and infidelities

SAME-SEX MARRIAGE: PRO AND CON

Celebrated as "romance," culminating in
divorce, or worse, routine denial
Understood as normal, modern, mundane
Entertainment

Disguising the essential horror
Distracting from the pain, breath-taking

Of the basic whirlpool drowning tragedy:
That anyone should ever have to wait for
That anyone should ever choose to look to
Another
For her own (for his own)
Boundless, immutable, miraculous personal worth. . . .

After my father died, December 1984,
my mother took me aside, not in sheer grief,
But in a statement of abiding and lifelong belief,
Said:
I WAS NOTHING
TILL I MARRIED YOUR FATHER.

I rage and bawl and struggle to this moment
Against the awful truth and the awful lie
of this statement in Mother's life,
in so many women's lives.
I WAS NOTHING
TILL I MARRIED YOUR FATHER.

So, given the extreme force of the circular saw lie
That a woman is only as good as her marriage
This lie that worked to separate
Mother from her own life

The Debate on the Left

(And how many millions of others, I wonder)
Is it possible
Can it ever conceivably be

That the dreadful institution of marriage
that has broken all those girlchildren's souls
this idea that invalidates women, that
corrupts female identity into a product for men to buy

This monstrosity, marriage,

Could ever be tamed, changed, moved,
Transmogrified
By the love between two women
By the love between two men

Into a place of nurturing and shelter
For this most illegitimate of relationships
the lesbian couple
the gay partnership

this relationship so homeless and beaten down

Lifted into a place of succor and respect
For both, for each
Marriage without regard to gender
    by Church or State
    ("gender" saved for one's own appreciate regard
    and the lover's, total and tender)

Can we these most unwelcome outsiders
We these gay and lesbian lovers
Be let in?
And want to, choose to
Go?

Without destruction of all we have learned
Outside, feminist, hetero-
dox lessons
About the centrifuge's crush
and the untolled cost of the awful lie
For the question is not, finally,
    May we *marry*?

It is

    Can *we* marry? . . .

Why Marry?

FRANK   BROWNING

From The New York Times, *April 17, 1996*

*Browning, a leftist writer and National Public Radio contrib-
utor, prefers more diverse relationship models to marriage.*

Thursday morning, and it's my turn to move our cars for street
cleaning. Gene has already bribed the cats into silence with
food.

So begins the day here in Windsor Terrace, a quiet Brooklyn
neighborhood populated by many kinds of families: a lesbian
couple next door—and beyond them an Italian widow who rents

out rooms, an Irish-American grandmother who shares her house with her daughter's family, the multigenerational Korean family that owns the corner grocery.

We gay couples, of course, are not considered families under the law, a fact that the bishops and Buchananites insist will never change and that many gay activists have identified as America's next great civil rights struggle. Indeed, a court case in Hawaii may soon lead to that state's recognition of same-sex marriage.

I suppose it's a good thing for gay adults to be offered the basic nuptial rights afforded to others. We call that equal treatment before the law. But I'm not sure the marriage contract is such a good plan for us.

The trouble with gay marriage is not its recognition of our "unnatural unions." The problem is with the shape of marriage itself. What we might be better off seeking is civic and legal support for different kinds of families that can address the emotional, physical, and financial obligations of contemporary life. By rushing to embrace the standard marriage contract, we could stifle one of the richest and most creative laboratories of family experience.

We gay folk tend to organize our lives more like extended families than nuclear ones. We may love our mates one at a time, but our "primary families" are often our ex-lovers and our ex-lovers' ex-lovers.

The writer Edmund White noticed this about gay male life twenty years ago; he called it the "banyan tree" phenomenon, after the tree whose branches send off shoots that take root to form new trunks. Nowhere has the banyan-tree family proved stronger than in AIDS care, where often a large group of people—ex-mates and their friends and lovers—tend the sick and maintain the final watch.

Modern marriage, by comparison, tends to isolate couples from their larger families and sometimes from friends—especially if they are ex-lovers. And a nuclear family with working parents has often proved less than ideal in coping with daily stresses or serious illness.

The marriage model could prove especially problematic for rearing children. In a gay family, there are often three parents— a lesbian couple, say, and the biological father. Sometimes, four or five adults are committed to nurturing the children. In such cases, a marriage between two might bring second-class status to the rest of the extended family and diminish their parental roles.

(Those who think that only a father and mother can successfully raise a child should visit Italy, Japan, Greece, Thailand, or American family archives, which show that before World War II, grandparents, aunts, uncles, and older siblings had vital child-rearing roles.)

Precisely because homosexuals have resided outside the law, they have invented family forms that respond to late twentieth-century needs, while formulating social and moral codes that provide love, freedom, and fidelity (if not always monogamy).

All I need do is look up and down Windsor Terrace to see that the family includes all sorts of relationships and obligations.

Each of us, hetero or homo, has a stake in nurturing a diverse landscape of families. Only a minority of us have marriages like Donna Reed's or Harriet Nelson's. Even Pat Buchanan knows that.

Retying the Knot

E. J.   G R A F F

From the Nation, *June 24, 1996*

Lesbian intellectual E. J. Graff believes that same-sex mar-
riage represents the most radical step of all—a way to trans-
form one of the most powerful institutions in society.

The right wing gets it: Same-sex marriage is a breathtakingly
subversive idea. So it's weirdly dissonant when gay neocons
and feminist lesbians publicly insist—the former with enthusiasm, the latter with distaste—that same-sex marriage would be a
conservative move, confining sexual free radicals inside some
legal cellblock. It's almost as odd (although more understand-
able) when pro-marriage liberals ply the rhetoric of fairness and
love, as if no one will notice that for thousands of years marriage
has meant Boy+Girl=Babies. But same-sex marriage seems fair
only if you accept a philosophy of marriage that, although it's
gained ground in the past several centuries, still strikes many as
radical: the idea that marriage (and therefore sex) is justified not
by reproduction but by love.

Sound like old news? Not if you're the Christian Coalition,
the Pope or the Orthodox rabbinate, or if you simply live in one
of many pre-industrial countries. Same-sex marriage will be a direct hit against the religious right's goal of re-enshrining biology
as destiny. Marriage is an institution that towers on our social
horizon, defining how we think about one another, formalizing
contact with our families, neighborhoods, employers, insurers,

hospitals, governments. Allowing two people of the same sex to marry shifts that institution's message.

That's why the family-values crowd has trained its guns on us, from a new hate video called *The Ultimate Target of the Gay Agenda: Same-Sex Marriages* to the apocalyptically named Defense of Marriage Act. The right wing would much rather see outré urban queers throwing drunken kisses off bar floats than have two nice married girls move in next door, with or without papoose, demonstrating to every neighborhood kid that a good marriage is defined from the inside out, that sodomy is a sin only in the mind of the beholder.

Chilled by that coming shift, antimarriage conservatives have also been disingenuous in their arguments, which basically come down to crying "tradition!" like a Tevye chorus. Even a quick glance at social history shows what conservatives pretend isn't so: Very little about marriage is historically consistent enough to be "traditional." That it involves two people? Then forget the patriarch Jacob, whose two wives and two concubines produced the head of the twelve tribes. That it involves a religious blessing? Not early Christian marriages, before marriage was a sacrament. That it is recognized by law? Forget centuries of European prole "marriages" conducted outside the law, in which no property was involved. That it's about love, not money? So much for centuries of negotiation about medieval estates, bride-price, morning gift and dowry (not to mention bride-burnings in today's India). Those who tsk away such variety, insisting that everyone knows what marriage *really* is, miss the point. Marriage is—marriage always has been—variations on a theme. Each era's marriage institutionalizes the sexual bond in a way that makes sense for that society, that economy, that class.

So what makes sense in ours? Or, to put it another way, what is contemporary marriage for? That's the question underlying the debate as right-wing and gay activists prepare for Hawaii's aftermath. Its answer has to fit our economic lives. In a GNP based on how well each of us plumbs our talents and desires in deciding what to make, buy or sell, we can hardly instruct those same innards to shut up about our sexual lives—as people could in a pre-industrial society where job, home and religion were all dictated by history. The right wants it both ways: Adam Smith's economy *and* feudal sexual codes. If same-sex marriage becomes legal, that venerable institution will ever after stand for sexual choice, for cutting the link between sex and diapers.

Ah, but it already does. Formally, U.S. marriage hasn't been justified solely by reproduction since 1965, when the Supreme Court batted down the last laws forbidding birth control's sale to married couples. In Margaret Sanger's era, contraception was charged with "perversion of natural functions," "immorality" and "fostering egotism and enervating self-indulgence." Dire diseases were predicated for those who indulged. Those are, almost word for word, the charges hurled by every critic of homosexuality—and for the same reasons. Once their ideologies are economically outdated, what can conservatives invoke except the threat of divine judgment?

All of which is why same-sex marriage is being considered in every postindustrial country, and why it seems simply "fair" to so many, including Hawaii's Supreme Court. That sense of fairness also draws on the liberal idea that a pluralist democracy's institutions should be capacious, that civic marriage should be one-size-fits-all. But same-sex marriage does more than just fit; it announces that marriage has changed shape.

As with any social change, there will be more consequences, which look pretty progressive to me. There are practical benefits: the ability to share insurance and pension benefits, care for our ill partners, inherit automatically, protect our children from desperate custody battles. And marriage will end a negative: Our sexual lives can no longer be considered felonious, which stings us in fights ranging from child custody to civil rights.

A more notable progressive shift is that, since same-sex couples will enter the existing institution, not some back-of-the-bus version called "domestic partnership" or "queer marriage," marriage law will have to become gender-blind. Once we can marry, jurists will have to decide every marriage, divorce, and custody question (theoretically at least) for equal partners, neither having more historical authority. Our entrance might thus rock marriage more toward its egalitarian shore.

Some progressives, feminists, and queer nationalists nevertheless complain that instead of demanding access to the institution as it is, we should be dismantling marriage entirely. But lasting social change evolves within and alters society's existing institutions. No one will force same-sex couples to darken the institution's doors: we'll merely gain the choices available to heterosexual pairs. None of this will alter a hard fact of contemporary life: Every commitment—to job, spouse, community, religion—must be invented from the inside out. Making lesbians and gay men more visible legally will insist that there is no traditional escape: that our society survives not by rote but by heart.

Connubial Personae

CAMILLE PAGLIA

From 10 Percent *magazine, May–June* 1995

An interview with Camille Paglia, a writer who defies categorization. So, it seems, does her argument about same-sex marriage.

10 Percent: What's your position on same-sex marriage?

Paglia: I think that it's a flash point for antigay backlash. It's the word *marriage*, coming out of the Judeo-Christian tradition, that has caused so much resistance. My problem is that I'm not so sure that Judeo-Christianity could or should honor or legitimize gay marriages. If there are going to be unions between gays, they should be outside the orthodox religious line—maybe pagan in some way. I do feel that some sort of commitment ceremony or union is in the best interest of the whole society as a way to strengthen gay relationships.

10 Percent: So what sort of alternative marriage ceremony are you envisioning for gay people?

Paglia: The truly radical position would be that there should be a separate ceremony, not just for gay marriages, but for all marriages. Gay activism has been stupid in demanding that marriages be performed in churches and synagogues. The truly radical argument would have been for us to appeal to progressive straights and say to them, *Renounce* the marriage ceremony.

If you are really progressive, don't pay lip service to gay rights. Do what people did in the '60s: Don't get married! It's in our interest as gays to want to strengthen relationships, so we do want to return to the idea of ceremony and ritual again, but let's find something that's gender and sexual-orientation neutral. And we should invite all progressive straight people to join us in this new kind of ceremony—whatever it is.

10 Percent: What would a ceremony with you and Alison Maddex be like?

Paglia: If Hawaii does legalize gay marriage, Alison and I would certainly be going. The idea of travelling to a Pacific Island to have a wedding ceremony is wonderful. I love it. Pele the Volcano Goddess, presumably, would be the presiding deity of such a ceremony. I love the idea of making a voyage back to nature.

10 Percent: Would other lesbian and gay couples follow suit?

Paglia: I think there will be a stampede of major proportions, but it may cause a backlash. That's the problem: calling it a *marriage*. If you say to some working-class guy on the street, "Do you believe in gay *marriages*?" it makes him have an absolute convulsion of revulsion. Marriage was traditionally meant for male and female. It was a bond for the raising of children, so it always had a procreative meaning. It has a long, sacred tradition behind it. I hate any time that gay causes get mixed up with seeming to profane other people's sacred traditions. The gay activist leadership has been totally clumsy about that. Rather than treating religion in a serious way and saying, "We respect the tradition of marriage," gay activism is associated with throwing balloons full of blood at the steps of St. Patrick's Cathedral.

10 Percent: Will the lesbian and gay divorce rate resemble the straight one?

Paglia: Who knows? My experience is that gay men's idea of marriage or any kind of relationship is rather open. That's why a lot of people are a little skeptical. Gay men—they're "together for thirty years": what does that mean? That means they go out and pick up strangers every two weeks. That's a very sophisticated view of marriage. Lesbians aren't like that. Lesbians *nest* in one big cinnamon bun where they fuse and it's all very sweet and nice. I like the idea of marriage, but I'm not sure that gay relationships have been tested over time. If we can't convince each other about it, I don't know how we're going to convince the greater world.

Crossing the Threshold
EVAN WOLFSON

From the Review of Law and Social Change *no. 3*
(1994–1995)

Evan Wolfson was among the first advocates of same-sex marriage, and he is now the most tireless advocate on the issue. Here he discusses why, against conventional wisdom, the right to marry is widely popular among lesbians and gay men.

In an argument typical of many intra-community critics of marriage challenges, Nancy Polikoff contends: "[T]he desire to marry in the lesbian and gay community is an attempt to mimic the worst of mainstream society, an effort to fit into an inherently problematic institution that betrays the promise of both lesbian and gay liberation and radical feminism."

There are at least two disturbing premises embedded in this argument. . . .

First, why is a lesbian's aspiration to marry "an attempt to mimic," rather than a genuine expression of her desires? Professor Mary C. Dunlap quotes one lesbian's observation:

> [I]t was strange to me when people in our community talked about commitment ceremonies as mocking heterosexual experience, because for me the creation of our Brit Ahavah [Jewish wedding ritual] was so different from a heterosexual wedding. The fact that gays and lesbians do this against all odds makes the whole process completely different.

Nor is this woman's desire to get married unusual. In the words of one gay man, "if it is freely chosen, a marriage license is as fine an option as sexual license. All I ask is the right to choose for myself, but that is exactly the right that society has never granted. . . ." One historian generalizes that "[g]ays and lesbians are raised in the same culture as everyone else. When they settle down they want gold bands, they want legal documents, they want kids." Even though equal marriage rights, until recently, seemed a dream, all available evidence suggests that the vast majority of gay and non-gay people alike share such sentiments.

In a 1994 survey by *The Advocate,* the largest existing poll of gay men on the subject, nearly two-thirds of the respondents stated unequivocally that they would marry a man if they were legally able to; 85 percent responded "yes" or "maybe"; only 15 percent said they would not marry. A significantly smaller, earlier poll by another journal presented similar results: 83 percent of lesbians and gay men in the study said they would "definitely" get married if they could. . . .

Like non-gay people, many lesbians and gay men offer less romantic explanations of their desire for equal marriage rights. For instance, noting the difficulties that gay people experience in terminating relationships and securing legal assistance, one attorney remarks: "I used to say, 'Why do we want to get married? It doesn't work for straight people.'. . . But now I say we should care: They have the privilege of divorce and we don't. We're left out there to twirl around in pain.". . .

For several years now, Lambda's intake has reflected a constant, high level of interest in marriage within our communities. During the 1987 March on Washington, thousands of lesbians and gay men participated in an event pointedly billed "The Wedding," in which they celebrated their relationships by exchanging personal vows before an officiant in front of the Internal Revenue Service Building. In his travels across the United States and again around the world, Neil Miller chronicled gay person after person either seeking marriage or indeed, as far as possible, actually wedding their partners.

Consider, for example, the experience of one couple that Miller encountered:

> Des was reluctant. She didn't believe in marriage and was opposed to imitating what she viewed as the heterosexual model. "I had a women's studies point of view," she noted. But gradually Trinity convinced her that marriage simply represented an expression of love and commitment that was neither intrinsically heterosexual nor homosexual. . . .

The suggestion that lesbians and gay men who want equal marriage rights do not know what is best for them as gay people is not uncommon in the intra-community arguments against pursuing marriage. In the charge that the demand for equal marriage rights is insufficiently radical or liberationist, a contemnable desire to "mimic" or "emulate" the non-gay world, or a sell-out of less "assimilationist" or less "privileged" gay people, there is an inescapable whiff of imputed false consciousness. However, given the diversity and number of women and men within our communities who strongly want the equal right to marry, the imputation seems wrong, as well as unfair. . . .

What many gay people do not want is an all-or-nothing model imposed on their lesbian or gay identity; they want both to be gay *and* married, to be gay *and* part of the larger society. For these lesbians and gay men, being gay is not just about being different, it is also about being equal. Their deeply held convictions about how they want to live their lives and liberation are not mere mimicry. They are entitled to respect within our community as well as by the state. . . .

Reflections on Little Rock
HANNAH ARENDT

From Dissent 6, no. 1 (Winter 1959)

This may seem a quirky choice, but this short statement shows how marriage rights were also controversial within another civil rights movement—in the 1950s and 1960s. Here Arendt argues that ending antimiscegenation laws was more important than desegregating public schools.

The Debate on the Left

The right to marry whoever one wishes is an elementary human right compared to which "the right to attend an integrated school, the right to sit where one pleases on a bus, the right to go into any hotel or recreation area or place of amusement, regardless of one's skin or color or race" are minor indeed. Even political rights, like the right to vote, and nearly all other rights enumerated in the Constitution, are secondary to the inalienable human rights to "life, liberty and the pursuit of happiness" proclaimed in the Declaration of Independence; and to this category the right to home and marriage unquestionably belongs.

CHAPTER FIVE

How Conservative a Project?
THE DEBATE ON THE RIGHT

One of the earliest twists of the same-sex marriage debate was the argument that it was a conservative reform: it would promote stability and monogamy among homosexuals and responsibility in the society as a whole. One of the clearest statements of this argument was contained in an article I wrote in 1989 in The New Republic, *entitled "Here Comes the Groom: A Conservative Case for Gay Marriage." It subsequently formed a part of the third chapter of my book,* Virtually Normal. *I should apologize, perhaps, for including my own work at length, but it is, I think, still the most cited argument of its type, so it is a natural place to start.*

The arguments against this position were almost immediate, specifically from Hadley Arkes in the National Review *and later from James Q. Wilson in* Commentary. *While ceding some ground to my position, both nevertheless argued that putting an end to an exclusively heterosexual definition of marriage would have radically unconservative ramifications.*

Subsequently, the debate took off with Jonathan Rauch's elegant 1996 essay, also published in The New Republic, and the Economist editorial, which echoes Rauch's arguments. Two of the smartest conservative writers around have also chimed in—Richard Posner and William Safire. Both oppose same-sex marriage for quirkily different reasons. Observing this debate from outside the conservative fold, Amy Schwartz nevertheless celebrates the conservative rush toward equality between gays and straights. Finally, David Brooks embraces the traditional conservative argument favoring civil marriage for gays, while lesbian conservative Tammy Bruce argues that gays and lesbians don't need marriage.

The Conservative Case

ANDREW SULLIVAN

From Virtually Normal: An Argument About Homosexuality, 1995

In this excerpt from my book I try to show how every conservative argument against same-sex marriage collapses upon close examination. This passage concentrates on the conservative notion that legalizing same-sex marriage would undermine traditional heterosexual marriage.

The most common conservative argument against same-sex marriage is that the public acceptance of homosexuality subverts the stability and self-understanding of the heterosexual family. But here the conservative position undermines itself somewhat. Since most conservatives concede the presence of a number of involuntarily homosexual persons, they must also concede that these persons are already part of "heterosexual" families. They are sons and daughters, brothers and sisters, even mothers and fathers, of heterosexuals. The distinction between "families" and "homosexuals" is, to begin with, empirically false; and the stability of existing families is closely linked to how homosexuals are treated within them. Presumably, it is against the interest of heterosexual families to force homosexuals into roles they are not equipped to play and may disastrously perform. This is not an abstract matter. It is quite common that homosexual fathers and mothers who are encouraged into heterosexual marriages subsequently find the charade and dishonesty too great to bear: spouses are betrayed, children are abandoned, families are broken, and lives are ruined. It is also common that homosexual sons and daughters who are denied the love and support of their families are liable to turn against the institution of the family, to wound and destroy it, out of hurt and rejection. And that parents, inculcated in the kind of disdain of homosexuality conservatives claim is necessary to protect the family, react to the existence of gay children with unconscionable anger and pain, and actually help destroy loving families.

Still, conservatives may concede this and still say that it's worth it. The threat to the stability of the family posed by public disapproval of homosexuality is not as great as the threat posed by public approval. How does this argument work? Largely by saying that the lives saved by preventing wavering straights from becoming gay are more numerous than the lives saved by keeping gay people out of heterosexual relationships and allowing greater tolerance of gay members of families themselves; that the stability of the society is better served by the former than by the latter. Now, recall that conservatives are not attempting to assert absolute moral truths here. They are making an argument about social goods, in this case, social and familial stability. They are saying that a homosexual life is, on the face of it, worse than a heterosexual life, as far as society is concerned. In Harvard psychologist E. L. Pattullo's words,

> Though we acknowledge some influences—social and biological—beyond their control, we do not accept the idea that people of bad character had no choice. Further, we are concerned to maintain a social climate that will steer them in the direction of the good.

The issue here is bad character and the implied association of bad character with the life of homosexuals. Although many conservatives feel loath to articulate what they mean by this life, it's clear what lies behind it. So if they won't articulate it, allow me. They mean by "a homosexual life" one in which emotional commitments are fleeting, promiscuous sex is common, disease is rampant, social ostracism is common, and standards of public decency, propriety, and self-restraint are flaunted. They mean a way of life that deliberately subverts gender norms in order to unsettle the virtues that make family life possible, ridicules heterosexual life, and commits itself to an ethic of hedonism, loneliness, and deceit. They mean by all this "the other," against which any norm has to be defended and any cohesive society protected. So it is clear that whatever good might be served by preventing gay people from becoming parents or healing internal wounds within existing families, it is greatly outweighed by the dangers of unleashing this kind of ethic upon the society as a whole.

But the argument, of course, begs a question. Is this kind of life, according to conservatives, what a homosexual life *necessarily* is? Surely not. If homosexuality is often indeed involuntary, as conservatives believe, then homosexuals are not automatically the "other"; they are sprinkled randomly throughout society, into families that are very much like anybody else's, with characters and bodies and minds as varied as the rest of humanity. If all human beings are, as conservatives believe, subject to social inducements to lead better or worse lives, then there is nothing inevitable at all about a homosexual leading a depraved life. In some cases, he might even be a paragon of virtue. Why then is the choice of a waverer to live a homosexual rather than a heterosexual life necessarily a bad one, from the point of view of society? Why does it lead to any necessary social harm at all?

Of course, if you simply define "homosexual" as "depraved," you have an answer; but it's essentially a tautologous one. And if you argue that in our society at this time, homosexual lives simply *are* more depraved, you are also begging a question. There are very few social incentives of the kind conservatives like for homosexuals *not* to be depraved: there's little social or familial support, no institution to encourage fidelity or monogamy, precious little religious or moral outreach to guide homosexuals into more virtuous living. This is not to say that homosexuals are not responsible for their actions, merely that in a large part of homosexual subculture there is much a conservative would predict, when human beings are abandoned with extremely few social incentives for good or socially responsible behavior. But the proper conservative response to this is surely not to infer that this behavior is inevitable, or to use it as a reason to deter others from engaging in a responsible homosexual existence, if that is what they want; but rather to construct social institutions and guidelines to modify and change that behavior for the better. But that is what conservatives resolutely refuse to do.

Why? Maybe for conservatives, there is something inherent even in the most virtuous homosexual life that renders it less desirable than the virtuous heterosexual life, and therefore merits social discouragement to deter the waverers. Let's assume, from a conservative perspective, the best-case scenario for such a waverer: he can choose between a loving, stable, and responsible same-sex relationship and a loving, stable, and responsible opposite-sex relationship. Why should society preference the latter?

The most common response is along the lines of Hadley Arkes, the conservative commentator, who has written on this subject on occasion. It is that the heterosexual relationship is good for men not simply because it forces them to cooperate and share with other human beings on a daily basis but because it forces them into daily contact and partnership with *women:*

> It is not marriage that domesticates men; it is women. Left to themselves, these forked creatures follow a way of life that George Gilder once recounted in its precise, chilling measures: bachelors were twenty-two times more likely than married men to be committed to hospital for mental disease (and ten times more likely to suffer chronic diseases of all kinds). Single men had nearly double the mortality rate of married men and three times the mortality rate of single women. Divorced men were three times more likely than divorced women to commit suicide or die by murder, and they were six times more likely to die of heart disease.

I will leave aside the statistical difficulties here: it's perfectly possible that many of the problems Arkes recounts were reasons why the men didn't get married, rather than consequences of their failing to do so. Let's assume, for the sake of argument, that Arkes is right: that marriage to a woman is clearly preferable to being single for an adult man; that such a man is more likely to be emotionally stable, physically healthy, psychologically in balance; and that this is good for the society as a whole. There is in this argument a belief that women are naturally more prone to be stable, nurturing, supportive of stability, fiscally prudent, and family-oriented than men, and that their connection to as many men as possible is therefore clearly a social good. Let's assume also, for the sake of argument, that Arkes is right about that too. It's obvious, according to conservatives, that society should encourage a stable opposite-sex relationship over a stable same-sex relationship.

But the waverer has another option: *he can remain single.* Should society actually encourage him to do this rather than involve himself in a stable, loving same-sex relationship? Surely, even conservatives who think women are essential to the successful socialization of men would not deny that the discipline of domesticity, of shared duties and lives, of the inevitable give-and-take of cohabitation and love with anyone, even of the same sex, tends to benefit men more than the option of constant, free-wheeling, etiolating bachelorhood. But this would mean creating a public moral and social climate which preferred stable gay relationships to gay or straight bachelorhood. And it would require generating a notion of homosexual responsibility that would destroy the delicately balanced conservative politics of private discretion and undiscriminating public disapproval. So conservatives are stuck again: their refusal to embrace responsible public support for virtuous homosexuals runs counter to their entire social agenda.

Arkes's argument also leads to another (however ironic) possibility destabilizing to conservatism's delicate contemporary compromise on the homosexual question: that for a wavering woman, a lesbian relationship might actually be socially *preferable* to a heterosexual relationship. If the issue is not mere domesticity but the presence of women, why would two women not be better than one, for the sake of children's development and social stability? Since lesbianism seems to be more amenable to choice than male homosexuality in most studies and surveys, conservatism's emphasis on social encouragement of certain behaviors over others might be seen as even more relevant here. If conservatism is about the social benefits of feminizing society, there is no reason why it should not be an integral part of the movement for women to liberate themselves completely from men. Of course, I'm being facetious; conservatives would be terrified by all the single males such a society would leave rampaging around. But it's not inconceivable at all from conservative premises that, solely from the point of view of the wavering woman, the ascending priorities would be: remaining single, having a stable, loving opposite-sex relationship, and having a stable, loving same-sex relationship. And there is something deliciously ironic about the sensibility of Hadley Arkes and E. L. Pattullo finding its full fruition in a lesbian collective.

Still, the conservative has another option. He might argue that removing the taboo on homosexuality would unravel an entire fabric of self-understanding in the society at large that could potentially destabilize the whole system of incentives for stable family relationships. He might argue that now, of all times, when families are in an unprecedented state of collapse, is not the occasion for further tinkering with this system; that the pride of heterosexual men and women is at stake; that their self-esteem and self-understanding would be undermined if society saw them as equivalent to homosexuals. In this view, the stigmatization of homosexuals is the necessary corollary to the celebration of traditional family life.

Does this ring true? To begin with, it's not at all clear why, if public disapproval of homosexuals is indeed necessary to keep families together, homosexuals of all people should bear the primary brunt of the task. But it's also not clear why the corollary really works to start with. Those homosexuals who have no choice at all to be homosexual, whom conservatives do not want to be in a heterosexual family in the first place, are clearly no threat to the heterosexual family. Why would accepting that such people exist, encouraging them to live virtuous lives, incorporating their difference into society as a whole, necessarily devalue the traditional family? It is not a zero-sum game. Because they have no choice but to be homosexual, they are not choosing that option over heterosexual marriage; and so they are not sending any social signals that heterosexual family life should be denigrated.

The more difficult case, of course, pertains to Arkes's "waverers." Would allowing them the option of a stable same-sex relationship as a preferable social option to being single really undermine the institution of the family? Is it inconceivable that a society can be subtle in its public indications of what is and what is not socially preferable? Surely, society can offer a hierarchy of choices, which, while preferencing one, does not necessarily denigrate the others, but accords them some degree of calibrated respect. It does this in many other areas. Why not in sexual arrangements?

You see this already in many families with homosexual members. While some parents are disappointed that their son or daughter will not marry someone of the opposite sex, provide grandchildren and sustain the family line for another generation, they still prefer to see that child find someone to love and live with and share his or her life with. That child's siblings, who may be heterosexual, need feel no disapproval attached to their own marriage by the simple fact of their sibling's difference. Why should society as a whole find it an impossible task to share in the same maturity? Even in the most homosexualized culture, conservatives would still expect over eighty percent of couples to be heterosexual: why is their self-esteem likely to be threatened by a paltry twenty percent—especially when, according to conservatives, the homosexual life is so self-evidently inferior?

In fact, it's perfectly possible to combine a celebration of the traditional family with the celebration of a stable homosexual relationship. The one, after all, is modeled on the other. If constructed carefully as a conservative social ideology, the notion of stable gay relationships might even serve to buttress the ethic of heterosexual marriage, by showing how even those excluded from it can wish to model themselves on its shape and structure. This very truth, of course, is why liberationists are so hostile to the entire notion. Rather than liberating society from asphyxiating conventions it actually harnesses one minority group—homosexuals—and enlists them in the conservative structures that liberationists find so inimical. One can indeed see the liberationists' reasons for opposing such a move. But why should conservatives oppose it?

The Closet Straight

HADLEY ARKES

From National Review, *July 5, 1993*

This early response to the arguments outlined in "The Politics of Homosexuality," an essay I wrote for The New Republic *in May 1993 and elaborated in* Virtually Normal, *hit on several subsequent conservative themes. But the most important is the inherently heterosexual nature of the marriage bond. Arkes believes that homosexuals who want the right to marry essentially want the right to be straight.*

What Andrew Sullivan wants, most of all, is marriage. And he wants it for reasons that could not have been stated more powerfully by any heterosexual who had been raised, as Sullivan was, in the Catholic tradition and schooled in political philosophy. "The apex of emotional life," says Sullivan, "is found in the marital bond." The erotic interest may seek out copulation, but the fulfillment of eros depends on the integrity of a bond woven of sentiment and confirmed by law. Marriage is more than a private contract; it is "the highest public recognition of our personal integrity." Its equivalent will not be supplied by a string of sensual nights, accumulated over many years of "living together." The very existence of marriage "premises the core of our emotional development. It is the architectonic institution that frames our emotional life."

No one could doubt for a moment: as much as any of the "guys" in the Damon Runyon stories, the man who wrote those lines is headed, irresistibly, for marriage. What he craves—homosexual marriage—would indeed require the approval conferred by law. It would also require a benediction conferred by straight people, who would have to consent to that vast, new modeling of our laws. That project will not be undertaken readily, and it may not be undertaken at all. Still, there is something, rooted in the nature of Andrew Sullivan, that must needs marriage.

But as Mona Charen pointed out, in an encounter with Sullivan at the National Review Institute conference this winter (*NR*, March 29), it is not marriage that domesticates men; it is women. I had the chance to see my own younger son, settled with three of his closest friends in a townhouse in Georgetown during his college years. The labors of the kitchen and the household were divided with a concern for domestic order, and the abrasions of living together were softened by the ties of friendship. And yet, no one, entering that house, could doubt for a moment that he was in a camp occupied for a while by young males, with their hormones flowing.

This is not to deny, of course, that men may truly love men, or commit themselves to a life of steady friendship. But many of us have continued to wonder just why any of these relations would be enhanced in any way by adding to them the ingredients of penetration—or marriage. The purpose of this alliance, after all, could not be the generation of children, and a marriage would not be needed then as the stable framework for welcoming and sheltering children. For gays, the ceremony of marriage could have the function of proclaiming to the world an exclusive love, a special dedication, which comes along with a solemn promise to forgo all other, competing loves. In short, it would draw its power from the romance of monogamy. But is that the vision that drives the movement for "gay rights"? An excruciating yearning for monogamy?

That may indeed be Andrew Sullivan's own yearning, but his position is already marking him as a curious figure in the camp of gay activists. When Sullivan commends the ideal of marriage for gays, he would seem to be pleading merely for the inclusion of gay "couples" in an institution that is indeed confined to pairs, of adults, in monogamous unions. But that is not exactly the vision of gay sex.

For many activists and connoisseurs, Sullivan would represent a rather wimpish, constricted view of the world they would open to themselves through sexual liberation. After all, the permissions for this new sexual freedom have been cast to that amorphous formula of "sexual orientation": the demand of gay rights is that we should recede from casting moral judgments on the way that people find their pleasure in engagements they regard as "sexual." In its strange abstraction, "sexual orientation" could take in sex with animals or the steamier versions of sadomasochism. The devotees of S&M were much in evidence during the recent march in Washington, but we may put aside for a moment these interests, to consider others which are even more exotic yet. There is, for example, the North American Man-Boy Love Association, a contingent of gay activists who identify themselves, unashamedly, as pedophiles. They insist that nothing in their "sexual orientation" should disqualify them to work as professional counselors, say, in the schools of New York, and to counsel young boys. And since they respect themselves, they will not hold back from commending their own way of life to their young charges. If there is to be gay marriage, would it be confined then only to adults? And if men are inclined to a life of multiple partners, why should marriage be confined to two persons? Why indeed should the notion of gay marriage be scaled down to fit the notions held by Andrew Sullivan?

The sources of anguish run even deeper here than Sullivan may suspect, for his dilemma may be crystallized in this way: If he would preserve the traditional understanding of marriage and monogamy, he would not speak for much of a constituency among gays. But if the notion of "marriage" were enlarged and redefined—if it could take in a plurality of people and shifting combinations—it could hardly be the kind of marriage that Sullivan devoutly wishes as "the apex of emotional life" and "the highest public recognition of our personal integrity."

In traditional marriage, the understanding of monogamy was originally tied to the "natural teleology" of the body—to the recognition that only two people, no more and no fewer, can generate children. To that understanding of a union, or a "marriage," the alliance of two men would offer such an implausible want of resemblance that it would appear almost as a mocking burlesque. It would be rather like confounding, as Lincoln used to say, a "horse chestnut" and a "chestnut horse." The mockery would be avoided if the notion of marriage could be opened, or broadened, to accommodate the varieties of sexual experience. The most notable accommodation would be the acceptance of several partners, and the change could be readily reckoned precisely because it would hardly be novel: the proposal for gay marriage would compel us to look again—to look anew with eyes unclouded by prejudice—to the ancient appeal of polygamy. After all, there would be an Equal Protection problem now: we could scarcely confine this new "marital" arrangement only to members of one gender. But then, once the arrangement is opened simply to "consenting adults," on what ground would we object to the mature couplings of aunts and nephews, or even fathers and daughters—couplings that show a remarkable persistence in our own age, even against the barriers of law and sentiment that have been cast up over centuries? All kinds of questions, once placed in a merciful repose, may reasonably be opened again. They become live issues once we are willing to ponder that simple question, Why should marriage be confined, after all, to couples, and to pairs drawn from different sexes?

That question, if it comes to be treated as open and problematic, will not readily be closed, or not at least on the terms that Andrew Sullivan seeks. The melancholy news then is this: We cannot deliver to him what he wants without introducing, into our laws, notions that must surely undercut the rationale and the justification for marriage. The marriage that he wants, he cannot practicably have; but in seeking it, he runs the risk of weakening even further the opinion that sustains marriage as "the architectonic institution that frames our emotional life." . . .

Against Homosexual Marriage

JAMES Q. WILSON

From Commentary, *March 1996*

In a rigorous point-by-point engagement with the arguments of Virtually Normal, *James Q. Wilson expresses the conservative desire not to impose change against the moral sensibilities of a heterosexual majority.*

Sullivan recounts three main arguments concerning homosexual marriage, two against and one for. He labels them prohibitionist, conservative, and liberal. I think it easier to grasp the origins of the three main arguments by referring to the principles on which they are based.

The prohibitionist argument is in fact a biblical one; the heart of it was stated by Dennis Prager in an essay reprinted in the *Public Interest* ("Homosexuality, the Bible, and Us," Summer 1993). When the first books of the Bible were written, and for a long time thereafter, heterosexual love is what seemed at risk. In many cultures—not only in Egypt or among the Canaanite tribes surrounding ancient Israel but later in Greece, Rome, and the Arab world, to say nothing of large parts of China, Japan, and elsewhere—homosexual practices were common and widely tolerated or even exalted. The Torah reversed this, making the family the central unit of life, the obligation to marry one of the first responsibilities of man, and the linkage of sex to procreation the highest standard by which to judge sexual relations. Leviticus puts the matter sharply and apparently beyond quibble.

Thou shalt not live with mankind as with womankind; it is an
abomination. . . . If a man also lie with mankind, as he lieth
with a woman, both of them have committed an abomination;
they shall surely be put to death; their blood shall be upon
them.

Sullivan acknowledges the power of Leviticus but deals with
it by placing it in a relative context. What is the nature of this
"abomination"? Is it like killing your mother or stealing a neighbor's bread, or is it more like refusing to eat shellfish or having
sex during menstruation? Sullivan suggests that all of these injunctions were written on the same moral level and hence can
be accepted or ignored *as a whole*. He does not fully sustain this
view, and in fact a refutation of it can be found in Prager's essay.
In Prager's opinion and mine, people at the time of Moses, and
for centuries before him, understood that there was a fundamental difference between whom you killed and what you ate,
and in all likelihood people then and for centuries earlier linked
whom you could marry closer to the principles that defined life
than they did to the rules that defined diets.

The New Testament contains an equally vigorous attack on
homosexuality by St. Paul. Sullivan partially deflects it by noting
Paul's conviction that the earth was about to end and the Second
Coming was near; under these conditions, all forms of sex were
suspect. But Sullivan cannot deny that Paul singled out homosexuality as deserving of special criticism. He seems to pass over
this obstacle without effective retort.

Instead, he takes up a different theme, namely, that on
grounds of consistency many heterosexual practices—adultery,
sodomy, premarital sex, and divorce, among others—should be
outlawed equally with homosexual acts of the same character.
The difficulty with this is that it mistakes the distinction alive in

most people's minds between marriage as an institution and marriage as a practice. As an institution, it deserves unqualified support; as a practice, we recognize that married people are as imperfect as anyone else. Sullivan's understanding of the prohibitionist argument suffers from his unwillingness to acknowledge this distinction.

The second argument against homosexual marriage—Sullivan's conservative category—is based on natural law as originally set forth by Aristotle and Thomas Aquinas and more recently restated by Hadley Arkes, John Finnis, Robert George, Harry V. Jaffa, and others. How it is phrased varies a bit, but in general its advocates support a position like the following: man cannot live without the care and support of other people; natural law is the distillation of what thoughtful people have learned about the conditions of that care. The first thing they have learned is the supreme importance of marriage, for without it the newborn infant is unlikely to survive or, if he survives, to prosper. The necessary conditions of a decent family life are the acknowledgment by its members that a man will not sleep with his daughter or a woman with her son and that neither will openly choose sex outside marriage.

Now, some of these conditions are violated, but there is a penalty in each case that is supported by the moral convictions of almost all who witness the violation. On simple utilitarian grounds it may be hard to object to incest or adultery; if both parties to such an act welcome it and if it is secret, what differences does it make? But very few people, and then only ones among the overeducated, seem to care much about mounting a utilitarian assault on the family. To this assault, natural-law theorists respond much as would the average citizen—never mind "utility," what counts is what is right. In particular, homosexual uses of the reproductive organs violate the condition that sex serve solely as the basis of heterosexual marriage.

To Sullivan, what is defective about the natural-law thesis is that it assumes different purposes in heterosexual and homosexual love: moral consummation in the first case and pure utility or pleasure alone in the second. But in fact, Sullivan suggests, homosexual love can be as consummatory as heterosexual. He notes that as the Roman Catholic Church has deepened its understanding of the involuntary—that is, in some sense genetic—basis of homosexuality, it has attempted to keep homosexuals in the church as objects of affection and nurture, while banning homosexual acts as perverse.

But this, though better than nothing, will not work, Sullivan writes. To show why, he adduces an analogy to a sterile person. Such a person is permitted to serve in the military or enter an unproductive marriage; why not homosexuals? If homosexuals marry without procreation, they are no different (he suggests) from a sterile man or woman who marries without hope of procreation. Yet people, I think, want the form observed even when the practice varies; a sterile marriage, whether from choice or necessity, remains a marriage of a man and a woman. To this Sullivan offers essentially an aesthetic response. Just as albinos remind us of the brilliance of color and genius teaches us about moderation, homosexuals are a "natural foil" to the heterosexual union, "a variation that does not eclipse the theme." Moreover, the threat posed by the foil to the theme is slight as compared to the threats posed by adultery, divorce, and prostitution. To be consistent, Sullivan once again reminds us, society would have to ban adulterers from the military as it now bans confessed homosexuals.

But again this misses the point. It would make more sense to ask why an alternative to marriage should be invented and praised when we are having enough trouble maintaining the institution at all. Suppose that gay or lesbian marriage were authorized; rather than producing a "natural foil" that would "not eclipse the theme," I suspect such a move would call even more seriously into question the role of marriage at a time when the threats to it, ranging from single-parent families to common divorces, have hit record highs. Kenneth Minogue recently wrote of Sullivan's book that support for homosexual marriage would strike most people as "mere parody," one that could further weaken an already strained institution.

To me, the chief limitation of Sullivan's view is that it presupposes that marriage would have the same, domesticating, effect on homosexual members as it has on heterosexuals, while leaving the latter largely unaffected. Those are very large assumptions that no modern society has ever tested.

Nor does it seem plausible to me that a modern society resists homosexual marriages entirely out of irrational prejudice. Marriage is a union, sacred to most, that unites a man and woman together for life. It is a sacrament of the Catholic Church and central to every other faith. Is it out of misinformation that every modern society has embraced this view and rejected the alternative? Societies differ greatly in their attitude toward the income people may have, the relations among their various races, and the distribution of political power. But they differ scarcely at all over the distinctions between heterosexual and homosexual couples. The former are overwhelmingly preferred over the latter. The reason, I believe, is that these distinctions involve the nature of marriage and thus the very meaning—even more, the very possibility—of society.

The final argument over homosexual marriage is the liberal one, based on civil rights.

As we have seen, the Hawaiian Supreme Court ruled that any state-imposed sexual distinction would have to meet the test of strict scrutiny, a term used by the U.S. Supreme Court only for racial and similar classifications. In doing this, the Hawaiian court distanced itself from every other state court decision—there are several—in this area so far. A variant of the suspect-class argument, though, has been suggested by some scholars who contend that denying access to a marriage license by two people of the same sex is no different from denying access to two people of different sexes but also different races. The Hawaiian Supreme Court embraced this argument as well, explicitly comparing its decision to that of the U.S. Supreme Court when it overturned state laws banning marriages involving miscegenation.

But the comparison with black-white marriages is itself suspect. Beginning around 1964, and no doubt powerfully affected by the passage of the Civil Rights Act of that year, public attitudes toward race began to change dramatically. Even allowing for exaggerated statements to pollsters, there is little doubt that people in fact acquired a new view of blacks. Not so with homosexuals. Though the campaign to aid them has been going on vigorously for about a quarter of a century, it has produced few, if any, gains in public acceptance, and the greatest resistance, I think, has been with respect to homosexual marriages.

Consider the difference. What has been at issue in race relations is not marriage among blacks (for over a century, that right has been universally granted) or even miscegenation (long before the civil-rights movement, many Southern states had repealed such laws). Rather, it has been the routine contact between the races in schools, jobs, and neighborhoods. Our own history, in other words, has long made it clear that marriage is a different issue from the issue of social integration.

There is another way, too, in which the comparison with race is less than helpful, as Sullivan himself points out. Thanks to the changes in public attitudes I mentioned a moment ago, gradually race was held to be not central to decisions about hiring, firing, promoting, and schooling, and blacks began to make extraordinary advances in society. But then, in an effort to enforce this new view, liberals came to embrace affirmative action, a policy that said that race *was* central to just such issues, in order to ensure that *real* mixing occurred. This move created a crisis, for liberalism had always been based on the proposition that a liberal political system should encourage, as John Stuart Mill put it, "experiments in living" free of religious or political direction. To contemporary liberals, however, being neutral about race was tantamount to being neutral about a set of human preferences that in such matters as neighborhood and schooling left groups largely (but not entirely) separate.

Sullivan, who wisely sees that hardly anybody is really prepared to ignore a political opportunity to change lives, is not disposed to have much of this either in the area of race or in that of sex. And he points out with great clarity that popular attitudes toward sexuality are anyway quite different from those about race, as is evident from the fact that wherever sexual orientation is subject to local regulations, such regulations are rarely invoked. Why? Because homosexuals can "pass" or not, as they wish; they can and do accumulate education and wealth; they exercise political power. The two things a homosexual cannot do are join the military as an avowed homosexual or marry another homosexual.

The result, Sullivan asserts, is a wrenching paradox. On the one hand, society has historically tolerated the brutalization inflicted on people because of the color of their skin, but freely allowed them to marry; on the other hand, it has given equal opportunity to homosexuals, while denying them the right to marry. This, indeed, is where Sullivan draws the line. A black or Hispanic child, if heterosexual, has many friends, he writes, but a gay child "generally has no one." And that is why the social stigma attached to homosexuality is different from that attached to race or ethnicity—"because it attacks the very heart of what makes a human being human: the ability to love and be loved." Here is the essence of Sullivan's case. It is a powerful one, even if (as I suspect) his pro-marriage sentiments are not shared by all homosexuals.

Let us assume for the moment that a chance to live openly and legally with another homosexual is desirable. To believe that, we must set aside biblical injunctions, a difficult matter in a profoundly religious nation. But suppose we manage the diversion, perhaps on the grounds that if most Americans skip church, they can as readily avoid other errors of (possibly) equal magnitude. Then we must ask on what terms the union shall be arranged. There are two alternatives—marriage or domestic partnership.

Sullivan acknowledges the choice, but disparages the domestic-partnership laws that have evolved in some foreign countries and in some American localities. His reasons, essentially conservative ones, are that domestic partnerships are too easily formed and too easily broken. Only real marriages matter. But—aside from the fact that marriage is in serious decline, and that only slightly more than half of all marriages performed in the United States this year will be between never-before-married heterosexuals—what is distinctive about marriage is that it is an institution created to sustain child-rearing. Whatever losses it has suffered in *this* respect, its function remains what it has always been.

The role of raising children is entrusted in principle to married heterosexual couples because after much experimentation—several thousand years, more or less—we have found nothing else that works as well. Neither a gay nor a lesbian couple can of its own resources produce a child; another party must be involved. What do we call this third party? A friend? A sperm or egg bank? An anonymous donor? There is no settled language for even describing, much less approving of, such persons.

Suppose we allowed homosexual couples to raise children who were created out of a prior heterosexual union or adopted from someone else's heterosexual contact. What would we think of this? There is very little research on the matter. Charlotte Patterson's famous essay, "Children of Gay and Lesbian Parents" (*Journal of Child Development*, 1992), begins by conceding that the existing studies focus on children born into a heterosexual union that ended in divorce or that was transformed when the mother or father "came out" as a homosexual. Hardly any research has been done on children acquired at the outset by a homosexual couple. We therefore have no way of knowing how they would behave. And even if we had such studies, they might tell us rather little unless they were conducted over a very long period of time.

But it is one thing to be born into an apparently heterosexual family and then many years later to learn that one of your parents is homosexual. It is quite another to be acquired as an infant from an adoption agency or a parent-for-hire and learn from the first years of life that you are, because of your family's position, radically different from almost all other children you will meet. No one can now say how grievous this would be. We know that young children tease one another unmercifully; adding this dimension does not seem to be a step in the right direction.

Of course, homosexual "families," with or without children, might be rather few in number. Just how few, it is hard to say. Perhaps Sullivan himself would marry, but, given the great tendency of homosexual males to be promiscuous, many more like him would not, or if they did, would not marry with as much seriousness. . . .

The courts in Hawaii and in the nation's capital must struggle with all these issues under the added encumbrance of a contemporary outlook that makes law the search for rights, and responsibility the recognition of rights. Indeed, thinking of laws about marriage as documents that confer or withhold rights is itself an error of fundamental importance—one that the highest court in Hawaii has already committed. "Marriage," it wrote, "is a state-conferred legal-partnership status, the existence of which gives rise to a multiplicity of rights and benefits. . . ." A state-conferred legal partnership? To lawyers, perhaps; to mankind, I think not. The Hawaiian court has thus set itself on the same course of action as the misguided Supreme Court in 1973 when it thought that laws about abortion were merely an assertion of the rights of a living mother and an unborn fetus.

I have few favorable things to say about the political systems of other modern nations, but on these fundamental matters—abortion, marriage, military service—they often do better by allowing legislatures to operate than we do by deferring to courts. Our challenge is to find a way of formulating a policy with respect to homosexual unions that is not the result of a reflexive act of judicial rights-conferring, but is instead a considered expression of the moral convictions of a people.

For Better or Worse?

J O N A T H A N   R A U C H

From The New Republic, *May 6, 1996*

Rauch delivers an almost Jesuitical analysis of why same-sex marriage makes sense for conservatives. He is particularly acute in making a social as well as a political argument for the virtues that marriage inculcates—especially in gay men. He is quite comfortable about using the threat of stigma to bring more social order into gay men's lives.

Whether gay marriage makes sense—and whether straight marriage makes sense—depends on what marriage is actually for. Current secular thinking on this question is shockingly sketchy. Gay activists say: marriage is for love, and we love each other, therefore we should be able to marry. Traditionalists say: marriage is for children, and homosexuals do not (or should not) have children, therefore you should not be able to marry. That, unfortunately, pretty well covers the spectrum. I say "unfortunately" because both views are wrong. They misunderstand and impoverish the social meaning of marriage.

So what is marriage for? Modern marriage is, of course, based upon traditions that religion helped to codify and enforce. But religious doctrine has no special standing in the world of secular law and policy (the "Christian nation" crowd notwithstanding). If we want to know what and whom marriage is for in modern America, we need a sensible secular doctrine.

At one point, marriage in secular society was largely a matter of business: cementing family ties, providing social status for men and economic support for women, conferring dowries, and so on. Marriages were typically arranged, and "love" in the modern sense was no prerequisite. In Japan, remnants of this system remain, and it works surprisingly well. Couples stay together because they view their marriage as a partnership: an investment in social stability for themselves and their children. Because Japanese couples don't expect as much emotional fulfillment as we do, they are less inclined to break up. They also take a somewhat more relaxed attitude toward adultery. What's a little extracurricular love provided that each partner is fulfilling his or her many other marital duties?

In the West, of course, love is a defining element. The notion of lifelong love is charming, if ambitious, and certainly love is a desirable element of marriage. In society's eyes, however, it cannot be the defining element. You may or may not love your husband, but the two of you are just as married either way. You may love your mistress, but that certainly doesn't make her your spouse. Love helps make sense of marriage emotionally, but it is not terribly important in making sense of marriage from the point of view of social policy.

If love does not define the purpose of secular marriage, what does? Neither the law nor secular thinking provides a clear answer. Today marriage is almost entirely a voluntary arrangement whose contents are up to the people making the deal. There are few if any behaviors that automatically end a marriage. If a man beats his wife, which is about the worst thing he can do to her, he may be convicted of assault, but his marriage is not automatically dissolved. Couples can be adulterous ("open") yet remain married. They can be celibate, too; consummation is not required. All in all, it is an impressive and also rather astonishing victory for modern individualism that so important an institution should be so bereft of formal social instruction as to what should go on inside of it.

Secular society tells us only a few things about marriage. First, marriage depends on the consent of the parties. Second, the parties are not children. Third, the number of parties is two. Fourth, one is a man and the other a woman. Within those rules a marriage is whatever anyone says it is.

Perhaps it is enough simply to say that marriage is as it is and should not be tampered with. This sounds like a crudely reactionary position. In fact, however, of all the arguments against reforming marriage, it is probably the most powerful.

Call it a Hayekian argument, after the great libertarian economist F. A. Hayek, who developed this line of thinking in his book *The Fatal Conceit.* In a market system, the prices generated by impersonal forces may not make sense from any one person's point of view, but they encode far more information than even the cleverest person could ever gather. In a similar fashion, human societies evolve rich and complicated webs of nonlegal rules in the form of customs, traditions and institutions. Like prices, they may seem irrational or arbitrary. But the very fact that they are the customs that have evolved implies that they embody a practical logic that may not be apparent to even a sophisticated analyst. And the web of custom cannot be torn apart and reordered at will because once its internal logic is violated it falls apart. Intellectuals, such as Marxists or feminists, who seek to deconstruct and rationally rebuild social traditions, will produce not better order but chaos.

So the Hayekian view argues strongly against gay marriage. It says that the current rules may not be best and may even be unfair. But they are all we have, and, once you say that marriage need not be male-female, soon marriage will stop being anything at all. You can't mess with the formula without causing unforeseen consequences, possibly including the implosion of the institution of marriage itself.

However, there are problems with the Hayekian position. It

is untenable in its extreme form and unhelpful in its milder version. In its extreme form, it implies that no social reforms should ever be undertaken. Indeed, no laws should be passed, because they interfere with the natural evolution of social mores. How could Hayekians abolish slavery? They would probably note that slavery violates fundamental moral principles. But in so doing they would establish a moral platform from which to judge social rules, and thus acknowledge that abstracting social debate from moral concerns is not possible.

If the ban on gay marriage were only mildly unfair, and if the costs of changing it were certain to be enormous, then the ban could stand on Hayekian grounds. But, if there is any social policy today that has a fair claim to be scaldingly inhumane, it is the ban on gay marriage. As conservatives tirelessly and rightly point out, marriage is society's most fundamental institution. To bar any class of people from marrying as they choose is an extraordinary deprivation. When not so long ago it was illegal in parts of America for blacks to marry whites, no one could claim that this was a trivial disenfranchisement. Granted, gay marriage raises issues that interracial marriage does not; but no one can argue that the deprivation is a minor one.

To outweigh such a serious claim it is not enough to say that gay marriage might lead to bad things. Bad things happened as a result of legalizing contraception, but that did not make it the wrong thing to do. Besides, it seems doubtful that extending marriage to, say, another 3 or 5 percent of the population would have anything like the effects that no-fault divorce has had, to say nothing of contraception. By now, the "traditional" understanding of marriage has been sullied in all kinds of ways. It is hard to think of a bigger affront to tradition, for instance, than allowing married women to own property independently of their husbands or allowing them to charge their husbands with rape. Surely it is unfair to say that marriage may be reformed for the sake of anyone and everyone except homosexuals, who must respect the dictates of tradition.

Faced with these problems, the milder version of the Hayekian argument says not that social traditions shouldn't be tampered with at all, but that they shouldn't be tampered with lightly. Fine. In this case, no one is talking about casual messing around; both sides have marshaled their arguments with deadly seriousness. Hayekians surely have to recognize that appeals to blind tradition and to the risks inherent in social change do not, a priori, settle anything in this instance. They merely warn against frivolous change.

So we turn to what has become the standard view of marriage's purpose. Its proponents would probably like to call it a child-centered view, but it is actually an anti-gay view, as will become clear. Whatever you call it, it is the view of marriage that is heard most often, and in the context of the debate over gay marriage it is heard almost exclusively. In its most straightforward form it goes as follows (I quote from James Q. Wilson's fine book *The Moral Sense*):

> A family is not an association of independent people; it is a human commitment designed to make possible the rearing of moral and healthy children. Governments care—or ought to care—about families for this reason, and scarcely for any other.

Wilson speaks about "family" rather than "marriage" as such, but one may, I think, read him as speaking of marriage without doing any injustice to his meaning. The resulting proposition—government ought to care about marriage almost entirely because of children—seems reasonable. But there are problems. The first, obviously, is that gay couples may have children, whether through adoption, prior marriage or (for lesbians) artificial insemination. Leaving aside the thorny issue of gay adoption, the point is that if the mere presence of children is the test, then homosexual relationships can certainly pass it.

You might note, correctly, that heterosexual marriages are more likely to produce children than homosexual ones. When granting marriage licenses to heterosexuals, however, we do not ask how likely the couple is to have children. We assume that they are entitled to get married whether or not they end up with children. Understanding this, conservatives often make an interesting move. In seeking to justify the state's interest in marriage, they shift from the actual presence of children to the anatomical possibility of making them. Hadley Arkes, a political science professor and prominent opponent of homosexual marriage, makes the case this way:

> The traditional understanding of marriage is grounded in the "natural teleology of the body"—in the inescapable fact that only a man and a woman, and only two people, not three, can generate a child. Once marriage is detached from that natural teleology of the body, what ground of principle would thereafter confine marriage to two people rather than some larger grouping? That is, on what ground of principle would the law reject the claim of a gay couple that their love is not confined to a coupling of two, but that they are woven into a larger ensemble with yet another person or two?

What he seems to be saying is that, where the possibility of natural children is nil, the meaning of marriage is nil. If marriage is allowed between members of the same sex, then the concept of marriage has been emptied of content except to ask whether the parties love each other. Then anything goes, including polygamy. This reasoning presumably is what those opposed to gay marriage have in mind when they claim that, once gay marriage is legal, marriage to pets will follow close behind.

But Arkes and his sympathizers make two mistakes. To see them, break down the claim into two components: (1) Two-person marriage derives its special status from the anatomical possibility that the partners can create natural children; and (2) apart from (1), two-person marriage has no purpose sufficiently strong to justify its special status. That is, absent justification (1), anything goes.

The first proposition is wholly at odds with the way society actually views marriage. Leave aside the insistence that natural, as opposed to adopted, children define the importance of marriage. The deeper problem, apparent right away, is the issue of sterile heterosexual couples. Here the "anatomical possibility" crowd has a problem, for a homosexual union is, anatomically speaking, nothing but one variety of sterile union and no different even in principle: a woman without a uterus has no more potential for giving birth than a man without a vagina.

It may sound like carping to stress the case of barren heterosexual marriage: the vast majority of newlywed heterosexual couples, after all, can have children and probably will. But the point here is fundamental. There are far more sterile heterosexual unions in America than homosexual ones. The "anatomical possibility" crowd cannot have it both ways. If the possibility of children is what gives meaning to marriage, then a postmenopausal woman who applies for a marriage license should be turned away at the courthouse door. What's more, she should be hooted at and condemned for stretching the meaning of marriage beyond its natural basis and so reducing the institution to frivolity. People at the Family Research Council or Concerned Women for America should point at her and say, "If she can marry, why not polygamy?"

Obviously, the "anatomical" conservatives do not say this, because they are sane. They instead flail around, saying that sterile men and women were at least born with the right-shaped parts for making children, and so on. Their position is really a nonposition. It says that the "natural children" rationale defines marriage when homosexuals are involved but not when hetero-sexuals are involved. When the parties to union are sterile het-erosexuals, the justification for marriage must be something else. But what?

Now arises the oddest part of the "anatomical" argument. Look at proposition (2) above. It says that, absent the anatomical justification for marriage, anything goes. In other words, it dis-misses the idea that there might be other good reasons for soci-ety to sanctify marriage above other kinds of relationships. Why would anybody make this move? I'll hazard a guess: to exclude homosexuals. Any rationale that justifies sterile heterosexual marriages can also apply to homosexual ones. For instance, mar-riage makes women more financially secure. Very nice, say the conservatives. But that rationale could be applied to lesbians, so it's definitely out.

The end result of this stratagem is perverse to the point of being funny. The attempt to ground marriage in children (or the anatomical possibility thereof) falls flat. But, having lost that rea-son for marriage, the antigay people can offer no other. In their fixation on excluding homosexuals, they leave themselves no consistent justification for the privileged status of *heterosexual* marriage. They thus tear away any coherent foundation that sec-ular marriage might have, which is precisely the opposite of what they claim they want to do. If they have to undercut mar-riage to save it from homosexuals, so be it!

For the record, I would be the last to deny that children are one central reason for the privileged status of marriage. When men and women get together, children are a likely outcome; and, as we are learning in ever more unpleasant ways, when children grow up without two parents, trouble ensues. Children are not a trivial reason for marriage; they just cannot be the only reason.

What are the others? It seems to me that the two strongest candidates are these: domesticating men and providing reliable caregivers. Both purposes are critical to the functioning of a humane and stable society, and both are much better served by marriage—that is, by one-to-one lifelong commitment—than by any other institution.

Civilizing young males is one of any society's biggest problems. Whenever unattached males gather in packs, you see no end of trouble; wildings in Central Park, gangs in Los Angeles, soccer hooligans in Britain, skinheads in Germany, fraternity hazings in universities, grope-lines in the military and, in a different but ultimately no less tragic way, the bathhouses and wanton sex of gay San Francisco or New York in the 1970s.

For taming men, marriage is unmatched. "Of all the institutions through which men may pass—schools, factories, the military—marriage has the largest effect," Wilson writes in *The Moral Sense*. (A token of the casualness of current thinking about marriage is that the man who wrote those words could, later in the very same book, say that government should care about fostering families for "scarcely any other" reason than children.) If marriage—that is, the binding of men into couples—did nothing else, its power to settle men, to keep them at home and out of trouble, would be ample justification for its special status.

Of course, women and older men don't generally travel in marauding or orgiastic packs. But in their case the second rationale comes into play. A second enormous problem for society is what to do when someone is beset by some sort of burdensome contingency. It could be cancer, a broken back, unemployment or depression; it could be exhaustion from work or stress under pressure. If marriage has any meaning at all, it is that, when you collapse from a stroke, there will be at least one other person whose "job" is to drop everything and come to your aid; or that when you come home after being fired by the postal service there will be someone to persuade you not to kill the supervisor.

Obviously, both rationales—the need to settle males and the need to have people looked after—apply to sterile people as well as fertile ones, and apply to childless couples as well as to ones with children. The first explains why everybody feels relieved when the town delinquent gets married, and the second explains why everybody feels happy when an aging widow takes a second husband. From a social point of view, it seems to me, both rationales are far more compelling as justifications of marriage's special status than, say, love. And both of them apply to homosexuals as well as to heterosexuals.

Take the matter of settling men. It is probably true that women and children, more than just the fact of marriage, help civilize men. But that hardly means that the settling effect of marriage on homosexual men is negligible. To the contrary, being tied to a committed relationship plainly helps stabilize gay men. Even without marriage, coupled gay men have steady sex partners and relationships that they value and therefore tend to be less wanton. Add marriage, and you bring a further array of stabilizing influences. One of the main benefits of publicly recognized marriage is that it binds couples together not only in their own eyes but also in the eyes of society at large. Around the partners is woven a web of expectations that they will spend nights together, go to parties together, take out mortgages together, buy furniture at Ikea together, and so on—all of which helps tie them together and keep them off the streets and at home. Surely that is a very good thing, especially as compared to the closet-gay culture of furtive sex with innumerable partners in parks and bathhouses.

The other benefit of marriage—caretaking—clearly applies to homosexuals. One of the first things many people worry about when coming to terms with their homosexuality is: Who will take care of me when I'm ailing or old? Society needs to care about this, too, as the AIDS crisis has made horribly clear. If that crisis has shown anything, it is that homosexuals can and will take care of each other, sometimes with breathtaking devotion—and that no institution can begin to match the care of a devoted partner. Legally speaking, marriage creates kin. Surely society's interest in kin-creation is strongest of all for people who are unlikely to be supported by children in old age and who may well be rejected by their own parents in youth.

Gay marriage, then, is far from being a mere exercise in political point-making or rights-mongering. On the contrary, it serves two of the three social purposes that make marriage so indispensable and irreplaceable for heterosexuals. Two out of three may not be the whole ball of wax, but it is more than enough to give society a compelling interest in marrying off homosexuals.

There is no substitute. Marriage is the *only* institution that adequately serves these purposes. The power of marriage is not just legal but social. It seals its promise with the smiles and tears of family, friends, and neighbors. It shrewdly exploits ceremony (big, public weddings) and money (expensive gifts, dowries) to deter casual commitment and to make bailing out embarrassing. Stag parties and bridal showers signal that what is beginning is not just a legal arrangement but a whole new stage of life. "Domestic partner" laws do none of these things.

I'll go further: far from being a substitute for the real thing, marriage-lite may undermine it. Marriage is a deal between a couple and society, not just between two people: society recognizes the sanctity and autonomy of the pair-bond, and in exchange each spouse commits to being the other's nurse, social worker and policeman of first resort. Each marriage is its own little society within society. Any step that weakens the deal by granting the legal benefits of marriage without also requiring the public commitment is begging for trouble.

So gay marriage makes sense for several of the same reasons that straight marriage makes sense. That would seem a natural and dangerous: frivolous because it blesses unions in which society has no particular interest; dangerous because anything which trivialises marriage undermines this most basic of institutions. Traditionalists are right about the importance of marriage. But they are wrong to see gay marriage as trivial or frivolous.

It is true that the single most important reason society cares about marriage is for the sake of children. But society's stake in stable, long-term partnerships hardly ends there. Marriage remains an economic bulwark. Single people (especially women) are economically vulnerable, and much more likely to fall into the arms of the welfare state. Furthermore, they call sooner upon public support when they need care—and, indeed, are likelier to fall ill (married people, the numbers show, are not only happier but considerably healthier). Not least important, marriage is a great social stabiliser of men.

Homosexuals need emotional and economic stability no less than heterosexuals—and society surely benefits when they have it. "Then let them 'unchoose' homosexuality and marry someone of the opposite sex," was the old answer. Today that reply is untenable. Homosexuals do not choose their condition; indeed, they often try desperately hard, sometimes to the point of suicide, to avoid it. However, they are less and less willing either to hide or to lead lives of celibacy. For society, the real choice is between homosexual marriage and homosexual alienation. No social interest is served by choosing the latter.

To this principle of social policy, add a principle of government. Barring a compelling reason, governments should not discriminate between classes of citizens. As recently as 1967, blacks and whites in some American states could not wed. No one but a crude racist would defend such a rule now. Even granting that the case of homosexuals is more complex than the case of miscegenation, the state should presume against discriminating—especially when handing out something as important as a marriage

place to stop. But the logic of the argument compels one to go a twist further. If it is good for society to have people attached, then it is not enough just to make marriage available. Marriage should also be *expected*. This, too, is just as true for homosexuals as for heterosexuals. So, if homosexuals are justified in expecting access to marriage, society is equally justified in expecting them to use it. I'm not saying that out-of-wedlock sex should be scandalous or that people should be coerced into marrying. The mechanisms of expectation are more subtle. When grandma cluck-clucks over a still-unmarried young man, or when mom says she wishes her little girl would settle down, she is expressing a strong and well-justified preference: one that is quietly echoed in a thousand ways throughout society and that produces subtle but important pressure to form and sustain unions. This is a good and necessary thing, and it will be as necessary for homosexuals as heterosexuals. If gay marriage is recognized, single gay people over a certain age should not be surprised when they are disapproved of or pitied. That is a vital part of what makes marriage work. It's stigma as social policy.

If marriage is to work it cannot be merely a "lifestyle option." It must be privileged. That is, it must be understood to be better, on average, than other ways of living. Not mandatory, not good where everything else is bad, but better: a general norm, rather than a personal taste. The biggest worry about gay marriage, I think is, is that homosexuals might get it but then mostly not use it. Gay neglect of marriage wouldn't greatly erode the bonding power of heterosexual marriage (remember, homosexuals are only a tiny fraction of the population)—but it would certainly not help. And heterosexual society would rightly feel betrayed if, after legalization, homosexuals treated marriage as a minority taste rather than as a core institution of life. It is not enough, I think, for gay people to say we want the right to marry. If we do not use it, shame on us.

Let Them Wed
THE EDITORS

From The Economist, *January 6, 1996*

The sober, unsentimental, free market conservative British magazine weighs in—for the gay rights movement.

Marriage may be for the ages—but it changes by the year. And never, perhaps, has it changed as quickly as since the 1960s. In western law, wives are now equal rather than subordinate partners; interracial marriage is now widely accepted both in statute and in society; marital failure itself, rather than the fault of one partner, may be grounds for a split. With change, alas, has come strain. In the twenty-five years from 1960, divorce rates soared throughout the West—more than sextupled in Britain, where divorce appears inevitable for the world's most celebrated marriage, that of Charles and Diana Windsor. Struggling to keep law apace with reality, Britain's Tory government is even now advancing another marriage reform, seeking, on the whole sensibly, to make quick or impulsive divorce harder but no-fault divorce easier.

That, however, is not the kind of reform which some decidedly un-Tory people are seeking— and have begun to achieve. Denmark, Norway, and Sweden now allow homosexual partners to register with the state and to claim many (though not all) of the prerogatives of marriage. The Dutch are moving in the same direction. In France and Belgium, cities and local governments have begun recognising gay partnerships. And, in the American

state of Hawaii, a court case may legalise homosexual marriage itself.

As of today, however, there is no country which gives homosexuals the full right of marriage. And that is what gay activists in more and more places are seeking. Marriage, one might think, is in turbulent enough waters already. Can gay marriage be a good idea—now?

To understand why the answer is yes, first set aside a view whose appealing simplicity is its undoing. "Governments are not elected to arrange nuptial liaisons, much less to untangle them," writes Joe Rogaly in the *Financial Times.* "It is a purely private matter." On this libertarian view, the terms of a marriage contract should be the partners' business, not the state's. With the help of lawyers and sympathetic churchmen, homosexuals can create for themselves what is in all practical respects a marriage; if they lack a government licence, so what?

The government-limiting impulse motivating this view is admirable. But, in truth, the state's involvement in marriage is both inevitable and indispensable. Although many kinds of human pairings are possible, state-sanctioned marriage is, tautologically, the only one which binds couples together in the eyes of the law. By doing so it confers upon partners unique rights to make life-or-death medical decisions, rights to inheritance, rights to share pensions and medical benefits; just as important, it confers upon each the legal responsibilities of guardianship and care of the other. Far from being frills, these benefits and duties go to the very core of the marriage contract; no church or employer or "commitment ceremony" can bestow them at one blow. If marriage is to do all the things that society demands of it, then the state must set some rules.

Just so, say traditionalists: and those rules should exclude homosexuals. Gay marriage, goes the argument, is both frivolous licence. Thus the question becomes: is there a compelling reason to bar homosexuals from marriage?

One objection is simply that both would-be spouses are of the same sex. That is no answer; it merely repeats the question. Perhaps, then, once homosexuals can marry, marital anarchy will follow? That might be true if homosexual unions were arbitrary configurations, mere parodies of "real" marriage. But the truth is that countless homosexual couples, especially lesbian ones, have shown that they are as capable of fidelity, responsibility and devotion as are heterosexual couples—and this despite having to keep their unions secret, at least until recently. Would gay marriage weaken the standard variety? There is little reason to think so. Indeed, the opposite seems at least as likely: permitting gay marriage could reaffirm society's hope that people of all kinds settle down into stable unions.

The question of children in homosexual households—adoption, especially—is thorny. That question, however, is mainly separate from the matter of marriage as such. In settling a child with guardians who are not the natural parents, the courts and adoption agencies will consider a variety of factors, just as they do now; a couple's homosexuality may be one such factor (though it need not, by itself, be decisive).

In the end, leaving aside (as secular governments should) objections that may be held by particular religions, the case against homosexual marriage is this: people are unaccustomed to it. It is strange and radical. That is a sound argument for not pushing change along precipitously. Certainly it is an argument for legalising homosexual marriage through consensual politics (as in Denmark), rather than by court order (as may happen in America). But the direction of change is clear. If marriage is to fulfill its aspirations, it must be defined by the commitment of one to another for richer for poorer, in sickness and in health—not by the people it excludes.

Homosexuality: The Policy Questions
RICHARD A. POSNER

From Sex and Reason, *by Richard A. Posner,* 1992

*Posner, a legal theorist best known for his pioneering work
in law and economics, makes a case for limited tolerance—
abolishing sodomy laws but retaining marriage rights as
exclusively heterosexual. Even so, Posner is tentative in opposing marriage rights, and he puts great store by the settled in-
stincts of a conservative populace.*

There are three differences between punishing sodomy and confining the right to marry to heterosexuals. The first is that permitting homosexual marriage would be widely interpreted as placing a stamp of approval on homosexuality, while decriminalizing sodomy would not, at least not to anywhere near the same extent. To say that an act is not a crime is not to commend it; a great deal of behavior that is disgusting or immoral or both is nevertheless not criminal. But marriage, even though considered sacramental only by Catholics, is believed by most people in our society to be not merely a license to reproduce but also a desirable, even a noble, condition in which to live. To permit persons of the same sex to marry is to declare, or more precisely to be understood by many people to be declaring, that homosexual marriage is a desirable, even a noble, condition in which to live. This is not what most people in this society believe; and for reasons stated earlier it would be misleading to suggest that homosexual marriages are likely to be as stable or rewarding as heterosexual marriages, even granting as one must that a sizable fraction of heterosexual marriages in our society are not stable and are not rewarding. I do not suggest that government's pronouncing homosexual marriage a beatific state would cause heterosexuals to rethink their sexual preference. My concern lies elsewhere. It is that permitting homosexual marriage would place government in the dishonest position of propagating a false picture of the reality of homosexuals' lives.

Against this it can be argued that as heterosexual marriage becomes ever more unstable, temporary, and childless, the suggestion that it differs fundamentally from what homosexual marriages could be expected to be like becomes ever more implausible. And this is true. But it is a point in favor not of homosexual marriage but of chucking the whole institution of marriage in favor of an explicitly contractual approach that would make the current realities of marriage transparent.

The second difference between the sodomy and marriage issues will strike many readers as a trivial addendum to the first. It is that the more broadly *marriage* is defined, the less information it and related terms convey. When we read that Mr. X is married or that Ms. Y is married, we know immediately that X's spouse is a woman and Y's a man. If we invite people to a party and ask them to bring their spouses, we know that each man will either come alone or bring a woman and that each woman will either come alone or bring a man. So a homosexual man will come alone and likewise a homosexual woman. If we do not care to limit the additional guests to spouses, we ask the invitees to bring not their spouses but their "guests." If our son or daughter tells us that he or she is getting married, we know the sex of the prospective spouse. All these understandings would be upset by permitting homosexual marriage. This of course is one reason homosexual rights advocates want homosexual marriage to be permitted. All I wish to emphasize is that there is an information cost to the proposal.

But there is also an information benefit. The denial of marriage to homosexuals prevents a homosexual couple from signaling the extent of their commitment. If marriage were abolished, heterosexual cohabitation would denote indifferently the briefest and the most permanent of relationships. If the "freedom to marry" of which the Supreme Court spoke in *Loving v. Virginia* were taken seriously, the deprivation to the homosexual couple denied the right to marry would carry a heavy weight; but of course the Court was thinking of heterosexual marriage.

The third difference between the sodomy and marriage issues is the most important. Abolishing the sodomy laws would have few collateral effects, though I have suggested that it would have one: it would make it easier for homosexuals to obtain jobs in fields at present closed to them. Authorizing homosexual marriage would have many collateral effects, simply because marriage is a status rich in entitlements. It would have effects on inheritance, social security, income tax, welfare payments, adoption, the division of property upon termination of the relationship, medical benefits, life insurance, immigration, and even testimonial privilege. (The *Commercial-News* of Danville, Ohio, carried an article under the intriguing banner "Homosexual Loses Court Battle over Use of Mate's Testimony." The mate in question was another man.) These incidents of marriage were designed with heterosexual marriage in mind, more specifically heterosexual marriages resulting in children. They may or may not fit the case of homosexual marriage; they are unlikely to fit it perfectly. Do we want homosexual couples to have the same rights of adoption and custody as heterosexual couples? Should we worry that a homosexual might marry a succession of dying AIDS patients in order to entitle them to spouse's medical benefits? These questions ought to be faced one by one rather than elided by conferring all the rights of marriage in a lump on homosexuals willing to undergo a wedding ceremony.

None of these points is decisive against permitting homosexual marriage. All together may not be. The benefits of such marriage may outweigh the costs. Nonetheless, since the public hostility to homosexuals in this country is too widespread to make homosexual marriage a feasible proposal even if it is on balance cost-justified, maybe the focus should be shifted to an intermediate solution that would give homosexuals most of what they want but at the same time meet the three objections I have advanced.

Denmark and Sweden, not surprisingly, provide the model. What in Denmark is called registered partnership and in Sweden homosexual cohabitation is in effect a form contract that homosexuals can use to create a simulacrum of marriage. The Danish law goes further than the Swedish: it places the registered partners under all the provisions of the marriage code except those relating to children, although a question has arisen whether the registered partner has the same beneficial rights in his (or her) partner's private pension that a spouse would have. Sweden, which already has defined a quasi-marital status for cohabitating heterosexuals, allows cohabiting homosexuals to elect that status, the main feature of which is an even division, upon the dissolution of the relationship, of what in this country would be called community property. The Danish approach is mechanical in assuming that the presence of children is the only thing that distinguishes heterosexual from homosexual marriage. The Swedish approach assumes, realistically I think, that a homosexual relationship, even when meant to last, is more like heterosexual cohabitation than like heterosexual marriage, so the forms that the Swedes have worked out to regularize what is after all an extremely common relationship in their country provide the appropriate model for homosexuals who want to live together in ours. It may indeed offer an increasingly attractive model for heterosexuals as well. . . .

Same-Sex Marriage Nears

WILLIAM SAFIRE

From The New York Times, *April 29, 1996*

> *Conservative columnist William Safire comes out in favor of*
> *domestic partnerships—but draws the line at marriage. But*
> *notice his dismissal of some conservative arguments that the*
> *changes in Hawaii are a result of "hyperactivist judges."*

As the legislative session headed toward a midnight close Friday night, opponents of homosexual marriage insisted on a
recorded vote. Supporters of gay rights won. Hawaii's state senators voted 15 to 10 against the more conservative House's bill to
ban the licensing of marital unions of persons of the same sex.

As a result, the state's lawyers will find it harder to assert a
"compelling state interest" in limiting marriage to one man and
one woman. *Baehr v. Miike* comes before Judge Kevin Chang in
August; the likelihood increases that he will rule that the state
Constitution's provision against sex discrimination precludes the
state from refusing to issue marriage licenses to gay couples.

No longer can defenders of one-man, one-woman marriage
claim that the institution is being threatened by hyperactivist
judges. One state's duly elected representatives have just paved
the way, and under the U.S. Constitution's Full Faith and Credit
clause, a judicial proceeding held in one state is to be honored in
all states.

Nor is the movement limited to the United States. In The
Hague last week, a majority of the Dutch Parliament called on

the government to submit legislation permitting homosexual marriage. That would affect all members of the European Union; British gays could marry in Amsterdam and claim spousal status in London.

The Hawaii solons, in a tense conference just before the deadline, considered a compromise. Homosexuals in contracted "domestic partnerships" were not to be denied pension or insurance benefits or inheritance or other state tax deductions available to spouses, thereby assuring fairness as taxpayers and equal treatment as employees—but not including a state of matrimony. The compromise, which might have affected the outcome of the court case, failed. That was unfortunate because that is the way this issue should be resolved.

Libertarians like me have a tough time with same-sex marriage because we despise discrimination, cherish privacy and reject homophobia. When we express reluctance to rush to make a fundamental change in the legal and religious definition of a family, editorialists assail "entrenched anti-gay bigotry" and shrilly accuse all who fail to embrace S.S.M. of being "driven by social intolerance." Such straight-bashing neither contributes to civil discourse nor persuades us we are morally obtuse.

To the heart of the matter: Why break the age-old pattern of defining marriage as the union of one man, one woman? Or, to slant the question the other way: Why should heterosexuals have a lock on wedlock?

Serious arguments presented by supporters of same-sex marriage have force: In times of casual cohabitation, marriage would encourage homosexual couples to stay together and build stable, mutually supportive lives. Moreover, when so many children need loving parents, society's sanction of marriage would make adoption much easier, though not everyone agrees that gay adoptive parents would not influence the sexual orientation of a child.

Religion aside, the state's interest in marriage is to create a unit for mutual care and the bearing and rearing of children. Tax and inheritance incentives have long been offered to bolster these "family values," which are under great strain, and nothing should be done now to further weaken the traditional family.

Underlying this disagreement, and giving the debate its bitterness, is the belief that what is at stake is not just tax and pension fairness (in the works for domestic partners who take contractual vows) but the reach for unequivocal social and theological approbation. Gays understandably want not just equal economic treatment but equal moral status; most Americans are not ready to go beyond toleration to active approval. That division is not in dispute.

Will S.S.M. be a political issue? Hawaii, dominated by Democrats, has shown it already is. In the national campaign, Republicans will oppose gay marriage, perhaps in a platform plank; if Bill Clinton ever holds a press conference and is asked about this, he can be expected to straddle, saying he "personally" opposes same-gender legal liaison, but it is a state issue and he's for states' rights.

The nation and its gay minority would be best served by the compromise Hawaii just scorned.

Gay Marriages and the Affirmation of an Ideal

AMY E. SCHWARTZ

From The Washington Post, *June 3, 1996*

A straight woman argues that gay marriage would be far more likely to make homosexuals like heterosexuals than the other way around.

When the Joe Camel character first started appearing on cigarette packs, along with mischievous rumors as to what the picture really showed, I yielded to prurient curiosity and bought a pack. Holding it in my hand, I discovered something peculiar: Though I had never in my life smoked a cigarette, let alone bought any, the sight of my own fingers clasped around a pack of Camels touched off an incredible wash of cultural familiarity, of rightness, that was utterly at odds with anything I'd heard about smoking in at least a decade.

Talk about a lesson in the workings of cultural pressure. Without knowing it, I had soaked up over the years—from ads, movies, who knows?—a terrific subconscious sense that the society around me supported this purchase, that I was doing what people do. It was ridiculous, of course; the feeling went away when I put the cigarettes out of sight in a drawer. But it left me with a healthy respect for the anti-tobacco people's arguments about the cumulative beneath-the-surface power of advertising (who knew that this, of all things, was still sloshing around in the zeitgeist?) and in general for the proposition that you can be unaware of a powerful, mostly invisible undertow of social reinforcement until you happen to stumble into it by mistake.

I wish something of the sort would happen to the people who have spent this political season wailing and gnashing their teeth over the lack of societal support for and the need to "defend" and "strengthen" the institution of marriage. Some of these worries appear heartfelt; others, like the "defense of marriage" tag stuck on the congressional bill to block legalization of gay marriages, seem transparent efforts to harness the societal interest in marriage to assertions of a "harm" both implausible and theoretical. To get engaged to be married in the midst of this debate, as I recently did, is a little like picking up that Camel pack. First, you immediately become aware of a fierce river of support that is totally at odds with the public plaints. Second, you get a glimpse, from feeling it, of how the support mechanism actually works, a close-up of the culture cranking itself efficiently from generation to generation.

And that glimpsed close-up in turn makes killingly clear—in case I had had any doubts to begin with—that the assertions about gay marriage hurting that mechanism, undermining that support, assume a process that has the mechanism exactly backward.

Conservative critics on every side wail that marriage and the family are under attack or in disrepute, succumbing to the onslaught of divorce, self-indulgence and the collapse of traditional sexual norms, not to mention the perfidious influence of gay rights. Are they kidding? The society is marriage-mad. Being single and considering whether to marry some particular person is like standing in a gale; say yes, and the gale picks you up and flings you through the air like one of those cows in *Twister.* The announcement of one's intention to marry brings floods of warmth and pleasure not just from friends and loved ones but from casual acquaintances and even strangers, as if (and on some level it's obviously true) you're doing something not just for yourselves but for everybody.

Signature purchases like rings touch off an internal buzz of recognition one hundred times as deafening as that of the Camel pack. As you plunge into the fervid territory controlled by the bridal industry you notice that much of what it does is ideally suited to ease you up and over large personal transitions, siphoning off your anxieties into details about reception halls, propelling you forward to the goal like those cheering spectators who line the last mile of marathons.

And it works. Some serious-minded critics worried about divorce statistics actually think the mechanism propelling couples forward from engagement to ceremony is a bit too strong. One rabbi of my acquaintance will occasionally refuse to perform a wedding ceremony for a couple she doesn't think is ready; she tells them they are welcome to seek another officiant, she says, but several such couples, on hearing so unexpected a challenge from their rabbi, have taken the escape hatch thus offered and have split up.

Though perhaps less inclined to such direct action, many of the people whose worries about the state of marriage are heartfelt—as distinct from those using those worries as a club to beat gay visibility—would agree that all this support for forming new marriages isn't their point; rather, what is needed is more help in sustaining the marriages once they're formed. What you need, in other words, isn't a lot of cheering at the marathon starting point but more of it on the uphill stretches and from other, more experienced runners.

Which is why the "defense of marriage" argument against gay marriage strikes me as so perverse, because, if the adult world's response to an engagement amounts to a burst of sustained cheering for the serious task ahead—Go for it, you can do it, we did it, everyone should do it, go for it!—then it is hard to see anything but destructiveness in substituting the message: Some people must never be allowed to do this.

Better, surely, to cheer the common denominator, to think what helped this rushing river of support might give gay couples in the struggle for serious goals like monogamy and fidelity—and.also what their achievement of those goals might give back to the rest of us. The evidence of a gay couple's desire to leap into lifelong commitment seems to me yet another bridge to that couple's humanity, an affirmation for the ideal of marriage that underlines a previously unnoticed kinship. Doesn't every successfully, publicly monogamous couple committed for life bolster the resolve of every other couple that aspires to that achievement?

The Power of Marriage
DAVID BROOKS

From The New York Times, *November 22, 2003*

A conservative argues not simply that gays should have the right to marry—but that society should insist that they do.

Anybody who has several sexual partners in a year is committing spiritual suicide. He or she is ripping the veil from all that is private and delicate in oneself, and pulverizing it in an assembly line of selfish sensations.

But marriage is the opposite. Marriage joins two people in a sacred bond. It demands that they make an exclusive commitment to each other and thereby takes two discrete individuals and turns them into kin.

Few of us work as hard at the vocation of marriage as we should. But marriage makes us better than we deserve to be. Even in the chores of daily life, married couples find themselves, over the years, coming closer together, fusing into one flesh. Married people who remain committed to each other find that they reorganize and deepen each other's lives. They may eventually come to the point when they can say to each other: "Love you? I am you."

Today marriage is in crisis. Nearly half of all marriages end in divorce. Worse, in some circles, marriage is not even expected. Men and women shack up for a while, produce children and then float off to shack up with someone else.

Marriage is in crisis because marriage, which relies on a culture of fidelity, is now asked to survive in a culture of contingency. Today, individual choice is held up as the highest value: choice of lifestyles, choice of identities, choice of cellphone rate plans. Freedom is a wonderful thing, but the culture of contingency means that the marriage bond, which is supposed to be a sacred vow till death do us part, is now more likely to be seen as an easily canceled contract.

Men are more likely to want to trade up, when a younger trophy wife comes along. Men and women are quicker to opt out of marriages, even marriages that are not fatally flawed, when their "needs" don't seem to be met at that moment.

Still, even in this time of crisis, every human being in the United States has the chance to move from the path of contingency to the path of marital fidelity—except homosexuals. Gays and lesbians are banned from marriage and forbidden to enter into this powerful and ennobling institution. A gay or lesbian couple may love each other as deeply as any two people, but when you meet a member of such a couple at a party, he or she then introduces you to a "partner," a word that reeks of contingency.

You would think that faced with this marriage crisis, we conservatives would do everything in our power to move as many people as possible from the path of contingency to the path of fidelity. But instead, many argue that gays must be banished from matrimony because gay marriage would weaken all marriage. A marriage is between a man and a woman, they say. It is women who domesticate men and make marriage work.

Well, if women really domesticated men, heterosexual marriage wouldn't be in crisis. In truth, it's moral commitment, renewed every day through faithfulness, that "domesticates" all people.

Some conservatives may have latched onto biological determinism (men are savages who need women to tame them) as a convenient way to oppose gay marriage. But in fact we are not animals whose lives are bounded by our flesh and by our gender. We're moral creatures with souls, endowed with the ability to make covenants, such as the one Ruth made with Naomi: "Where you go I will go, and where you stay I will stay. Your people will be my people and your God my God. Where you die I will die, and there I will be buried."

The conservative course is not to banish gay people from making such commitments. It is to expect that they make such commitments. We shouldn't just allow gay marriage. We should insist on gay marriage. We should regard it as scandalous that two people could claim to love each other and not want to sanctify their love with marriage and fidelity.

When liberals argue for gay marriage, they make it sound like a really good employee benefits plan. Or they frame it as a civil rights issue, like extending the right to vote.

Marriage is not voting. It's going to be up to conservatives to make the important, moral case for marriage, including gay marriage. Not making it means drifting further into the culture of contingency, which, when it comes to intimate and sacred relations, is an abomination.

Respecting Marriage and Equal Rights

TAMMY BRUCE

From FrontPage Magazine, *Febraury 25, 2004*

Lesbian conservative Tammy Bruce wants equality under the law but is happy to leave the "M-word" to heterosexuals.

Whoever thought that there would be actual voiced concerns about men in America wanting to marry their goats? Is there something going on in our great Heartland that I've missed? Instead of "The L Word" does Showtime have a special series just for the Midwest called "The G Word"?

Of course not.

But the debate over the idea of gay marriage has brought out concerns by one extremist end that it will lead to people marrying their livestock to Gay Gestapo charges of homophobic bigotry against those opposed to same-sex nuptials.

Neither accusation is valid, so as an independent gay woman, I think it's time to make a few things clear. First of all, despite what you hear from the Gay Elite, there is not a consensus in the gay community about this issue. We do not all operate in the cultural or political equivalent of a Vulcan mind-meld.

I, one among many, respect and understand the growing concern about the disintegration of our traditions and values. I am so concerned, it is the heart and soul of my second book, *The Death of Right and Wrong.*

Consequently, I respect the majority of Americans and their opinion that marriage should be defined as between one man and one woman.

At the same time, as an American, I also believe that every American deserves the same rights and protections as every other. Most of you do, too. The very same polls that show how united Americans are against "gay marriage" indicate a majority approving of civil unions.

That doesn't surprise me. It is consistent with the American belief that we can have fair play and equality while recognizing the need to honor traditional institutions.

Frankly, I believe the cultural trouble and moral vapidity in our society today—the moral relativism I write about in *DRW*—has sprung from the "liberation" movements of the '60s and '70s. It was then that the Left began to attack the traditional in the name of liberation and equality.

Anything that would strike a pose against authority and social norms, ranging from promiscuous sex to drug abuse to adultery to riotous violence, was embraced and encouraged by leftist leadership. The "Counter Culture" was born.

Courtesy of cultural Incrementalism (which I explained in my previous column) what it became has rivaled Rosemary's Baby.

Today's struggle with single-parent families, drug addiction, the epidemic of sexually transmitted diseases among the young, suicide rates, the devaluing of the family, and even the extraordinarily high divorce rate, I contend, can be traced back to the time which lionized the destruction of the traditional and the elevation of moral relativism.

Despite this, American society remains committed to equality, but it's apparent that we don't like the aftermath of taking our traditions for granted. So, yes, we've decided to maintain the idea of "marriage" as it has stood, while finding another way to guarantee the rights of gay people.

While this should actually be a relatively easy situation to resolve (heck, Bush, Kerry, and Edwards all hold the same position—against gay marriage, for civil unions), all Hell seems to have broken loose—not only in San Francisco, but in Washington, D.C., as well.

On one hand you have the reckless law-breaking behavior of San Francisco mayor Gavin Newsom bestowing marriage licenses on gay couples. A few of my gay friends have voiced their support for this. I reminded these friends, who are also pro-choice, that Fresno, California, has a pro-life mayor. How would they feel if that mayor decided to ignore the law and keep women from accessing their legal abortion rights?

They heard me, but it was disturbing that I had to put this into perspective.

Now, in Washington, D.C., the President has declared the need to amend the U.S. Constitution! Really now—that appears to be as much of a stunt as the rogue gay marriages in San Francisco. And this from a man (who along with Cheney) in the last election who said it should be a matter left to the states. It seems, though, only if the states do what you like.

Clearly, the Constitution should be amended as a last resort. Regardless of how you feel about gay marriage, or abortion, or saving the spotted owl (or not), the Constitution is not made of silly putty—to be twisted and shaped and torn apart depending on our national mood. It is written in a way that makes us have to struggle with issues we face.

After all, if we are truly committed to wanting to save and not tamper with our traditional institutions, which represent the core of the American value system, doesn't the Constitution fall into that category as well?

I am heartened by a few true conservatives, including Representative David Dreier (whom I got to know on the Schwarzenegger Transition Team), who have voiced concerns about the rush to amend.

We've been through worse; we've survived and found solutions. We'll survive this too, but the gay community must come to terms with a few issues first.

Gays ultimately need to stop looking to government for unconditional love and approval of who we are. Andrew Sullivan, a political commentator and writer many of you know and respect, wrote a piece for *Time* magazine where he actually equated governmental recognition of gay marriage as a necessary element to all gay people feeling accepted and wanted. He claimed that anything other than marriage will "build a wall between gay people and their own families."

While his story was personal and moving, the argument was, frankly, nonsense, and representative of the general mentality among the gay elite. It also gives the government and other people's opinions far too much power over the quality of our lives and effectively eliminates our own responsibility for our happiness.

Part of the fight for gay marriage is based in Sullivan's lament—that it is only governmental recognition of who are that will make us whole. Let's get real—the only thing that will make gay people whole is personal acceptance of ourselves by ourselves. Instead, we are still looking to Mommy or Daddy, now in the form of Society, to tell us we're "okay"—to sanctify, if you will, our lives and relationships.

Society has been the benevolent parent for a very long time. And it has been amazing, and a testament to the American character, that despite being a people of faith who have legitimate concerns about the gay lifestyle, Americans have made this the best place on Earth for gays and lesbians, where we are free to live incomparably rich lives.

Now, when Americans have said through polls and voting, that they do not want to give up the meaning of marriage but support a comparable alternative, how do the gay elite respond?

When you ask for one cultural thing to be left untouched, the Gay Elite become the Gay Gestapo.

It's a very fast change from the polo shirt to the brown shirt these days.

In classic Thought Police fashion and like children throwing a tantrum, the name-calling flies—those who oppose gay marriage are "homophobes," "haters" and, the label du jour, "bigots." Once again, the Left, unable to answer critics with respect, resort to name-calling only to further the divide they need to validate their inevitable victimhood.

Marriage is worth protecting, in more ways than one. It's also worth noting the cavalier way in which heterosexuals have handled marriage has lent fuel to the fire of this issue.

How seriously can any of us take the president's vow to "protect the sanctity of marriage" when Britney Spears indulges in it for five minutes in Vegas? Marriage has become a television reality game show. And protecting children? Before amending the Constitution, perhaps the Feds should make divorce a little harder to get. It's divorce that is ruining children's lives at the moment, not a couple of lesbians who want to get married (no matter how scary some of those pictures were out of San Francisco).

If George W. Bush is serious about "saving the institution," he has his hands full and he's running late.

CHAPTER SIX

The Defense of Marriage Act?
THE NATIONAL DEBATE BEGINS

In some sense all the debate on same-sex marriage that went on before the advent of the Defense of Marriage Act was a warm-up. This legislation was introduced in May 1996 in the U.S. House of Representatives to ensure that legal same-sex marriages in Hawaii could not be upheld in other states under the Full Faith and Credit clause of the U.S. Constitution. As a matter of law, it seems highly implausible that states would have been compelled to uphold same-sex marriages by such means, as the arguments of Chapter 10 make clear. But the mere threat was enough to provoke uproar in Washington and around the country. Was such a law necessary—or even constitutional? And was the country ready for same-sex marriage anywhere?

This chapter begins with the arguments for (Jay Alan Sekulow) and against (Cass Sunstein) the constitutionality of the Defense of Marriage Act—or DOMA, as it became known. Transcripts from the House hearings are excerpted: Congressman Barney Frank's passionate attack on the political animus behind the bill; Congressman Henry Hyde's defense of informal living arrangements between gay people; Congressman Bob Inglis's explosion about the miscegenation analogy. But perhaps the most telling exchange of the entire debate is between Congressmen Sonny Bono and Barney Frank as Bono wrestles with his own conflicts between his gut and his conscience. Finally, Congressman John Lewis expresses his opposition to the bill from a traditional civil rights perspective, and Senator John Kerry charts out his own position between opposing civil marriage on the one hand and opposing the legislation on the other.

The Defense of Marriage Act was passed by overwhelming margins in both the House and the Senate and was signed into law by President Clinton in September 1996 in the middle of the night.

H.R. 3396: To Define and Protect the Institution of Marriage

May 7, 1996

The text of the Defense of Marriage Act. There are two sections: the first outlines states' rights not to recognize the same-sex marriages of other states; the second defines marriage, for federal purposes, as an arrangement made between a man and a woman. This bill was the first in the nation's history to define marriage at a federal level. The issue had previously always been left to the states to decide.

SAME-SEX MARRIAGE: PRO AND CON

H.R. 3396

To define and protect the institution of marriage.

IN THE HOUSE OF REPRESENTATIVES
MAY 7, 1996

Mr. BARR of Georgia (for himself, Mr. LARGENT, Mr. SENSENBRENNER, Mrs. MYRICK, Mr. VOLKMER, Mr. SKELTON, Mr. BRYANT of Tennessee, and Mr. EMERSON) introduced the following bill; which was referred to the Committee on the Judiciary.

A BILL

To define and protect the institution of marriage.

Be it enacted by the Senate and House of Representatives of the United States of America in Congress assembled,

SECTION 1. SHORT TITLE.

This Act may be cited as the "Defense of Marriage Act."

SEC. 2. POWERS RESERVED TO THE STATES.

(a) IN GENERAL.—Chapter 115 of title 28, United States Code, is amended by adding after section 1738B the following:

"§ 1738C. CERTAIN ACTS, RECORDS, AND PROCEEDINGS AND THE EFFECT THEREOF

"No State, territory, or possession of the United States, or Indian tribe, shall be required to give effect to any public act, record, or judicial proceeding of any other State, territory, possession, or tribe respecting a relationship between persons of the same sex that is treated as a marriage under the laws of such other State, territory, possession, or tribe, or a right or claim arising from such relationship."

(b) CLERICAL AMENDMENT.—The table of sections at the beginning of chapter 115 of title 28, United States Code, is amended by inserting after the item relating to section 1738B the following new item:

"1738C. Certain acts, records, and proceedings and the effect thereof."

SEC. 3. DEFINITION OF MARRIAGE.

(a) IN GENERAL.—Chapter 1 of title 1, United States Code, is amended by adding at the end the following:

"§ 7. DEFINITION OF 'MARRIAGE' AND 'SPOUSE'

"In determining the meaning of any Act of Congress, or of any ruling, regulation, or interpretation of the various administrative bureaus and agencies of the United States, the word 'marriage' means only a legal union between one man and one woman as husband and wife, and the word 'spouse' refers only to a person of the opposite sex who is a husband or a wife."

(b) CLERICAL AMENDMENT.—The table of sections at the beginning of chapter 1 of title 1, United States Code, is amended by inserting after the item relating to section 6 the following new item:

"7. Definition of 'marriage' and 'spouse'."

Defending Marriage

JAY ALAN SEKULOW

*From the written testimony provided to the House
Judiciary Committee from the American Center for
Law and Justice, May 15, 1996*

*Here the chief lawyer for the Religious Right defends the De-
fense of Marriage Act (DOMA). Deflecting the accusation that
DOMA was a purely political ploy, Sekulow claims that without it the Constitution would soon have wreaked havoc on the
marriage laws of the nation.*

A decision for the same-sex couples who are plaintiffs in Baehr
will, very likely, have nationwide ramifications. Those ramifications are due to one provision of the United States Constitution, and its role in a directed nationwide effort to change the
laws of fifty states regarding the nature of a legal relationship,
marriage. The constitutional provision states:

Full faith and credit shall be given in each state to the public
acts, records, and judicial proceedings of every other state.
And the Congress may by general laws prescribe the manner
in which such Acts, Records, and proceedings shall be proved,
and the effect thereof.

It is possible, because nationally organized efforts are intent
on pushing the issue to the limits, that under the Full Faith and
Credit Clause, other states will have to recognize as valid Hawaiian "marriages" between same-sex couples, and thus accord

those couples all the benefits and protections accorded any other married couples. Several writers already have advanced, or at least discussed, this argument in law review articles. . . .

The threat that same-sex couples married in Hawaii will seek to have their marriages recognized in other states is real. Indeed, given the intensity with which the homosexual community has been focusing on the developments in *Baehr*, it is no exaggeration to suggest that *Baehr* simply is part of an orchestrated attempt to gain nationwide recognition (ultimately, acceptance) of same-sex marriages.

This strategy is not a figment of an overwrought imagination, whether mine or another's. The evidence of such a strategy is plain, for its proponents disdain to hide their purposes. The Marriage Project of the Lambda Legal Defense and Education Fund puts its goal in its name.

That organization, LLDEF, and its Marriage Project have been closely involved in the *Baehr* litigation. If successful, according to Lambda, "[c]ommon sense, constitutional doctrines, and legal precedent suggest that when [same-sex] marriages are lawfully performed in Hawaii, they will have to be recognized by other states. . . ."

Other statements show that homosexuals are eagerly awaiting the decision in *Baehr* to take advantage of the opportunity for "marriage" that a decision in *Baehr* may offer. For example, lesbian columnist Deb Price, referring to the plans she has with her lesbian partner, wrote, "We'll be on the first plane out! So many of us are just waiting for the day that our relationships are legally recognized.". . .

Moreover,

Gays and lesbians . . . eagerly wait word from Hawaii and many plan to head for the islands once and if licenses become available. "We'd go right away," John Holden and Michael

Galluccio said. "We've even asked my mother to be prepared to watch the baby at a moment's notice. And if it doesn't become legal until next year, we'll take Adam along, because by then he'll be old enough for the trip.". . .

Some have predicted not a trickle of such Hawaii same-sex marriage junkets, but a flood. And one magazine targeted to the gay and lesbian community reported in 1990 that eighty-three percent of the reader-respondents to a survey stated that if same-sex marriage was legalized they would marry. . . .

For Mr. Wolfson, who heads up Lambda's Marriage Project, the question of winning the right of same-sex couples to marry is apparently rather more than just being allowed to marry. In a recent article, Mr. Wolfson set the tone for his piece by quoting the lyrics of a song. Those lyrics allow us to peek behind the facade of the Marriage Project's stated goal of obtaining equal marriage rights for homosexuals to the deeper and more disturbing motivations behind Mr. Wolfson's press for legalization: "How can the world change, It can change like that, Due to one little word: 'Married.'"

Like the vapors Pandora had wished not to have let loose, Mr. Wolfson is clear about one thing: his goal of revolutionizing society, served in part by revolutionizing marriage, is a no-holds-barred, take-no-prisoners struggle: "[A]s [Martin Luther King, Jr.] put it, 'In this Revolution, no plans have been written for retreat,' we must ready ourselves to defend our victory and advance toward other goals.". . .

The point of this strategy, for homosexuals, was stated by Michelangelo Signorile in *Out* magazine:

[Homosexuals must] fight for same-sex marriage and its benefits and then, once granted, redefine the institution of marriage completely . . . to debunk a myth and radically alter an archaic institution. . . . The most subversive action lesbians and gays can undertake—and one that would perhaps benefit all of society—is to transform the notion of "family."

Thus, the strategy to recognize same-sex marriage is nothing less than a strategy to discard the traditional idea of "family" that has served to hold this society together. . . .

Will this strategy succeed? Can it be that over two hundred years of national unity and previous centuries of common law regarding the nature of marriage and the matrimonial relationship would fall victim to the latest round of judicial retrofitting of a *state* constitutional requirement of equality under the law? Right now, that is an open question. Clearly there are those who argue that, under the Full Faith and Credit Clause, states would be required to recognize same-sex marriages performed in Hawaii. To those arguments it is a fair response that there is a "public policy" exception to the Full Faith and Credit requirement. According to the *Restatement (Second) of Conflict of Laws* § 283 (1971), a state that had a "significant relationship to the spouses and the marriage at the time of the marriage" need not recognize a marriage if the marriage contravenes "the strong public policy" of that state.

It is not possible to predict with certainty, however, how courts will apply this exception to same-sex marriages. Section 2 of the Defense of Marriage Act removes this uncertainty by providing in essence that states are not bound, as a matter of federal law, to recognize same-sex marriages performed in another state. But that certainty does not come at the expense of state prerogatives. DOMA does not prevent states from choosing to recognize same-sex marriages. A state still would be free, as a matter of state law, to accord those marriages whatever status the state wishes. By removing the confusion surrounding the application of the Full Faith and Credit clause, the states will be free and empowered to develop their own policy on same-sex marriages. In this respect, Congress eschews any role in compelling states to adopt Hawaii's policy as their own, and insures that neither Hawaii nor any other state can cause this intended revolution through "ordinary litigation between parties. . . ."

Beyond the direct and odious consequences of a certain Supreme Court decision with which he disagreed, Abraham Lincoln had rather more to say about a role for the judiciary that he feared the citizenry might pass to it by default. In his first inaugural address, he explained:

> At the same time the candid citizen must confess that if the policy of the government, upon vital questions, affecting the whole people, is to be irrevocably fixed, by decisions of the Supreme Court, the instant they are made, in ordinary litigation between parties, in personal action, the people will have ceased, to be their own rulers, having, to that extent, practically resigned their government, into the hands of that eminent tribunal. Nor is there, in this view, any assault upon the court, or the judges. It is a duty, from which they may not shrink, to decide cases properly brought before them; and it is no fault of theirs, if others seek to turn their decisions to political purposes.

The only real question here is whether Congress has the power, under the Full Faith and Credit Clause, to define what effect a same-sex marriage validly created in one jurisdiction will have in another. For these purposes, the key language of the clause states, "Congress may by general laws prescribe the manner in which such acts, records, and proceedings [of every state] shall be proved [in every other state], and the effect thereof." While this language enables Congress to regulate the effect of proofs of foreign, that is, sister-state judgments under the Full Faith and Credit Clause, Congress has only exercised this authority three times.

The first usage was in 1790 when Congress codified the functions of the Full Faith and Credit clause. . . , again in 1980 with the Parental Kidnapping Prevention Act. . . , and finally, with the Full Faith and Credit Child Support Orders Act of 1994. . . . This bill would create . . . and allow for a further exercise of Congress' authority to "prescribe the manner in which . . . acts, records, and proceedings" of one state are proved in another state.

The fact that the authority is rarely used does not mean that the authority does not exist. The enabling language is clear; it has been noted, however, that "there are few clauses of the Constitution, the literal possibilities of which have been so little developed as the Full Faith and Credit clause.". . .

Don't Panic

CASS SUNSTEIN

From oral testimony given by the professor of jurisprudence at the University of Chicago Law School at the hearings held by the Senate Judiciary Committee, July 11, 1996

Here Sunstein argues that DOMA is unnecessary, and its claim of authority to regulate marriage federally under the Full Faith and Credit clause is probably unconstitutional.

I'm going to be talking . . . about the constitutional issues, the question of congressional power. I won't say a word about the policy questions or the underlying issues about the nature or definition of marriage. The first point to note about this legislation is that it's remarkably unprecedented. In the nation's entire history, now well over two hundred years, Congress has never passed legislation whose purpose in effect was to negate the application of one state's judgment in other states. Congress has legislated under the full faith and credit clause. This negating or nullifying power has never been exercised once.

This legislation risks two dangers. One is it may well be pointless, and if it's not pointless, it raises very serious constitutional problems.

If it's pointless, it's because states have grappled with this problem for a long time. This is an old problem, not a new one; it's familiar. And states that have significant geographical connections with people don't have to recognize marriages among people when those marriages violate the public policy of the state. In cases involving incest, polygamy, adultery, and more, states have grappled successfully with this problem without national intervention. This particular issue, the issue of same-sex marriages, falls into a class of cases with which the federal system has dealt successfully without national legislation.

If the statute isn't pointless, it's very problematic from the constitutional point of view. There's a good reason to think that the full faith and credit clause gives Congress broad power to extend the application of judgments in one state. There's good reason to think that Congress has not been given the power to negate judgments by one state insofar as they're applied in other states. If Congress does have the power to do this under the full faith and credit clause, there's a big problem under the equal protection of the components of the due process clause, as construed just a few weeks ago by the Supreme Court in *Romer v. Evans*. If Congress does this, it seems like a limited measure just involving same-sex marriage, there could be very large future consequences in areas involving product liability, punitive damages, marriage, and divorce, where there are interest groups all over the nation who would be extremely thrilled to see the possibility that Congress can nullify the extraterritorial application of one state's judgments.

Let me just say a few words now by way of elaboration. On pointlessness, as I say, this is not a new problem, it's an old one. In areas involving minors, incestuous or bigamous marriages, states have dealt with this very successfully and very frequently. There are volumes and volumes of cases. They don't involve congressional legislation. When a marriage violates a state's policy and when the state has a geographical connection with the parties, the state is not obliged to recognize the marriage. That is the tradition. It's extremely well settled law. It's in (both restatements?) of the conflicts of law. It suggests the very serious possibility that this legislation has no purpose. If it does have a purpose, it is problematic from the constitutional point of view. There has been no serious suggestion that this is okay under the commerce clause. It would be an exotic understanding of the commerce clause to say that marriage falls within that domain.

The full faith and credit clause does, as you say, Senator Hatch, have the word "effects" in it, and Congress does have power to prescribe the effect of a judgment, and that might seem textually to give Congress power here, but I think there are some reasons to think that that is more word play or a verbal trick than an accurate understanding of the Constitution.

The full faith and credit clause, above all, has a unifying purpose, not a disunifying purpose. It's part of the move from the Articles of Confederation to the Constitution. If you look at the purpose of the clause, it's not to allow nullification, it's to allow extension of judgments, not to negate them. If you look at the history of the clause back when the framers were writing, Madison and the others, they spoke about congressional extension and enforcement of judgments. They spoke not at all about congressional nullification of judgments. There's a big dog that didn't bark in the framer's night, and that's the bark of nullification.

If history and purpose aren't conclusive, let's look just at Congress's practice for now well over two hundred years. Congress has never once nullified the extraterritorial application of a state judgment. Congress has acted under the full faith and credit clause a fair bit. It's always been in the interest of extension. The consequences of nullifying rather than extension could be very extreme. Californian divorces, Idaho punitive damage judgments, Illinois product liability judgments, all of them would henceforth be up for grabs.

That's why from the standpoint of federalism this is a very large as well as a very new bit of legislation. If for the first time in the country Congress is going to act to nullify a judgment in its extraterritorial applications, there is a problem under the equal protection clause. The Court said just a few weeks ago that Congress may not enact measures that have the peculiar property of imposing a broad disability on a single group. This is an invalid form of legislation. If Congress hasn't legislated for polygamous, incestuous marriages or marriages among minors, then it has raised the question of discrimination. In conclusion, this legislation has never been—nothing like it has ever been done. It's unprecedented. It may well be pointless. This problem has been handled by the states for well over two hundred years. If it has a point, it risks unconstitutionality. From the standpoint of federalism and constitutional law, it is ill advised.

The Hearings of the House Judiciary Committee on the Defense of Marriage Act

May 15, 1996

The Hearings of the House Judiciary Committee proved to be memorable. The raw emotions of gay men and lesbians and of House members and others on both sides of the issue electrified Capitol Hill for a day. It was the first time in history that the real lives of homosexuals were addressed so forthrightly in the halls of Congress. What follows is an edited transcript of the highlights. The featured speakers are Congressman Barney Frank of Massachusetts, one of two openly gay members of Congress; Hadley Arkes, an Amherst College professor; Congressman Henry Hyde, a Republican of fervent Roman Catholic faith; the highly conservative Republican Congressman from South Carolina, Bob Inglis; and the executive director of the Human Rights Campaign, the nation's largest gay rights lobby, Elizabeth Birch.

Rep. Barney Frank: We are dealing with a couple of related events today. This legislation and Senator Dole's apparent resignation from the Senate. They are both indications that the Republican national campaign is not doing very well, and there is a significant effort to change the subject. There are issues that ought to be discussed around the question of marriage, same-sex marriage. They ought to be discussed in a reasonable and unhurried way. First, let's be clear that the crisis that is being invoked to justify this drafting of this committee into the Republican campaign effort is greatly exaggerated. Same-sex marriage is nowhere legal in America today, and is not likely to become legal within the next couple of months in a final and binding way.

Why the hurry then? Particularly why the hurry in a Congress which has not been known for its capacity rapidly to dispose of important issues? Because we have a campaign that is hurting, and this is part of that effort. That's reflected, in part, in the very nature of the bill. There is a desperate effort here to find an issue. So we are apparently going to be asked to give the states a power which everybody who is for the bill thinks the states already have. We are told we must empower the states to reject, under their exception to the full faith and credit clause, marriages in Hawaii. But everybody who is talking about giving the states that power, in fact, thinks the states already have it.

What my friends have here is an elephant stick. Now, an elephant stick is the big stick someone is carrying walking around the White House. And when asked what it's for, he says, "Well, it keeps all the elephants off Pennsylvania Avenue." And when the answer is "There are no elephants," they say, "See, my stick worked."

Well, that's what they've got. They seek to empower to do what they believe the states can already do. In fact, if you took this seriously, it would be undermining the states' power. Because if, in fact, you accept as a reality that the states have the power to do this, . . . what we are now saying to the states is, "Oh, no, you must get permission from us."

Authors of this bill have written and said, "This is a bill to allow the states to do this." Well, passing a bill that allows the states to do something logically assumes that the states cannot do it in the absence of that permission. If we need to pass a bill to allow the states, then the states apparently can't do it without us.

Now, no one thinks that. So, why are we passing a bill to do what the people who want the bill passed think the states can already do? Because what they are worried about is not what the states decide to do with regard to marriage. They are worried about how the state decides to allocate its electoral votes. And this is an effort to influence not marriage in the states, but whether the Democratic or Republican tickets win. We'll deal with that more. But I also want to talk about the substance.

This is entitled, "Protect the institution of marriage," to "define and protect." "Define," I would have no semantic objection. We could debate this. But the notion that same-sex marriage somehow constitutes an assault on marriage between a man and a woman is very bizarre.

Apparently, the only logic I could think of is that people are afraid that men and women who are now married or contemplating marriage will, if they learn that they could get a tax advantage from marrying someone of the same sex, change their minds about marrying someone of the opposite sex and go off and marry someone of the same sex.

Because how can it be? Against what are you protecting marriage? I mean, those who believe in the importance of a man and a woman in love coming together in a union that is emotional and reinforced legally, how in the world is it a threat? And I will say, in terms of the priorities here—and I understand why they want to change the subject, things aren't going well with regard to Medicare or the environment or education and a lot of other issues. I talk, obviously as others do, to people in my district, and I have people tell me:

> "I am worried about losing my Medicare."
> "I am worried about losing my job."
> "I am worried about the lack of safety on the
>   streets."

"I am worried that there is not enough money
now to continue with toxic waste cleanup."

Never yet has someone come to me and said, "Congressman, I am terribly threatened. There are two women who are deeply in love a couple of miles away from me. And if you do not prevent them from formalizing their union, this will be terrible for me, and, in fact, will threaten my marriage." I know of no heterosexual marriage, the form of marriage that we have that has sustained us, that is threatened by this.

Herb and I entertained on Sunday 21 members of my family. A large majority of them were, in fact, heterosexual couples and the children of those heterosexual couples. I must tell you that having spent several hours in Herb's and my company none of them left with their marriages in jeopardy. In no case were the marital bonds any weaker than before. In no case did these people, who range in age from a couple of toddlers who might be too young, but from a four-year-old to a twenty-year-old on to Herb's parents, in no case was this disruptive. So that's why I reiterate that this is largely political in motivation. There is no need to empower the states to do what the states want. I do believe there is a constitutional issue here. But the constitutional issue is not one for the role of the Congress. There are people who believe that under the full faith and credit clause the states must accept same-sex marriage if any state does it. There are other people who believe that under the public policy exceptions that states have been allowed to have that would not be binding.

That is something that will be litigated directly between the states and the Supreme Court. There is no constitutional role for the Congress in this, whether or not—I mean, apparently what this is, is an amicus brief. I've never heard of Congress passing an amicus brief and calling it a law. Because that's all it could mean.

So this part about the states is either a nullity, if you believe that the states have no such power, or if you believe that the Supreme Court would uphold the states' rights here, as it has in other cases, then it's totally unnecessary.

So we have a totally unnecessary bill to ward off something, which is now, in effect, being rushed through a Congress which is unable to even get the gas tax repealed because they are unable to function, and therefore they are looking desperately for an alternative political issue. And that's it. And it is, I think, an issue which in addition is exaggerated in its defense. Because the notion that two men who have an emotional bond live together, or two women, threatens marriage is of a piece with the illogic of the rest of this bill . . .

Mr. Hadley Arkes: There was a family, a situation in Virginia not long ago, of a forty-year-old mother married to her nineteen-year-old son. They were forced to separate. I suppose people could argue that their presence wasn't going to disintegrate the institution of marriage.

To make our point, again, we are not predicting that there is going to be an erosion of marriage, but I think the melancholy point is this, that the notion of marriage may not be extended to take in, to accommodate the concern for gay marriage without setting off many other kinds of changes, and as a result of those changes, I think we would find that marriage would not have that special kind of significance that makes it an object right now of such craving. As Dennis [Prager] suggested, it is not that you are going to sort of undercut families that exist, but as the society keeps offering many alternatives and notions of sexuality outside of the framework of marriage, we move away from the sense that there is something portentous about the generation of new life, something that commands that this be pursued within a framework of commitment where the child understands that her parents are committed to her nurturance for the same reason that they are committed to one another. That they have quit their freedom to be rid of that relationship when it no longer suits their convenience. Now, if you think that all of this might undercut in time, or erode our conviction about the importance of that framework, about the generation of children as opposed to the notion that our children are simply spawned with no particular responsibility, remind ourselves that even in those melancholy situations when marriages dissolve, the framework of lawfulness at least has this advantage, that it fixes the question of who bears responsibility for the children.

Another point, I just might say that in response to Andrew [Sullivan] and, again, Andrew is a man of just impeccable arguments and I respect his judgments on many things, but I thought the concern here is about the debate being stifled by being drawn into the cloister of the courts, where it is handled, according to the formulas that are familiar to lawyer and judges, and that I thought it would be quite consistent with the spirit of liberalism, as Justice Brennan used to say, that robust arena of public discussion that we bring things out of the cloister of the courts, and bring them back into the public arena of discussion where it is matter of discussion not merely for lawyers.

Rep. Henry Hyde: Professor, I have known people in my life who have been deeply in love, not married, men and women, an enduring love, a powerful love, into their old age. What is stopping people, two men who love each other, or two women, from having that commitment of the soul as well as of the body, what do they need marriage for to solemnize it? Why can't they have this relationship which can be as fulfilling as if they have gotten a marriage license and taken an oath, and that is all marriage is, you are swearing to each other before an official witness, that they will love, honor and obey, or cherish, or whatever the word is. You can see how long ago it was that I got married. But what is the big deal?

Mr. Hadley Arkes: I think you are inviting me to, I don't want to go [over] ground I have already traversed, but to point out that, as I said, we understand that there are many relations of deep love between men and men, between women and women, grandparents and grandchildren, and, as I said, in the nature of things, not merely a matter of opinion, in the nature of things, those loves cannot be diminished as loves because they are not manifested properly in marriage. So I think I would agree with that wholly. . . .

Rep. Inglis: I must tell you that it offends me tremendously to have homosexuals compare themselves to the historic struggle for civil rights among black people.

Ms. Birch: Why?

Rep. Inglis: Because black people were economically disenfranchised and cut out of this society, whereas homosexuals, by most studies that I am aware of, have a higher standard of living than heterosexuals. So the comparison offends me tremendously—

Ms. Birch: Yeah, well, your information, sir, is inaccurate.

Rep. Inglis: —that you can persist in this comparison to this historic struggle of blacks to achieve equality in this country. The fact is, that [it] is not a choice to be black, but it is a choice—I know you don't like this, but it is obviously a choice to be homosexual.

Ms. Birch: Wrong.

Rep. Inglis: And that is simply, you are wrong to assert that it is not a choice.

Ms. Birch: Representative, I don't think you know anything about it.

Rep. Inglis: You are absolutely wrong to assert that. So therefore—

Ms. Birch: And if you would like to talk about the law, I would like to respond to that. I don't think you know anything about the struggle of African-Americans in this country *vis-à-vis* gay Americans.

Rep. Inglis: I know, because you are the head victim, I know, you are in charge of victims, so you will decide who can speak for that, not anybody else.

Ms. Birch: I would expect a little dignity and respect.

Rep. Inglis: But I think that the point that should be made here, and really what this all boils down to is, is it a choice or is it a condition? And if you would please make the honest argument—you would say, listen, it is a wonderful condition, let's all be gay, but you are not making that argument. You are making the argument, we are poor and pitiful and you must accept us the way we are, so you are admitting that it is not a desirable lifestyle, and there is something wrong with it, by arguing that it is not a choice. So I think if you analyze that honestly, it is essential to me because I hope that many can be rescued from that lifestyle and returned to where they can have a happy lifestyle because I think it is inherently destructive.

Ms. Birch: Mr. Chairman, may I respond?

Rep. Canady: I am sorry, the thirty minutes has gone—I am sorry the thirty seconds has gone.

Transcript of the Mark-Up Record of the Defense of Marriage Act
House Judiciary Committee, June 12, 1996

Every so often in a public debate, an interchange occurs that seems to encapsulate all the tensions surrounding the issue. This dialogue between Congressmen Sonny Bono and Barney Frank is one of those moments. Bono seems to concede Frank's arguments in defense of same-sex marriage, but emotionally holds something back. Since Bono was the father of a lesbian, his conflicts were even deeper than most—and his honesty truly remarkable.

Mr. Bono: I . . . this has been an amazing experience for me because I'm immersed in legal rhetoric that is interpreting the Constitution, and it's staggering how brilliant everyone is and how well they know their craft, and I wouldn't dare venture into their craft.

And it's clear to me, Mr. Chairman, that your job here, or my job here, is to try to interpret the Constitution and then act on that interpretation, representing the people. But it seems like the rhetoric has gone on to a point—sometimes things go way beyond where they should go, and an impasse is an impasse. And if there was ever an obvious impasse, this is it.

And what seems to have occurred here is that this subject is a rough subject because, if you're not a homosexual, you have strong feelings one way; if you are a homosexual, you have strong feelings the other way. But I would just like to go on the record and say this: that when things like this come out, it certainly makes a minority feel like everyone thinks they're less. And I think for someone to defend that is absolutely natural.

And Barney's a good friend of mine—or I consider him a good friend of mine. And I see his point of view, and I appreciate his fight. He's fighting as hard as he can because he's a human being; he has these feelings; he's gay; my daughter's gay. He has to live this way. So society hasn't quite accepted all of this.

So I think we go beyond the Constitution here. I think we go beyond all these brilliant interpretations here, and I think we have hit feelings, and we've hit what people can handle and what they can't handle, and it's that simple. And no matter how you justify what you say legally or whether it represents the Constitution, I think it breaks down to whether you're able to handle something or whether you're not able to handle something. I don't love my daughter any less because she's gay, and I don't dislike Barney any more because he's gay. I have, again, a tremendous respect.

And I want to reiterate that, no matter how strong of a person you are, these kind of bills and this kind of legislation is going to make someone defensive and going to make them feel like other people are trying to make them less, and Barney's not less.

And so I think that sometimes we have to now go beyond the law and get into a sensitivity and just say it like it is, tell the truth, and go on with it. I mean, what is obvious here is the votes are going to be the way they're going to be. And we can talk for hours and hours and hours, and you'll hear both sides brilliantly discussed—

Mr. Gekas: Will the gentleman yield for a moment?

Mr. Bono: Let me just finish, and I'll be happy to yield.

I just want to say this; I owe this to Barney, and I want to go on record that I'm not homophobic; I'm not a bigot, and I'm not pandering to hatred, and I like—I like Barney, and I love my daughter. I simply can't handle it yet, Barney. It's nothing—nothing else, but at least I want to honestly say that to you, and throw aside all the legal rhetoric. I wish I was ready, but I can't tell my son it's okay, or I don't think I can yet. So if I could—

Mr. Frank: Would you yield to me?

Mr. Bono: Yes.

Mr. Frank: I would ask that the gentleman have an additional minute, and I thank the gentleman and I appreciate candor and the decency that motivates it.

I would say two things. It's not that I feel less. This bill says I and many others are less. It says that—and no one is asking for a stamp of approval. What we're saying is, if we pay taxes, if we work, we simply want to be able to get the same financial benefits and the same responses other people do.

And, secondly, in terms of handling it—and I understand that, but no one is asking you or any of the others to do any more than leave us alone and let us have the same rights as anyone else. Let us have the rights in any State that decides, because that's all this amendment says. If the State—if we can persuade a State legislature to do it, if we can win a referendum, if we can have a court decision not be overturned, let us be like anyone else. So no one is asking you to do anything else, and if it bothers people, turn your head, but don't inflict legal disabilities that carry out that feeling.

Mr. Bono: I ask for an additional thirty seconds.

Chairman Hyde: Without objection.

Mr. Bono: I hear you. I really do hear you. And my response back to you is, you're absolutely right, but the other side of it is this has taken people to as far as they can go, and then no justifiers—I don't want to justify it because I can't. You just go as far as you can go, and then that's why I want to say to you again, honestly, I can't go this far as you deserve even, but—and I'm sorry, but I think that's the whole situation here, and I think we could argue it legally for hours and days, but that's what it's going to get down to.

House Debate on the Defense of Marriage Act

July 11, 1996

In arguing against the oppression of homosexuals through what he refers to as a "mean-spirited bigots act," African-American congressman John Lewis cites the Declaration of Independence to invoke the rights of homosexuals to "life, liberty, and the pursuit of happiness" and quotes Martin Luther King, Jr.'s, sentiments on the subject of interracial marriage, too.

Congressman John Lewis of Georgia

Let me say that when I was growing up in the south during the 1940s and the 1950s, the great majority of the people in that region believed that black people should not be able to enter places of public accommodation, and they felt that black people should not be able to register to vote, and many people felt that was right but that was wrong. I think as politicians, as elected officials, we should not only follow but we must lead, lead our districts, not put our fingers into the wind to see which way the air is blowing but be leaders.

Mr. Chairman, this is a mean bill. It is cruel. This bill seeks to divide our nation, turn Americans against Americans, sow the seeds of fear, hatred and intolerance. Let us remember the Preamble of the Declaration of Independence: We hold these truths self-evident that all people are endowed by their creator with certain inalienable rights. Among these are life, liberty, and the pursuit of happiness.

This bill is a slap in the face of the Declaration of Independence. It denies gay men and women the right to liberty and the pursuit of happiness. Marriage is a basic human right. You cannot tell people they cannot fall in love. Dr. Martin Luther King, Jr., used to say when people talked about interracial marriage and I quote, "Races do not fall in love and get married. Individuals fall in love and get married."

Why do you not want your fellow men and women, your fellow Americans to be happy? Why do you attack them? Why do you want to destroy the love they hold in their hearts? Why do you want to crush their hopes, their dreams, their longings, their aspirations?

We are talking about human beings, people like you, people who want to get married, buy a house, and spend their lives with the one they love. They have done no wrong.

I will not turn my back on another American. I will not oppress my fellow human being. I have fought too hard and too long against discrimination based on race and color not to stand up against discrimination based on sexual orientation.

Mr. Chairman, I have known racism. I have known bigotry. This bill stinks of the same fear, hatred, and intolerance. It should not be called the Defense of Marriage Act. It should be called the defense of mean-spirited bigots act.

I urge my colleagues to oppose this bill, to have the courage to do what is right. This bill appeals to our worst fears and emotions. It encourages hatred of our fellow Americans for political advantage. Every word, every purpose, every message is wrong. It is not the right thing to do, to divide Americans.

We are moving toward the twenty-first century. Let us come together and create one nation, one people, one family, one house, the American house, the American family, the American nation.

Senate Debate on the Defense of Marriage Act

September 10, 1996

In the election year of 1996, Senator John F. Kerry was one of fourteen senators opposed to the Defense of Marriage Act. He opposed it not because he favored or favors equal marriage rights for gays and lesbians, but because he felt the act was premature, unnecessary, and bigoted in its intent. Here is his speech in full—a speech that Republican supporters of president George W. Bush hope to use against the Democratic nominee in 2004.

John Kerry Takes a Stand

Madam President, I listened to my colleague, the Senator from Texas—and we will hear from others on this floor—talk about the need to defend marriages and to affirm a traditional marriage and to assert that this vote is somehow a vote that will define who is for traditional marriage and who is not.

Well, I don't agree with that definition of what this vote is about, and I do not want my feelings about, or opinions about, marriage or traditional marriage to be somehow tailored by political definitions. I am not for same-sex marriage. I have said that publicly. I would not vote for same-sex marriage.

I do not believe that this vote is specifically about defending marriage in America. I am going to vote against this bill. I will vote against this bill, though I am not for same-sex marriage, because I believe that this debate is fundamentally ugly, and it is fundamentally political, and it is fundamentally flawed.

The Defense of Marriage Act declares today on the floor of the Senate what most Americans think is pretty obvious. It declares what no State has adopted to the contrary, and won't, I imagine, for some time. In fact, the trend among States is to the contrary, no State withstanding that trend. Therefore, I suppose we really should not be surprised that the U.S. Senate is spending its time in an exercise of this kind, which ought to properly feed the cynicism that already attaches to so much of what we do in Washington.

The truth that we know, which today's exercise ignores, is that marriages fall apart in the United States, not because men and women are under siege by a mass movement of men marrying men or women marrying women. Marriages fall apart because men and women don't stay married. The real threat comes from the attitudes of many men and women married to each other and from the relationships of people in the opposite sex, not the same sex. Yet, this legislation is directed at something that has not happened and which needs no Federal intervention.

Obviously, the results of this bill will not be to preserve anything, but will serve to attack a group of people out of various motives and rationales, and certainly out of a lack of understanding and a lack of tolerance, and will only serve the purposes of the political season.

If this were truly a defense of marriage act, it would expand the learning experience for would-be husbands and wives. It would provide for counseling for all troubled marriages, not just for those who can afford it. It would provide treatment on demand for those with alcohol and substance abuse, or with the pernicious and endless invasions of their own abuse as children that they never break away from. It would expand the Violence Against Women Act. It would guarantee day care for every family that struggles and needs it. It would expand the curriculum in schools to expose high school students to a greater set of practical life choices. It would guarantee that our children would be able to read when they leave high school. It would expand the opportunity for adoptions. It would expand the protection of abused children. It would help children do things after school other than to go out and perhaps have unwanted teenage pregnancies. It would help augment Boys Clubs and Girls Clubs, YMCA's and YWCA's, school-to-work, and other alternatives so young people can grow into healthy, productive adults and have healthy adult relationships. But we all know the truth. The truth is that mistakes will be made and marriages will fail. But these are ways that we could truly defend marriage in America.

Mr. President, this bill is not necessary. No State has adopted same-sex marriage. We have a judicial question before the court in Hawaii, and it is astonishing to me that the very people who make the loudest and most continuous arguments about Federal mandates and Federal intrusion and leaving the States to their own devices and let the States work their will, before any State in the country has made a choice to do otherwise—those very people are leading the charge to have the Federal Government not just intervene, but intervene with a power grab that reaches, unconstitutionally, to do things that you cannot do by statute.

I oppose this legislation because not only is it meant to divide Americans, but it is fundamentally unconstitutional, regardless of what your views are. DOMA is unconstitutional. There is no single Member of the U.S. Senate who believes that it is within the Senate's power to strip away the word or spirit of a constitutional clause by simple statute. DOMA would, de facto, add a section to our Constitution's full faith and credit clause, article IV, section 1, to allow the States not to recognize the legal marriage in another State. That is in direct conflict with the very specific understandings interpreted by the Supreme Court of the clause itself. The clause states—simple words—"Full faith and credit shall be given"—not "may be given," "shall be given"—"in each State to the public Acts, Records, and judicial Proceedings of every other State." It says:

> And the Congress may by general Laws prescribe the Manner in which such Acts, Records and Proceedings shall be proved, and the Effect thereof.

It doesn't say no effect. It doesn't say can nullify. It doesn't say can obviate or avoid. It says it has to show how you merely procedurally prove that the act spoken of has taken place, and if it has taken place, then what is the full effect of that act in giving full faith and credit to that State. I think any schoolchild could understand that allowing States to not accept the public act of another is the exact opposite of what the Founding Fathers laid forth in the clause itself. Let me repeat:

> Full faith and credit shall be given in each State to the public Acts, Records, and judicial Proceedings of every other State.

Now, if we intend to change it—and that is a different vote than having the constitutional process properly adhered to. But it seems to me that what Congress is doing is allowing a State to ignore another State's acts, and every law that Congress has ever passed has invoked the full faith and credit of another State's legislation.

All of these laws share a basic common denominator. They all implement the full faith and credit mandate. They do not restrict it. Not once has it been restricted in that way. For example, the Parental Kidnapping Prevention Act of 1990 provided the States have to enforce child custody determinations made by other States. The Full Faith and Credit for Child Support Orders of 1994 provided that States have to enforce child support determinations made by other States. It did not say you could not do it. It did not say you could avoid it. It did not diminish it. It said you have to enforce it. The Safe Homes for Women Act of 1994 required States to recognize protective orders issued in other States with regard to domestic violence. Those laws are the products of constitutional exercises of the appropriate congressional law in implementing the full faith and credit clause. The bill before us, a statute, is the exact opposite. It is an extreme unconstitutional attempt to restrict and undermine the basic fundamental approach which helps create the concept of a unified and single nation. Madam President, this bill is not just unconstitutional. It is not just unprecedented.

It is also unnecessary.

Right now, as we speak, there is no rash outbreak among the States to recognize same-sex marriage. In fact, States—one after another—are moving in the opposite direction. For example, the State of Michigan passed a law which defines marriage as the union between a man and a woman and declares Michigan will not recognize a same-sex marriage conducted in another State. This bill is a solution in search of a problem. Madam President, even if the Hawaiian Supreme Court decides to recognize same-sex marriage, Michigan and a dozen other States have spoken against it. Resolving this tension rests squarely with the judicial branch, not the Congress. This is a power grab into States' rights of monumental proportions.

Madam President, it is ironic that many of the arguments for this power grab are echoes of the discussion of interracial marriage a generation ago. Nearly thirty years ago, this country and this body heard similar arguments against striking State laws criminalizing interracial marriage. And, the issue was resolved by the Supreme Court in the case *Loving v. Virginia*. Until the *Loving* case was decided, many southern States had laws banning interracial marriage. When the Supreme Court ruled that this ban was unconstitutional, one Congressman from Louisiana felt compelled to come to the floor of the Senate and rail against the decision in addition to the nomination of Thurgood Marshall. He said, "this shows how far we are removed from the ideas of our Founding Fathers. The Justices of the Court interpret laws not on the basis of two centuries of wisdom, but rather in line with current social fads and their own personal theories on how to create the perfect society." But that Congressman was wrong thirty years ago. And, thankfully the Court exhibited wisdom in overturning the ban. What if they had not? Pointedly and poignantly, Leon Higginbotham, Chief Justice Emeritus of the Third U.S. Court of Appeals, answers the question for us. He states that "if the Virginia courts had been sustained by the United States Supreme Court, Clarence Thomas could have been in the penitentiary today rather than serving as an Associate Justice of the Supreme Court."

Madam President, as late as 1981, in the midst of a discrimination case, a U.S. Senator threw his support behind a university which banned interracial dating and marriage. Defending a ban on interracial marriage in the 1980s.

Madam President, DOMA is unconstitutional, unprecedented, and unnecessary. Again, I return to the original questions: What is its legislative purpose? What is its motivation? What does passage of this bill mean for the country? It is hard to believe that this bill is anything other than a thinly veiled attempt to score political debating points by scapegoating gay and lesbian Americans. That is politics at its worst, Mr. President. It is a perfect exemplar of the polarizing issues E. J. Dionne describes in his book, *Why Americans Hate Politics*. In the past few years, legislative attacks on gay people have increased in frequency and scope. Trying to keep gay men and lesbians out of the armed services. Trying to keep AIDS educational materials free of any mention of homosexuality. Trying to take away the children of gay parents. Certainly the struggle for civil rights is a long one and individual prejudices are difficult to overcome. The great civil rights teacher Martin Luther King observed:

> It is pretty difficult to like some people. Like is sentimental and it is pretty difficult to like someone bombing your home; it is pretty difficult to like somebody threatening your children; it is difficult to like congressmen who spend all of their time trying to defeat civil rights. But Jesus says love them, and love is greater than like.

Madam President, that is the ultimate irony. For a bill which purports to defend and regulate marriage, there has been so little talk of love here in this Chamber. Madam President, as we quickly approach the end of the millennium, the problems facing average Americans and the pressures experienced by the American family are overwhelming—personal debt and bankruptcies are at an all-time high, divorce rates are skyrocketing, schools are crumbling, education costs are astronomical, and health care costs continue to rise.

It is clear the Congress should be alleviating the pressures of the American family. That would be the best defense of marriage. If we want to defend marriage, we should be working to change the ugly reality of spousal abuse. We should be redoubling our efforts to eradicate alcohol, drug, and other forms of substance abuse. We should acknowledge the pernicious ramifications of abandonment.

And we should commit our collective resources to creating educational opportunities for Americans, to securing health care, and to easing the economic burden too many people feel today.

We should bring Americans together with common purpose and empower individuals and communities to ease the pressure of today's increasingly complicated everyday life. This bill does not bring people together. In fact, it does the exact opposite. It divides Americans. It is a stark reminder that all citizens who play by the rules, who pay their taxes and who contribute to the economic, social, and political vibrancy of this great melting pot do not have equal rights.

I would have thought that the other side would have learned by now that there is a nasty boomerang effect to the politics of division. It rends the social and political fabric. It divides the country. I have some experience with divided countries. I fought in one. I have looked into the eyes of hatred, bigotry, ignorance, of raw unbridled passion for conflict. Look to Northern Ireland, look to Bosnia, look to the Middle East—and see the end-product of the politics of division.

Let us stop this division. Let us balance the budget. Let us provide health security and retirement security. Let us protect our environment.

And, most of all, Madam President, let us give everyone a chance for an education. Education is the key to overcoming ignorance, to keeping families together, to providing a glimpse of the American dream. Bolstering education would do more to defend marriage than anything in this bill.

This is an unconstitutional, unprecedented, unnecessary, and mean-spirited bill. I urge my colleagues to oppose it.

CHAPTER SEVEN

Not in Front of the Children?

SAME-SEX MARRIAGE AND PARENTHOOD

Much of the argument against extending civil marriages to gays and lesbians has centered on the effect such unions would have on children. And, indeed, when the issue of homosexuality is raised, the problem of parenting is rarely far behind. Legalizing same-sex marriage would logically mean granting homosexuals adoption and parenting rights, and the implications of such a move have yet to be fleshed out. Unfortunately, most of the existing studies of children born of lesbian or gay parents have consisted of small samples of dubious extraction. Nevertheless, the unanimity of such studies is striking: there seems to be no appreciable difference between children brought up in stable homosexual homes and those brought up in stable heterosexual ones.

Many of these studies are laborious to read, laden with social science jargon and statistics. The best summary, however, is Professor Charlotte Patterson's account for the American Psychological Association; it begins this section. Also included is by far the best recent study comparing children in stable two-parent heterosexual homes with those in stable two-parent lesbian homes. Following these pieces is a telling critique by a group of scholars, from the Journal of Divorce and Remarriage, arguing that almost all the studies Patterson cites do not meet basic guidelines for statistical validity, and the few that do support conclusions somewhat different than Patterson's. The chapter finishes with real-life accounts of the extreme tensions, difficulties, and triumphs of gay and lesbian family units— and Maggie Gallagher's case for protecting a traditional definition of marriage.

Children of Lesbian and Gay Parents: Summary of Research Findings

CHARLOTTE PATTERSON

From Lesbian and Gay Parenting: A Resource for Psychologists, *American Psychological Association, 1995*

Patterson provides the most comprehensive survey of most of the existing social science studies on the adjustment of children brought up in lesbian or gay families.

One belief that often underlies both judicial decision-making in custody litigation and public policies governing foster care and adoption has been the belief that lesbians and gay men are not fit to be parents. In particular, courts have sometimes assumed that gay men and lesbians are mentally ill, that lesbians are less maternal than heterosexual women, and that lesbians' and gay men's relationships with sexual partners leave little time for ongoing parent-child interactions. Results of research to date have failed to confirm any of these beliefs. . . .

The first general concern is that development of sexual identity will be impaired among children of lesbian or gay parents—for instance, that children brought up by gay fathers or lesbian mothers will show disturbances in gender identity and/or in gender role behavior. It has also been suggested that children brought up by lesbian mothers or gay fathers will themselves become gay or lesbian.

A second category of concerns involves aspects of children's personal development other than sexual identity (Falk, 1989; Editors of the *Harvard Law Review*, 1990; Kleber et al., 1986). For example, courts have expressed fears that children in the custody of gay or lesbian parents will be more vulnerable to mental breakdown, will exhibit more adjustment difficulties and behavior problems, and will be less psychologically healthy than children growing up in homes with heterosexual parents.

A third category of specific fears expressed by the courts is that children of lesbian and gay parents may experience difficulties in social relationships. For example, judges have repeatedly expressed concern that children living with lesbian mothers may be stigmatized, teased, or otherwise traumatized by peers. Another common fear is that children living with gay or lesbian parents may be more likely to be sexually abused by the parent or by the parent's friends or acquaintances.

Three aspects of sexual identity are considered in the research: gender identity concerns a person's self-identification as male or female; gender-role behavior concerns the extent to which a person's activities, occupations, and the like are regarded by the culture as masculine, feminine, or both; sexual orientation refers to a person's choice of sexual partners—i.e., heterosexual, homosexual, or bisexual (Money & Earhardt, 1972; Stein, 1993). To examine the possibility that children in the custody of lesbian mothers or gay fathers experience disruptions of sexual identity, research relevant to each of these three major areas of concern is summarized below.

Gender Identity. In studies of children ranging in age from five to fourteen, results of projective testing and related interview procedures have revealed normal development of gender identity among children of lesbian mothers (Green, 1978; Green, Mandel, Hotvedt, Gray, & Smith, 1986; Kirkpatrick, Smith, & Roy, 1981). More direct assessment techniques to assess gender identity have been used by Golombok, Spencer, and Rutter (1983) with the same result: all children in this study reported that they were happy with their gender, and that they had no wish to be a member of the opposite sex. There was no evidence in any of the studies of gender identity difficulties among children of lesbian mothers. No data have been reported in this area for children of gay fathers.

Gender-Role Behavior. A number of studies have examined gender-role behavior among the offspring of lesbian mothers (Golombok et al., 1983; Gottman, 1990; Green, 1978; Hoeffer, 1981; Kirkpatrick et al., 1981; Patterson, 1994a). These studies reported that such behavior among children of lesbian mothers fell within typical limits for conventional sex roles. For instance, Kirkpatrick and her colleagues (1981) found no differences between children of lesbian versus heterosexual mothers in toy preferences, activities, interests, or occupational choices.

Rees (1979) administered the Bem Sex Role Inventory (BSRI) to 24 adolescents, half of whom had divorced lesbian and half of whom had divorced heterosexual mothers. The BSRI yields scores on masculinity and femininity as independent factors and an androgyny score from the ratio of masculinity to femininity. Children of lesbian and heterosexual mothers did not differ on masculinity or on androgyny, but children of lesbian mothers reported greater psychological femininity than did those of heterosexual mothers. This result would seem to run counter to expectations based on stereotypes of lesbians as lacking in femininity, both in their own demeanor and in their likely influences on children.

Sex role behavior of children was also assessed by Green and his colleagues (1986). In interviews with the children, no differences between 56 children of lesbian and 48 children of heterosexual mothers were found with respect to favorite television programs, favorite television characters, or favorite games or toys. There was some indication in interviews with children themselves that the offspring of lesbian mothers had less sex-typed preferences for activities at school and in their neighborhoods than did children of heterosexual mothers. Consistent with this result, lesbian mothers were also more likely than heterosexual mothers to report that their daughters often participated in rough-and-tumble play or occasionally played with "masculine" toys such as trucks or guns; however, they reported no differences in these areas for sons. Lesbian mothers were no more or less likely than heterosexual mothers to report that their children often played with "feminine" toys such as dolls. In both family types, however, children's sex-role behavior was seen as falling within normal limits.

In summary, the research suggests that children of lesbian mothers develop patterns of gender-role behavior that are much like those of other children. No data are available as yet in this area for children of gay fathers.

Sexual Orientation. A number of investigators have also studied a third component of sexual identity: sexual orientation (Bailey,

Bobrow, Wolfe, & Mikach, 1995; Bozett, 1980, 1982, 1987, 1989; Gottman, 1990; Golombok et al., 1983; Green, 1978; Huggins, 1989; Miller, 1979; Paul, 1986; Rees, 1979). In all studies, the great majority of offspring of both gay fathers and lesbian mothers described themselves as heterosexual. Taken together, the data do not suggest elevated rates of homosexuality among the offspring of lesbian or gay parents. For instance, Huggins (1989) interviewed 36 teenagers, half of whom were offspring of lesbian mothers and half of heterosexual mothers. No children of lesbian mothers identified themselves as lesbian or gay, but one child of a heterosexual mother did; this difference was not statistically significant. In a recent study, Bailey and his colleagues (1995) studied adult sons of gay fathers and found more than 90 percent of the sons to be heterosexual. Because the heterosexual and nonheterosexual sons did not differ in the length of time they had resided with their fathers, the effects of the exposure to the fathers' sexual orientation on the sons' sexual orientation must have been either very small or nonexistent. . . .

Studies assessing potential differences between children of gay and lesbian versus heterosexual parents have sometimes included assessments of children's social relationships. The most common focus of attention has been on peer relations, but some information on children's relationships with adults has also been collected. Research findings that address the likelihood of sexual abuse are also summarized in this section.

Research on peer relations among children of lesbian mothers has been reported by Golombok and her colleagues (1983), Green (1978), and by Green and his colleagues (1986). Reports by both parents and children suggest normal development of peer relationships. For example, as would be expected, most school-aged children reported same-sex best friends and predominantly same-sex peer groups (Golombok et al., 1983; Green, 1978). The quality of children's peer relations was described, on average, in positive terms by researchers (Golombok et al., 1983) as well as by lesbian mothers and their children (Green et al., 1986). No data on the children of gay fathers have been reported in this area.

Studies of relationships with adults among the offspring of lesbian and gay parents have also yielded a generally positive picture (Golombok et al., 1983; Harris & Turner, 1985/86; Kirkpatrick et al., 1981). For example, Golombok and her colleagues (1983) found that children of divorced lesbian mothers were more likely to have had recent contact with their fathers than were children of divorced heterosexual mothers. Another study, however, found no differences in this regard (Kirkpatrick et al., 1981). Harris and Turner (1985/86) studied the offspring of gay fathers as well as those of lesbian mothers; parent-child relationships were described in positive terms by parents in their sample. One significant difference between lesbian and gay parents, on the one hand, and heterosexual parents, on the other, was that heterosexual parents were more likely to say that their children's visits with the other parent presented problems for them (Harris & Turner, 1985/86).

In the Golombok et al. (1983) study, children's contacts with adult friends of their lesbian mothers were also assessed. All of the children were reported to have contact with adult friends of their mothers, and the majority of lesbian mothers reported that their adult friends were a mixture of homosexual and heterosexual adults.

Lesbians Choosing Motherhood:
A Comparative Study of Lesbian and
Heterosexual Parents and Their Children

DAVID K. FLAKS ET AL.

From Developmental Psychology *31, no. 1 (1995)*

This is the best recent survey on lesbian mothering. The results of its comparison of heterosexual and lesbian mothers are striking. If anything, Flaks finds lesbian mothers to be more conscientious than their heterosexual counterparts.

It is within the context of the developing literature on planned lesbian-mother families that the present research project was conducted. Its purpose was to expand what is known about these families, with an eye toward addressing the expressed concerns of family court judges and legislators (Falk, 1989). This study focused specifically on lesbian couples raising children born to them through donor insemination. By defining the experimental sample in this way, we eliminated the potentially confounding variables of single parenting, parental separation, and adoption.

Several features of this study make it unique among research on planned lesbian-mother families. First, this is the only study to separately assess the impact on boys and girls of being raised in a lesbian home. In addition, in the area of planned lesbian-mother families, this is only the second study to compare lesbian mothers and their children with a matched control group of heterosexual parents and their children and to corroborate parental assessments of the children by soliciting independent teacher ratings. Furthermore, this study represents the first effort to examine lesbian-mother families by using a broad range of outcome measures, including intellectual and behavioral assessments of the children, as well as evaluations of the parents' relationship quality and parenting skills. Each of these areas was chosen because it has been the subject of negative judicial assumptions about lesbian-mother families. . . .

In all, 15 lesbian-mother families and 15 heterosexual-parent families participated in this study, most of whom resided in the Pennsylvania area. . . . [M]ost of the parents in both groups were well-educated, and almost all had at least part-time employment outside of the home. The lesbian parents were somewhat older on average than the heterosexual parents. In addition, the lesbian and heterosexual couples had relationships of similar length, with the lesbian couples having been together for an average of 12.7 years (ranging from 7.5 to 18 years), and the heterosexual couples had been together for an average of 12.8 years (ranging from 8 to 20.5 years). The couples had also lived together for similar amounts of time: The lesbian couples had shared a residence for an average of 11.9 years (ranging from 5.5 to 18 years), and the heterosexual couples had lived together for an average of 11.2 years (ranging from 6 to 17 years).

Demographics of the 15 focal children in the lesbian- and heterosexual-parent samples were also similar. Both groups consisted of 8 girls and 7 boys. The focal children in both groups had a mean age of 5.8 years, with a range of 3.1 to 8.3 years, respectively, in the lesbian-mother group and 3.2 to 7.9 years, respectively, in the heterosexual-parent group. . . .

Notwithstanding this study's specific features, its results are entirely consistent with prior research on planned lesbian-mother families (McCandish, 1987; Patterson, 1994; Steckel, 1985, 1987). Like earlier research, results of this study are consistent with the conclusion that the children of lesbian and heterosexual parents are remarkably similar, specifically in the areas of intellectual functioning and behavioral adjustment. In each of these areas, no gender differences were found; scores for both boys and girls in the lesbian- and heterosexual-parent groups were extremely similar, and each group compared favorably with the standardization samples for the instruments used. Furthermore, of the 24 comparisons made between the children in the two groups, 17 actually favored the children of lesbian parents, a fact that diminishes the likelihood that differences were not found because of problems associated with small sample size. Rather, given the direction and magnitude of these results, it is more probable that the two groups of children and parents were comparable in the areas assessed.

Like their children, the two groups of parents evaluated in this study also revealed similarities. In the area of relationship quality, no differences were found between the groups, although the lesbian couples received higher scores in every area of dyadic adjustment. Moreover, both the lesbian and heterosexual couples were comparable in overall dyadic adjustment to the married couples in Spanier's (1976) normative sample, suggesting satisfactory relationship quality in both groups.

Only in the domain of parenting skills awareness were differences found between the two groups of couples. Analysis using the Parent Awareness Skills Survey revealed that the lesbian couples were more aware of the skills necessary for effective parenting than were their heterosexual counterparts. Specifically, the lesbian couples proved to be superior in their ability to identify the critical issues in child-care situations and to formulate appropriate solutions to the problems they noticed. With further analysis, however, it was revealed that these differences were related to the parents' gender rather than to their sexual orientation: Both heterosexual and lesbian mothers demonstrated an awareness of parenting skills that was superior to that of heterosexual fathers. Although this result may suggest that the heterosexual fathers were less capable in their ability to handle child-care problems, it may also represent a gender difference in their likelihood to verbalize their ideas about parenting. The latter conclusion is supported by an examination of the actual responses of the participants on the parenting skills measure. The verbatim records of the fathers were substantially shorter than those of the three groups of mothers. Further research is necessary for one to compare the parenting skills of parents on the basis of gender, preferably relying on observational data.

What are the implications of these results? Healthy developmental outcomes for the children in this and other studies of lesbian families support the view of Patterson (1992) and others that neither father presence nor parental heterosexuality is crucial for healthy child development. Such a conclusion, although uncontroverted in the research literature, remains controversial because it challenges widely accepted psychoanalytic and social learning theories of child development. Because such theories rely on traditional family structures to define the factors that promote children's development, they are not able to account easily for successful outcomes in nontraditional families, particularly those in which there is no opposite-sex parent in the home. Evidence of the type presented here, which suggests that well-adjusted children of both sexes can be raised in families of varying configurations, will hopefully provide an impetus for a reevaluation of the parental qualities most important for optimal child development. To accommodate the findings of this and other studies of lesbian families, it would appear that theories of child development will have to take into account the preeminence of process variables over structural ones in predicting the most desirable family environment for raising children (Patterson, 1994). . . .

A Review of Data Based Studies Addressing the Effects of Homosexual Parenting on Children's Sexual and Social Functioning

PHILIP A. BELCASTRO ET AL.

From the Journal of Divorce and Remarriage 20
(1993)

An opposite view of the social science data. Belcastro and his colleagues see most of the studies as essentially useless, ruined by lack of external validity and the biases of their authors. The truth is, the authors argue, we still don't know for sure what effect gay parents have on the development of children.

Abstract Part of the intellectual and political movement to provide homosexuals equal rights and opportunities under the law extends to homosexuals and bisexuals seeking custody of their biological children after divorce and/or custody of an adopted child. Family courts take into consideration parents' sexual orientation when considering custody decisions. To date, the data based research on children reared by homosexual parents is sparse. A search of the published literature identified fourteen data based studies which addressed some aspect of homosexual parenting and its effects on children. Each study was evaluated according to accepted standards of scientific inquiry. The most impressive finding was that all of the studies lacked external validity, and not a single study represented any sub-population of homosexual parents. Three studies met minimal or higher standards of internal validity, while the remaining eleven presented moderate to fatal threats to internal validity. The conclusion that there are no significant differences in children reared by lesbian mothers versus heterosexual mothers is not supported by the published research data base.

As a preface to the discussion, we have an obligation to comment on the real and ideal standards of scientific research utilizing human subjects. It is easy for a critic to demand ideal scientific standards. However, the reality of inadequate funding, population inaccessibility and incomplete behavioral constructs renders the goal of pure validity an ideal. On the other hand, such limitations cannot be ignored when proposing cause and effect via the scientific method.

The most impressive finding is that all of the studies lacked external validity. Furthermore, not a single study remotely represented any sub-population of homosexual parents. This limitation, in terms of scientific inference, is imposing.

With only three exceptions (i.e., Green et al., 1986; Hoeffer, 1979; Puryear, 1983) the studies' designs presented moderate to fatal threats to their internal validity. Seven studies did not utilize a control group and only three studies satisfactorily attempted to match comparison groups (i.e., Green et al., 1986; Hoeffer, 1979; Puryear, 1983). All of the studies utilized marginally acceptable sample sizes. Also, it was possible for a bisexual to enter either the homosexual or heterosexual groups in each study. With only one exception (i.e., Rees, 1979), of those studies utilizing a control group matched to a lesbian group, a considerable proportion of the lesbians were cohabiting with sexual partners and this same factor, cohabitation, was not true for the comparison heterosexual group. Another mutual limitation of these studies was one identified by Rees (1979), namely, lesbians' political and legal desire to present a happy, well-adjusted family to the world.

An importune weakness for these studies was the construction of the independent variable. As pointed out there was no control for bisexuals being classified as homosexuals. Furthermore, there was no control, save Rees (1979), for establishing a single-parent household. The gay households samples were a pieced-together patchwork of gay lovers, former spouses, custody rights quirks, and extended genetic and step-family units. The contamination of the independent variable resulted in the absence of even a single study comprised of a group of single-parent homosexual households matched to a group of single-parent heterosexual households.

The majority of studies also suffered from internal validity flaws such as inadequate instrumentation and disparate testing conditions that, unlike the external validity problems, were well within the researchers' control. In some cases the researchers argued that any information, regardless of quality, is better than none. We disagree and contend that improperly gathered data is scientifically defective.

Finally, based upon the researchers' interpretation of the data and at least in one case censorship of the data, most were biased towards proving homosexual parents were fit parents. A disturbing revelation was that some of the published works had to disregard their own results in order to conclude the homosexuals were fit parents. We believe that the system of manuscript review by peers, for minimum scientific standards of research, was compromised in several of these studies.

On the positive side, three of the studies demonstrated a minimum or higher standard of internal validity; two of which were dissertations. Although additional faults could be cited for these studies, their basic design and analyses were acceptable. In the interest of economy, only the variables that discriminated between the groups statistically, and were directly related to the three general concerns of family courts, are noted.

Green et al., 1986

- Daughters of lesbian mothers were more likely to cross-dress than daughters of heterosexual mothers.
- Daughters of lesbian mothers were more likely to choose traditionally masculine jobs than daughters of heterosexual mothers.
- Daughters of lesbian mothers were more likely to be above average in rough-and-tumble play than daughters of heterosexual mothers.
- Daughters of lesbian mothers were more likely to play with trucks than daughters of heterosexual mothers.
- Daughters of lesbian mothers were more likely to play with guns than daughters of heterosexual mothers.
- Children of lesbian mothers were more likely to be interested in play-acting and role-taking than children of heterosexual mothers.
- Lesbians' daughters were more likely to choose male activities than daughters of heterosexual mothers.
- Lesbians' sons were more likely to have a strong preference for female activities than heterosexual mothers' sons.
- Daughters of mothers who were active in lesbianism or feminist organizations were more likely to be interested in male occupations and desired to be like a man when they grew up.

(Please note: The authors blocked on several variables resulting in cells with < 5 subjects, and these results were omitted from the above list.)

Hoeffer, 1979

- Lesbians' daughters were more likely to score higher on sex-typed masculine activities than daughters of heterosexual mothers.

- Lesbians' daughters were less likely to view themselves as androgynous than daughters of heterosexual mothers.
- Lesbians' daughters were less likely to have female valued traits than daughters of heterosexual mothers.
- Lesbian mothers were less likely to encourage their sons and more likely to encourage their daughters in sex-role behavior than heterosexual mothers.
- Lesbians' sons were more likely to have female-valued traits than sons of heterosexual mothers.
- Lesbian mothers were less likely to encourage play with sex-typed toys for their children than heterosexual mothers.
- Lesbian mothers were more likely to report male peers influencing their sons than heterosexual mothers.
- Lesbians' daughters were more likely to have significant contact with male teachers than daughters of heterosexual mothers.

Puryear, 1983
- Lesbian children were more likely to draw the family as involved in separate activities than children of heterosexual mothers.
- Lesbian children were less likely to draw the father as being involved in activities with themselves than children of heterosexual mothers.
- Lesbian children were less likely to draw activities between mother and child that showed cooperation than children of heterosexual mothers.
- Lesbian children were less likely to draw activities between father and child that showed cooperation between the two, than children of heterosexual mothers.
- Lesbian children were less likely to draw activities between child and "other adult" that showed cooperation, than children of heterosexual mothers.

- Lesbian mothers were less likely to rate their children's relationship with their father as good than children of heterosexual mothers.

A pitfall is to consciously or unconsciously judge these differences on a moral basis. That is not the intent of this review. What is possible, given the collective limitations of these three studies, is to conclude that there appears to be some significant differences between children raised by lesbian mothers versus heterosexual mothers in their family relationships, gender identity and gender behavior. The most defined trend is that daughters of lesbian mothers are more likely to value and exhibit male sex-typed traits than daughters of heterosexual mothers. A second trend is that children of lesbian mothers are less likely to perceive their family as an interactive family unit and their father as cooperative, than children of heterosexual mothers. One critical concern of the courts is whether children of gay parents are more likely to adopt a homosexual lifestyle. Unfortunately, only one study utilized a post-adolescent sample in order to render any estimate. Paul (1986) surveyed adult offspring of gay and bisexual households and reported 23.5 percent of the subjects homosexual. However, his sample was seriously flawed.

In our view, the statement that there are no significant differences in children reared by homosexual parents versus heterosexual parents is not supported by the published research base. The converse also remains unproven.

The ultimate outcome of answering these research questions is not just whether there are differences but whether those differences are desirable or undesirable societal outcomes. This leads to the moral decision of whether society has a right to prevent nurturing of children and ultimately adults who are more tolerant and personally receptive to (1) homosexuals; (2) homosexual behaviors; and (3) homosexual relationships.

Some essential refinements to the research question are necessary. We will not reiterate the recommendations for the reviewed studies with the exception of the need for representative samples, and adult offspring samples from homosexual households. Future studies need to isolate and precisely construct comparison groups that equate the homosexual rearing family unit with the heterosexual rearing family unit in all essential aspects of the experience including (1) parental lovers with parenting roles; (2) length of exposure to the homosexual family unit at various childhood developmental stages; and (3) divorced/separated parents' family role and contact with offspring. The classification of parents' sexual orientation should be qualitatively measured for the entire time frame of their children's lifetime. Parents' sexual orientation should be blocked on homosexual, heterosexual, or bisexual. A comprehensive lifetime sexual behavior profile should be constructed on children from homosexual households and their heterosexual cohorts. There is a pressing need to study children raised by homosexual fathers and in turn determine any differences in outcomes regarding children raised by lesbian mothers versus homosexual fathers, and also their heterosexual cohorts. Lastly, in order to address the question of whether homosexual parents rear homosexual children, it is necessary to examine the lineage of homosexuals.

Coming Out to My Children
ANTIGA

From Politics of the Heart: A Lesbian Parenting
Anthology, *1987*

A reflection on the rejection lesbian mothers sometimes experience at the hands of their own children.

COMING OUT TO MY CHILDREN

I thought that I was waiting
until
they could handle it
before telling them.

When I did
both daughters wondered why
it had taken me so long
both sons pretended that
they hadn't heard.

The pain
of the oldest daughter was spoken:
"Mom, I wish you weren't a Lesbian."
The pain
of the youngest son was hidden until
he was hospitalized

so drunk
he could not say his name.
When he could speak
they asked for my phone number
and he answered:
"Don't call her. She's a Lesbian."

Parenting by Gay Fathers

JERRY J. BIGNER AND
FREDERICK W. BOZETT

From Homosexuality and Family Relations, *edited by*
Frederick W. Bozett and Marvin B. Sussman, 1990

A recent sociological survey of gay fathers.

When gay fathers are compared with nongay fathers in their responses to the Iowa Parent Behavior Scale, the gay fathers
are found to be more strict and to consistently emphasize the
importance of setting limits on children's behavior (Bigner &
Jacobsen, 1989b). They report going to greater lengths than
nongay fathers in promoting cognitive skills of children by
explaining rules and regulations. As such, they may place greater
emphasis on verbal communication with children. Gay fathers
tend to be less traditional or more authoritative with children
and to be somewhat strict in the execution of their control over

children. Generally, gay fathers are found to be more sensitive and responsive to the perceived needs of children than nongay fathers. Gay fathers also appear to go to extra lengths to act as a resource for activities with children. They seem no different from nongay fathers in their expression of intimacy toward children except that they appear less willing to be demonstrative toward their partner in their children's presence than are nongay fathers (Bigner & Jacobsen, 1989b).

Several explanations can be suggested that address the differences and similarities in parenting behavior of gay and nongay fathers. First, gay fathers may feel additional pressures to be more proficient at their parenting role than nongay fathers. Factors that might motivate them to be "better" fathers could include (1) stronger feelings of guilt about their role in fathering children, based on an increased sensitivity about their sexuality; and (2) sensitivity to the belief that they are "in the spotlight" or expected to perform better due to a fear that visitation or custody decisions could be challenged because of their sexual orientation. Second, these findings suggest that gay fathers may be less conventional and more androgynous than nongay fathers. As such, they may incorporate a greater degree and combination of expressive role functions than more traditionally sex-role oriented nongay fathers. These expressive role functions are found more conventionally in the traditional female mothering role. The cultural stereotype of the father role among traditional males is that they (1) generally are not interested in children or in child-rearing issues; (2) view the occupational role as their primary parenting identity; (3) are less competent caregivers than women; and (4) are less nurturant than women toward children. It is possible that nongay fathers adopt this as their parenting style while gay fathers may demonstrate a blending of the qualities traditionally associated with both mother and father role images.

What is the quality of parent-child relations for those men who are gay and yet remain married and/or closeted and do not reveal their homosexuality to children? Researchers find that these relationships often are of less quality than those found among fathers who are open and honest with their children regarding their homosexuality (Bozett, 1987b; Miller, 1979a). Gay fathers who have disclosed their homosexuality to their children and to others tend to live a relatively stable lifestyle that may involve a domestic type of relationship with another man who often is a permanent partner, they tend to spend quality time with their children, and are dependable sources of caregiving (Miller, 1979a). . . .

Why I'm Glad I Grew Up in a Gay Family

PAULA FOMBY

From Mother Jones, *May/June 1991*

A voice rarely heard from in this context: the child's.

I grew up in the closet, waiting for my mother to come out first. When I was thirteen, she told me that she was a lesbian and confessed what I had assumed, that the woman who had lived with us for four years was her lover. I cried; when I remember it, I picture myself running away from her and down the street.

Being the child in a gay family, for me, meant telling lies. My mother asked me not to tell my friends that she was gay, comparing the embarrassment to a secret we shared about an eraser I had once stolen from a stationery store. There was little danger that I would say anything. Through high school, I constructed my social life around the fact that my mother and her lover were asleep by ten o'clock, making sure I had no guests in our house, who might see them go to bed. Should anyone actually see them disappear behind the same closed door, I was quick to invent an explanation. If my mother and Connie overheard the stories I made up, they never said anything, taking this, I suppose, as my method of defense.

Children have clear signals about what it means to be gay— where I lived, a limp wrist, a high-pitched voice, a purple polo shirt for boys, and anything leaning toward hippie fashion for girls. To be gay was to be stupid; the two words were literally synonymous. I was slow to understand that the shared bed in my house and the insults made in the cafeteria line were all supposed to be part of the same thing.

The hardest part of having a gay mother was accepting homosexuality and all its consequences before I even knew what that involved. I loved my mother and Connie, but I cringed at the mention of the Gay Pride parade, and I looked at their gay friends skeptically, eager for reasons to dislike them. I never said anything, valiantly trying to support a cause I didn't even want to discuss with my friends. As long as they kept it quiet, I was content; otherwise, I hated the danger their social lives posed to mine.

In order to live peaceably, I accepted my mother's lifestyle a long time ago; feeling comfortable with it has come more recently. My first efforts to defend gays were destructively self-conscious. I gave a speech to a high-school class about gay rights, but when a student asked if I was gay, I was quicker than I should have been to say no. In college, I alienated myself at a party by screaming at somebody who resented heterosexualhating gays. My argument lacked basis and logic, but I felt threatened, as if they were somehow pointing a finger at my mother. This constant tension between defending gays while defining myself as straight finally articulated itself when I realized that there are not simply gay couples with children; there are gay families, where everyone must deal with the prejudice surrounding homosexuality.

The fact that there is no real definition of the gay family is obvious when I try to explain Connie. To dismiss Connie as an entity existing in our house only for my mother's sake negates the impact she's had on more than half of my life. She has been a part of my decisions, she has purchased my groceries, she has entertained my ambitions. She has been far more than a roommate to me, and I love her, want to protect her, and make her happy. I know also what she means to my mother—they are wedded in everything but the legal sense.

Each person in my family has matured into what it means to be gay individually. My mother and Connie have become more involved in the gay community since I left home. Seeing them take pride in their relationship makes me more proud to talk about them, and I have met people who say "it's pretty cool" to come from such a unique family. My willingness to discuss coming from a gay family results as much from the support of friends and college teachers as it does from my unchanging belief, idealized in all families, that my mother always does the right thing. . . .

What Marriage Is For

M A G G I E   G A L L A G H E R

From the Weekly Standard, *August 4–11, 2003*

A conservative writer argues that marriage cannot be sepa-
rated from its procreative origins—and allowing gays to marry
would undermine the institution as a whole.

Gay marriage is no longer a theoretical issue. Canada has it.
Massachusetts is expected to get it any day. The *Goodridge*
decision there could set off a legal, political, and cultural battle
in the courts of fifty states and in the U.S. Congress. Every politician, every judge, every citizen has to decide: Does same-sex
marriage matter? If so, how and why?

The timing could not be worse. Marriage is in crisis, as everyone knows: High rates of divorce and illegitimacy have eroded
marriage norms and created millions of fatherless children, whole
neighborhoods where lifelong marriage is no longer customary,
driving up poverty, crime, teen pregnancy, welfare dependency,
drug abuse, and mental and physical health problems. And yet,
amid the broader negative trends, recent signs point to a modest
but significant recovery.

Divorce rates appear to have declined a little from historic
highs; illegitimacy rates, after doubling every decade from 1960 to
1990, appear to have leveled off, albeit at a high level (33 percent
of American births are to unmarried women); teen pregnancy and
sexual activity are down; the proportion of homemaking mothers
is up; marital fertility appears to be on the rise. Research suggests
that married adults are more committed to marital permanence

than they were twenty years ago. A new generation of children of divorce appears on the brink of making a commitment to lifelong marriage. In 1977, 55 percent of American teenagers thought a divorce should be harder to get; in 2001, 75 percent did.

A new marriage movement—a distinctively American phenomenon—has been born. The scholarly consensus on the importance of marriage has broadened and deepened; it is now the conventional wisdom among child welfare organizations. As a Child Trends research brief summed up: "Research clearly demonstrates that family structure matters for children, and the family structure that helps children the most is a family headed by two biological parents in a low-conflict marriage. Children in single-parent families, children born to unmarried mothers, and children in stepfamilies or cohabiting relationships face higher risks of poor outcomes. . . . There is thus value for children in promoting strong, stable marriages between biological parents."

What will court-imposed gay marriage do to this incipient recovery of marriage? For, even as support for marriage in general has been rising, the gay marriage debate has proceeded on a separate track. Now the time has come to decide: Will unisex marriage help or hurt marriage as a social institution?

Why should it do either, some may ask? How can Bill and Bob's marriage hurt Mary and Joe? In an exchange with me in the just-released book *Marriage and Same Sex Unions: A Debate,* Evan Wolfson, chief legal strategist for same-sex marriage in the Hawaii case, *Baehr v. Lewin,* argues there is "enough marriage to share." What counts, he says, "is not family structure, but the quality of dedication, commitment, self-sacrifice, and love in the household."

Family structure does not count. Then what is marriage for? Why have laws about it? Why care whether people get married or stay married? Do children need mothers and fathers, or will any sort of family do? When the sexual desires of adults clash with the interests of children, which carries more weight, socially and legally?

These are the questions that same-sex marriage raises. Our answers will affect not only gay and lesbian families, but marriage as a whole.

In ordering gay marriage on June 10, 2003, the highest court in Ontario, Canada, explicitly endorsed a brand new vision of marriage along the lines Wolfson suggests: "Marriage is, without dispute, one of the most significant forms of personal relationships. . . . Through the institution of marriage, individuals can publicly express their love and commitment to each other. Through this institution, society publicly recognizes expressions of love and commitment between individuals, granting them respect and legitimacy as a couple."

The Ontario court views marriage as a kind of Good Housekeeping Seal of Approval that government stamps on certain registered intimacies because, well, for no particular reason the court can articulate except that society likes to recognize expressions of love and commitment. In this view, endorsement of gay marriage is a no-brainer, for nothing really important rides on whether anyone gets married or stays married. Marriage is merely individual expressive conduct, and there is no obvious reason why some individuals' expression of gay love should hurt other individuals' expressions of non-gay love.

There is, however, a different view—indeed, a view that is radically opposed to this: Marriage is the fundamental, cross-cultural institution for bridging the male-female divide so that children have loving, committed mothers and fathers. Marriage is inherently normative: It is about holding out a certain kind of relationship as a social ideal, especially when there are children involved. Marriage is not simply an artifact of law; neither is it a mere delivery mechanism for a set of legal benefits that might as well be shared more broadly. The laws of marriage do not create marriage, but in societies ruled by law they help trace the boundaries and sustain the public meanings of marriage.

In other words, while individuals freely choose to enter marriage, society upholds the marriage option, formalizes its definition, and surrounds it with norms and reinforcements, so we can raise boys and girls who aspire to become the kind of men and women who can make successful marriages. Without this shared, public aspect, perpetuated generation after generation, marriage becomes what its critics say it is: a mere contract, a vessel with no particular content, one of a menu of sexual lifestyles, of no fundamental importance to anyone outside a given relationship.

The marriage idea is that children need mothers and fathers, that societies need babies, and that adults have an obligation to shape their sexual behavior so as to give their children stable families in which to grow up.

Which view of marriage is true? We have seen what has happened in our communities where marriage norms have failed. What has happened is not a flowering of libertarian freedom, but a breakdown of social and civic order that can reach frightening proportions. When law and culture retreat from sustaining the marriage idea, individuals cannot create marriage on their own.

In a complex society governed by positive law, social institutions require both social and legal support. To use an analogy, the government does not create private property. But to make a market system a reality requires the assistance of law as well as culture. People have to be raised to respect the property of others, and to value the traits of entrepreneurship, and to be law-abiding generally. The law cannot allow individuals to define for themselves what private property (or law-abiding conduct) means. The boundaries of certain institutions (such as the corporation) also need to be defined legally, and the definitions become socially shared knowledge. We need a shared system of meaning, publicly enforced, if market-based economies are to do their magic and individuals are to maximize their opportunities.

Successful social institutions generally function without people's having to think very much about how they work. But when a social institution is contested—as marriage is today—it becomes critically important to think and speak clearly about its public meanings.

Again, what is marriage for? Marriage is a virtually universal human institution. In all the wildly rich and various cultures flung throughout the ecosphere, in society after society, whether tribal or complex, and however bizarre, human beings have created systems of publicly approved sexual union between men and women that entail well-defined responsibilities of mothers and fathers. Not all these marriage systems look like our own, which is rooted in a fusion of Greek, Roman, Jewish, and Christian culture. Yet everywhere, in isolated mountain valleys, parched deserts, jungle thickets, and broad plains, people have come up with some version of this thing called marriage. Why?

Because sex between men and women makes babies, that's why. Even today, in our technologically advanced contraceptive culture, half of all pregnancies are unintended: Sex between men and women still makes babies. Most men and women are powerfully drawn to perform a sexual act that can and does generate life. Marriage is our attempt to reconcile and harmonize the erotic, social, sexual, and financial needs of men and women with the needs of their partner and their children.

How to reconcile the needs of children with the sexual desires of adults? Every society has to face that question, and some resolve it in ways that inflict horrendous cruelty on children born outside marriage. Some cultures decide these children don't matter: Men can have all the sex they want, and any children they create outside of marriage will be throwaway kids; marriage is for citizens—slaves and peasants need not apply. You can see a version of this elitist vision of marriage emerging in America under cover of acceptance of family diversity. Marriage will continue to exist as the social advantage of elite communities. The poor and the working class? Who cares whether their kids have dads? We can always import people from abroad to fill our need for disciplined, educated workers.

Our better tradition, and the only one consistent with democratic principles, is to hold up a single ideal for all parents, which is ultimately based on our deep cultural commitment to the equal dignity and social worth of all children. All kids need and deserve a married mom and dad. All parents are supposed to at least try to behave in ways that will give their own children this important protection. Privately, religiously, emotionally, individually, marriage may have many meanings. But this is the core of its public, shared meaning: Marriage is the place where having children is not only tolerated but welcomed and encouraged, because it gives children mothers and fathers.

Of course, many couples fail to live up to this ideal. Many of the things men and women have to do to sustain their own marriages, and a culture of marriage, are hard. Few people will do them consistently if the larger culture does not affirm the critical importance of marriage as a social institution. Why stick out a frustrating relationship, turn down a tempting new love, abstain from sex outside marriage, or even take pains not to conceive children out of wedlock if family structure does not matter? If marriage is not a shared norm, and if successful marriage is not socially valued, do not expect it to survive as the generally accepted context for raising children. If marriage is just a way of publicly celebrating private love, then there is no need to encourage couples to stick it out for the sake of the children. If family structure does not matter, why have marriage laws at all? Do adults, or do they not, have a basic obligation to control their desires so that children can have mothers and fathers?

The problem with endorsing gay marriage is not that it would allow a handful of people to choose alternative family forms, but that it would require society at large to gut marriage of its central presumptions about family in order to accommodate a few adults' desires.

The debate over same-sex marriage, then, is not some sideline discussion. It is the marriage debate. Either we win—or we lose the central meaning of marriage. The great threat unisex marriage poses to marriage as a social institution is not some distant or nearby slippery slope, it is an abyss at our feet. If we cannot explain why unisex marriage is, in itself, a disaster, we have already lost the marriage ideal.

Same-sex marriage would enshrine in law a public judgment that the desire of adults for families of choice outweighs the need of children for mothers and fathers. It would give sanction and approval to the creation of a motherless or fatherless family as a deliberately chosen "good." It would mean the law was neutral as to whether children had mothers and fathers. Motherless and fatherless families would be deemed just fine.

Same-sex marriage advocates are startlingly clear on this point. Marriage law, they repeatedly claim, has nothing to do with babies or procreation or getting mothers and fathers for children. In forcing the state legislature to create civil unions for gay couples, the high court of Vermont explicitly ruled that marriage in the state of Vermont has nothing to do with procreation. Evan Wolfson made the same point in *Marriage and Same Sex Unions:* "[I]sn't having the law pretend that there is only one family model that works (let alone exists) a lie?" He goes on to say that in law, "marriage is not just about procreation—indeed is not necessarily about procreation at all."

Wolfson is right that in the course of the sexual revolution the Supreme Court struck down many legal features designed to reinforce the connection of marriage to babies. The animus of elites (including legal elites) against the marriage idea is not brand new. It stretches back at least thirty years. That is part of the problem we face, part of the reason 40 percent of our children are growing up without their fathers.

It is also true, as gay-marriage advocates note, that we impose no fertility tests for marriage: Infertile and older couples marry, and not every fertile couple chooses procreation. But every marriage between a man and a woman is capable of giving any child they create or adopt a mother and a father. Every marriage between a man and a woman discourages either from creating fatherless children outside the marriage vow. In this sense, neither older married couples nor childless husbands and wives publicly challenge or dilute the core meaning of marriage. Even when a man marries an older woman and they do not adopt, his marriage helps protect children. How? His marriage means, if he keeps his vows, that he will not produce out-of-wedlock children.

Does marriage discriminate against gays and lesbians? Formally speaking, no. There are no sexual-orientation tests for marriage; many gays and lesbians do choose to marry members of the opposite sex, and some of these unions succeed. Our laws do not require a person to marry the individual to whom he or she is most erotically attracted, so long as he or she is willing to promise sexual fidelity, mutual caretaking, and shared parenting of any children of the marriage.

But marriage is unsuited to the wants and desires of many gays and lesbians, precisely because it is designed to bridge the male-female divide and sustain the idea that children need mothers and fathers. To make a marriage, what you need is a husband and a wife. Redefining marriage so that it suits gays and lesbians would require fundamentally changing our legal, public, and social conception of what marriage is in ways that threaten its core public purposes.

Some who criticize the refusal to embrace gay marriage liken it to the outlawing of interracial marriage, but the analogy is woefully false. The Supreme Court overturned anti-miscegenation laws because they frustrated the core purpose of marriage in order to sustain a racist legal order. Marriage laws, by contrast, were not invented to express animus toward homosexuals or anyone else. Their purpose is not negative, but positive: They uphold an institution that developed, over thousands of years, in thousands of cultures, to help direct the erotic desires of men and women into a relatively narrow but indispensably fruitful channel. We need men and women to marry and make babies for our society to survive. We have no similar public stake in any other family form—in the union of same-sex couples or the singleness of single moms.

Meanwhile, *cui bono?* To meet the desires of whom would we put our most basic social institution at risk? No good research on the marriage intentions of homosexual people exists. For what it's worth, the Census Bureau reports that 0.5 percent of households now consist of same-sex partners. To get a proxy for how many gay couples would avail themselves of the health insurance benefits marriage can provide, I asked the top ten companies listed on the Human Rights Campaign's website as providing same-sex insurance benefits how many of their employees use this option. Only one company, General Motors, released its data. Out of 1.3 million employees, 166 claimed benefits for a same-sex partner, one one-hundredth of one percent.

People who argue for creating gay marriage do so in the name of high ideals: justice, compassion, fairness. Their sincerity is not in question. Nevertheless, to take the already troubled institution most responsible for the protection of children and throw out its most basic presumption in order to further adult interests in sexual freedom would not be high-minded. It would be morally callous and socially irresponsible.

If we cannot stand and defend this ground, then face it: The marriage debate is over. Dan Quayle was wrong. We lost.

CHAPTER EIGHT

A Slippery Slope?
THE POLYGAMY AND ADULTERY DEBATE

Curiously, perhaps, a major subsidiary argument related to same-sex marriage turned into a full-scale fight. Several leading conservatives—including former education secretary Bill Bennett and Washington Post *columnist Charles Krauthammer—chose to oppose same-sex marriage partly on the grounds that they believed that there was no rational or moral distinction between sanctioning polygamy and legalizing same-sex marriage. Their arguments are reproduced below—as are impassioned responses from me and Jonathan Rauch.*

Linked to polygamy was the notion that gay men are inherently more promiscuous than straight men and that a same-sex marriage would therefore inevitably be more likely to involve adultery than would a heterosexual marriage; and so gay unions would demean the institution as a whole. So polygamy and adultery became part of a distinct line of argument against same-sex marriage that continues still.

This chapter concludes with an extract from The Homosexual-ization of America, *in which gay writer Dennis Altman celebrates precisely the polygamous gay male impulses that so alarm Bennett and Krauthammer. The essay appeared in 1982—before the AIDS epidemic exploded, and before the issue of same-sex marriage came to redefine the cultural and political self-understanding of many lesbian and gay Americans.*

Leave Marriage Alone
WILLIAM BENNETT

From Newsweek, *June 3, 1996*

If we allow same-sex marriage, why not polygamy? or incest?

There are at least two key issues that divide proponents and opponents of same-sex marriage. The first is whether legally recognizing same-sex unions would strengthen or weaken the institution. The second has to do with the basic understanding of marriage itself.

The advocates of same-sex marriage say that they seek to strengthen and celebrate marriage. That may be what some intend. But I am certain that it will not be the reality. Consider: the legal union of same-sex couples would shatter the conventional definition of marriage, change the rules which govern behavior, endorse practices which are completely antithetical to the tenets of all of the world's major religions, send conflicting signals about marriage and sexuality, particularly to the young, and obscure marriage's enormously consequential function—procreation and child rearing.

Broadening the definition of marriage to include same-sex unions would stretch it almost beyond recognition—and new attempts to expand the definition still further would surely follow. On what principled ground can Andrew Sullivan exclude others who most desperately want what he wants, legal recognition and social acceptance? Why on earth would Sullivan exclude from marriage a bisexual who wants to marry two other people? After all, exclusion would be a denial of that person's sexuality. The same holds true of a father and daughter who want to marry. Or two sisters. Or men who want (consensual) polygamous arrangements. Sullivan may think some of these arrangements are unwise. But having employed sexual relativism in his own defense, he has effectively lost the capacity to draw any lines and make moral distinctions.

Forsaking all others is an essential component of marriage. Obviously it is not always honored in practice. But it is the ideal to which we rightly aspire, and in most marriages the ideal is in fact the norm. Many advocates of same-sex marriage simply do not share this ideal; promiscuity among homosexual males is well known. Sullivan himself has written that gay male relationships are served by the "openness of the contract" and that homosexuals should resist allowing their "varied and complicated lives" to be flattened into a "single, moralistic model." But that "single, moralistic model" has served society exceedingly well. The burden of proof ought to be on those who propose untested arrangements for our most important institution. . . .

The Role of Nature

HADLEY ARKES

*From the hearing of the House Judiciary Committee,
May 15, 1996*

*Here Amherst political science professor Hadley Arkes makes
the same point as Bennett, but he defends it more philosophi-
cally. His point is that marriage is rooted in nature, not convention, and that nature requires the union to be procreative
in possibility. Lose that principle, and everything else is lost
with it.*

The categories of the Constitution must be filled in with a substance of what we are talking about, and it becomes impossible to speak about marriage and sexuality in these cases without
using the "N" word, nature. We understand that this is not about
love. There are abiding relations of love between brothers and
sisters, parents and children, and in the nature of things those
loves cannot be diminished as loves because they are not attended
by penetration or because they are not expressed in marriage.

Marriage has something to do preeminently with the estab-
lishment of a framework of lawfulness and commitment for the
begetting and nurturance of children. This is the plainest connection between the idea of marriage and what has been called
the natural teleology of the body, the fact that we are all, as the
saying goes, engendered. We are men and women, there are
only two people, not three, only a man and woman can beget a
child. There is a coherence in this scheme that is not impaired in
the least when the couple are incapable of bearing children.

But my main point is this, if we detach marriage from that natural teleology of the body, on what ground of principle to the law consigns marriage to couples, on what ground would the law say no to people who profess that their love is not confined to a coupling, but woven together in the larger ensemble of three or four. I think our previous speakers have already indicated they are not aware of any ground of principle in which the law would say no. If that arrangement were made available to ensembles of the same sex, it would have to be made available to ensembles of mixed sexes, which is to say we would be back, in principle, to the acceptance of polygamy.

I want to make clear that I am not offering a prediction. I am not saying that if we accept gay marriage we will be engulfed by polygamy and incest and other exotic arrangements. I am raising a question of principle about the ground on which the law says no. It couldn't simply say, that is not what we do here, because that answer suffices right now.

Let me go further. Let me say, I would not impute to the people on the other side of this question, even the remotest interest in promoting polygamy or anything more exotic, but this much can be said properly about their position, that it has at the heart of their rhetorical strategy and the logic of their arguments to deny that there is any defining ground in nature for sexuality, or any defining limits in nature for sexuality, and it is their strategy to keep pushing that to the limit to keep establishing the point that all these relations are ultimately matters of convention. That we know we can count upon, that there will be activists out there testing the limits and pushing it to the next level, and we know we can count on it precisely for the reasons expressed here, that no one on the panel seems to be quite clear about the ground of principle on which the law would say no. . . .

Three's a Crowd

ANDREW SULLIVAN

From The New Republic, *June 17, 1996*

A riposte to Arkes and Bennett. Note in particular the point that if promiscuity is the issue, then lesbian marriage—on conservative grounds—should have more moral legitimacy than heterosexual marriage.

It wasn't that we hadn't prepped. Testifying on the Hill was a first for me, and those of us opposing the "Defense of Marriage Act" had been chatting for days about possible questions. But we hadn't quite expected this one. If a person had an "insatiable desire" to marry more than one wife, Congressman Bob Inglis of South Carolina wanted to know, what argument did gay activists have to deny him a legal, polygamous marriage? It wasn't a stray question. Republican after Republican returned gleefully to a Democratic witness who, it turned out, was (kind of) in favor of polygamy. I hastily amended my testimony to deal with the question. Before long, we were busy debating on what terms Utah should have been allowed into the Union and whether bisexuals could have legal harems.

Riveting stuff, compared to the Subcommittee on the Constitution's usual fare. But also revealing. In succeeding days, polygamy dominated the same-sex marriage debate. Both Bill Bennett and George Will used the polygamy argument as a first line of defense against same-sex marriage. In the *Washington Post* and *Newsweek,* Bennett in particular accused the same-sex marriage brigade of engaging in a "sexual relativism" with no obvious stopping place and no "principled ground" to oppose the recognition of multiple spouses.

Well, here's an attempt at a principled ground. The polygamy argument rests, I think, on a couple of assumptions. The first is that polygamous impulses are morally and psychologically equivalent to homosexual impulses, since both are diversions from the healthy heterosexual norm, and that the government has a role to prevent such activities. But I wonder whether Bennett really agrees with this. Almost everyone seems to accept, even if they find homosexuality morally troublesome, that it occupies a deeper level of human consciousness than a polygamous impulse. Even the Catholic Church, which believes that homosexuality is an "objective disorder," concedes that it is a profound element of human identity. It speaks of "homosexual persons," for example, in a way it would never speak of "polygamous persons." And almost all of us tacitly assume this, even in the very use of the term "homosexuals." We accept also that multiple partners can be desired by gays and straights alike: that polygamy is an activity, whereas both homosexuality and heterosexuality are states.

So where is the logical connection between accepting same-sex marriage and sanctioning polygamy? Rationally, it's a completely separate question whether the government should extend the definition of marriage (same-sex or different-sex) to include more than one spouse or whether, in the existing institution between two unrelated adults, the government should continue to discriminate between its citizens. Politically speaking, the connection is even more tenuous. To the best of my knowledge, there is no polygamists' rights organization poised to exploit same-sex marriage to return the republic to polygamous abandon. Indeed, few in the same-sex marriage camp have anything but disdain for such an idea. And, as a matter of social policy, same-sex marriage is, of course, the opposite of Bennett's relativism. Far from opening up the possibilities of multiple partners for homosexuals, it actually closes them down.

Bennett might argue, I suppose, that any change in marriage opens up the possibility of any conceivable change in marriage. But this is not an argument, it's a panic. If we're worried about polygamy, why not the threat of legally sanctioned necrophilia? Or bestiality? The same panic occurred when interracial marriage became constitutional—a mere thirty years ago—and when women no longer had to be the legal property of their husbands. The truth is, marriage has changed many, many times over the centuries. Each change should be judged on its own terms, not as part of some seamless process of alleged disintegration.

So Bennett must move to his next point, which is that homosexuals understand the institution of marriage so differently than heterosexuals do that to admit them into it would be to alter the institution entirely. To argue this, he has to say that gay men are so naturally promiscuous that they are constitutively unable to sustain the monogamous requirements of marriage and so fail to meet the requirements of membership. He has even repeatedly—and misleadingly—quoted my book, *Virtually Normal,* to buttress this point.

Bennett claims that I believe male-male marriage would and should be adulterous—and cites a couple of sentences from the epilogue to that effect. In context, however, it's clear that the sentences he cites refer to some cultural differences between gay and straight relationships, as they exist today before same-sex marriage has been made legal. He ignores the two central chapters of my book—and several articles—in which I unequivocally argue for monogamy as central to all marriage, same-sex or opposite-sex.

That some contemporary gay male relationships are "open" doesn't undermine my point; it supports it. What I do concede, however, is that, in all probability, gay male marriage is not likely to be identical to lesbian marriage, which isn't likely to be identical to heterosexual marriage. The differences between the genders, the gap between gay and straight culture, the unique life experiences that divide as well as unite heterosexuals and homosexuals, will probably create an institution not easily squeezed into a completely uniform model. And a small minority of male-male marriages may perhaps fail to uphold monogamy as successfully as many opposite-sex marriages. But what implications does that assertion have for the same-sex marriage debate as a whole?

Bennett argues that nonmonogamous homosexual marriages will fatally undermine an already enfeebled institution. He makes this argument for one basic reason: men are naturally more promiscuous, and male-male marriages will legitimize such promiscuity. But this argument has some problems. If you believe that men are naturally more promiscuous than women, then it follows that lesbian marriages will actually be more monogamous than heterosexual ones. So the alleged damage male-male marriages might do to heterosexual marriage would be countered by the good example that lesbian marriages would provide. It's a wash. And if you take the other conservative argument—that marriage exists not to reward monogamy but to encourage it—then Bennett is also in trouble. There is surely no group in society, by this logic, more in need of marriage rights than gay men. They are the group that most needs incentives for responsible behavior, monogamy, fidelity, and the like.

I'm not trying to be facetious here. The truth is, I think, marriage acts both as an incentive for virtuous behavior—and as a social blessing for the effort. In the past, we have wisely not made nit-picking assessments as to who deserves the right to marry and who does not. We have provided it to anyone prepared to embrace it and hoped for the best. . . .

When John and Jim Say "I Do"
CHARLES KRAUTHAMMER

From Time, *July 22, 1996*

The wrangle continues, with Krauthammer (again) charging Sullivan with providing no coherent, moral basis for allowing same-sex marriage and not polygamous marriage.

Gay marriage is coming. Should it?

For the time being, marriage is defined as the union (1) of two people (2) of the opposite sex. Gay-marriage advocates claim that restriction No. 2 is discriminatory, a product of mere habit or tradition or, worse, prejudice. But what about restriction No. 1? If it is blind tradition or rank prejudice to insist that those who marry be of the opposite sex, is it not blind tradition or rank prejudice to insist that those who marry be just two?

In other words, if marriage is redefined to include two men in love, on what possible principled grounds can it be denied to three men in love?

This is traditionally called the polygamy challenge, but polygamy—one man marrying more than one woman—is the wrong way to pose the question. Polygamy, with its rank inequality and female subservience, is too easy a target. It invites exploitation of and degrading competition among wives, with often baleful social and familial consequences. (For those in doubt on this question, see Genesis: 26–35 on Joseph and his multimothered brothers.)

The question is better posed by imagining three people of the same sex in love with one another and wanting their love to be legally recognized and socially sanctioned by marriage.

Why not? Andrew Sullivan, author of *Virtually Normal: An Argument About Homosexuality,* offers this riposte to what he calls the polygamy diversion (*New Republic,* June 7): homosexuality is a "state," while polygamy is merely "an activity." Homosexuality is "morally and psychologically" superior to polygamy. Thus it deserves the state sanction of marriage, whereas polygamy does not.

But this distinction between state and activity makes no sense for same-sex love (even if you accept it for opposite-sex love). If John and Jim love each other, why is this an expression of some kind of existential state, while if John and Jim and Jack all love each other, this is a mere activity?

And why is the impulse to join with two people "morally and psychologically inferior" to the impulse to join with one? Because, insists Sullivan, homosexuality "occupies a deeper level of human consciousness than a polygamous impulse." Interesting: this is exactly the kind of moral hierarchy among sexual practices that homosexual advocates decry as arbitrary and prejudiced.

Finding, based on little more than "almost everyone seems to accept," the moral and psychological inferiority of polygamy, Sullivan would deny the validity of polygamist marriage. Well, it happens that most Americans, finding homosexuality morally and psychologically inferior to heterosexuality, would correspondingly deny the validity of homosexual marriage. Yet when they do, the gay-marriage advocates charge bigotry and discrimination.

Or consider another restriction built into the traditional definition of marriage: that the married couple be unrelated to each other. The Kings and Queens of Europe defied this taboo, merrily marrying their cousins, with tragic genetic consequences for their offspring. For gay marriage there are no such genetic consequences. The child of a gay couple would either be adopted or the biological product of only one parent. Therefore the fundamental basis for the incest taboo disappears in gay marriage.

Do gay-marriage advocates propose to permit the marriage of, say, two brothers, or of a mother and her (adult) daughter? If not, by what reason of logic or morality?

The problem here is not the slippery slope. It is not that if society allows gay marriage, society will then allow polygamy or incest. It won't. The people won't allow polygamy or incest. Even the gay-marriage advocates won't allow it.

The point is why they won't allow it. They won't allow it because they think polygamy and incest wrong or unnatural or perhaps harmful. At bottom, because they find these practices psychologically or morally abhorrent, certainly undeserving of society's blessing.

Well, that is how most Americans feel about homosexual marriage, which constitutes the ultimate societal declaration of the moral equality of homosexuality and heterosexuality. They don't feel that way, and they don't want society to say so. They don't want their schools, for example, to teach their daughters that society is entirely indifferent whether they marry a woman or a man. Given the choice between what Sullivan calls the virtually normal (homosexuality) and the normal, they choose for themselves, and hope for their children, the normal.

They do so because of various considerations: tradition, utility, religion, moral preference. Not good enough reasons, say the gay activists. No? Then show me yours for opposing polygamy and incest.

Marrying Somebody
JONATHAN RAUCH

Unpublished

In an essay submitted to Time *but rejected for publication, Rauch argues that marriage is inherently about uniting with one other person, and, given that definition, same-sex marriage does not represent a slippery slope at all.*

I'm not surprised—who could be?—by the furor over homosexual marriage, which Hawaii's courts may (or may not) legalize. . . .

What does surprise me is the line that opponents are taking. When the fuss about gay marriage began, I assumed the main case against it would revolve around adoption rights. In fact, the main objection has turned out to be, essentially, this: If homosexuals can get married because they love each other, why not polygamy? Why not incest? A man may love several women, after all, or his mother.

People who use this line of attack seem to regard it as a trump card, a devastating objection. In *Time* magazine, Charles Krauthammer declared that marriage is two-sex for the same reasons—tradition, religion, utility, morality—that it is two-person. "Not good enough reasons, say the gay activists," he gloated. "No? Then show me yours for opposing polygamy and incest." Ha!

All right, I'll show him, and it isn't difficult.

The hidden assumption of the argument which brackets gay marriage with polygamous or incestuous marriage is that homosexuals want the right to marry anybody they fall for. But, of course, heterosexuals are currently denied that right. They cannot marry their immediate family or all their sex partners. What homosexuals are asking for is the right to marry, not anybody they love, but *somebody* they love, which is not at all the same thing.

Heterosexuals can now marry any of millions of people; even if they can't marry their parents or siblings, they have plenty of choice. Homosexuals want the same freedom, subject to the same restrictions. Currently, however, they have zero marital choice (unless, of course, they try to fool heterosexuals into marrying them—a bad idea for a lot of reasons). To ask for a comparably, but not infinitely, broad choice of partners is not unreasonable.

Do homosexuals actually exist? I think so, and today even the Vatican accepts that some people are constitutively attracted only to members of the same sex. By contrast, no serious person claims there are people constitutively attracted only to relatives, or only to groups rather than individuals. Anyone who can love two women can also love one of them. People who insist on marrying their mother or several lovers want an additional (and weird) marital option. Homosexuals currently have no marital option at all. A demand for polygamous or incestuous marriage is thus frivolous in a way that the demand for gay marriage is not.

Suppose, though, that someone insists that he can't be happy without several husbands, and that this is a basic constitutive need for him. Or suppose he says he can't be happy unless he marries a close relative. For argument's sake, let's say we believe him. Shouldn't at least this person be allowed to marry two wives, or his father?

No. The reason is that, from society's point of view, the main purpose of marriage is not, and never has been, to sanctify love. If the point of marriage were to let everybody seek his ultimate amorous fulfillment, then adultery would be a standard part of the marital package. In fact, society doesn't much care whether spouses love each other, as long as they meet their marital obligations. The purpose of secular marriage, rather, is to bond as many people as possible into committed, stable relationships. Such little societies-within-society not only provide the best environment for raising children, they also domesticate men and ensure that most people have someone whose "job" is to look after them.

Polygamy radically undermines this goal, because if one man has two wives, it follows that some other man has no wife. As Robert Wright notes in his book *The Moral Animal,* the result is that many low-status males end up unable to wed and dangerously restless. Over time, a society can sanction polygamy only if it is prepared to use harsh measures to repress a menacing underclass of spouseless men. In that respect, the one-partner-each rule stands at the very core of a liberal society, by making marriage a goal that everyone can aspire to. Gay marriage, note, is fully in keeping with liberalism's inclusive aspirations. Polygamy absolutely is not.

Incest, of course, may produce impaired children. But incestuous marriage is a horrible idea for a much bigger reason than that, a reason that holds even for sterile (or homosexual) couples. Imagine a society where parents and children viewed each other as potential mates. Just for a start, every child would grow up wondering whether his parents had sexual designs on him, or were "grooming" him as a future spouse. Holding open the prospect of incestuous marriage would devastate family life by, effectively, legitimizing sexual predation within it.

Faced with such arguments, the Krauthammer school retreats to a last stand. OK, they say, "you still can't give any principled reason why adult *homosexuals* shouldn't be allowed to form legal unions of three or more. Once gay marriage is legal, how are you going to prevent that?" But no homosexuals that I know of want the right to marry two or more same-sex partners, and society has no earthly reason to sanction such a frivolous right anyway. This is like arguing, "Once gay marriage is legal, how can you stop people from marrying their dog?" To such an argument, the appropriate response is Don't be ridiculous.

The rather peculiar idea underlying the "If gay marriage, then polygamy" argument is that, at bottom, there really is no very good reason to be against polygamy—you just have to be blindly against it, and ditto for gay marriage. But there are ample grounds to oppose polygamous and incestuous marriage, grounds that have nothing to do with whether gay people will be allowed to partake of society's most stabilizing, civilizing institution. I don't ask to break the rules that we all depend on. I just want to be allowed to follow them.

Sexual Freedom and the End of Romance

DENNIS ALTMAN

From The Homosexualization of America,
1982

A pre-AIDS defense of the religious right's nightmare: a cul-
ture in which monogamy is not expected in relationships.
Note, however, that this describes gay male culture before
same-sex marriage became an imaginable option.

While the idea that all lesbians seek totally monogamous relationships while all gay men reject monogamy is clearly a
myth, it does seem clear that among gay men a long-lasting
monogamous relationship is almost unknown. Indeed both gay
women and gay men tend to be involved in what might be called
multiple relationships, though of somewhat different kinds. For
many lesbians, especially those affected by feminist precepts,
the very exaggeration of this paragraph by Charlotte Waters
sums it up:

> Once upon a time Deardra loved Carol. Deardra also loved
> Margo, Toni and Kathy, but was just coming out of a primary
> relationship with Jan and so didn't want to get into anything
> heavy with anyone. Carol loved Deardra and also Margo and
> sometimes Renalda, but she didn't give a hang about Toni and
> she hated Kathy's guts. Actually, Carol loved Deardra best,
> but Deardra wasn't into loving anyone best and claimed she
> was equally noncommitted to them all.

For gay men a parallel case is described by Edmund White:

> The gay male couple inhabiting the seventies is composed of
> two men who love each other, share the same friends and in-
> terests and fuck each other almost inadvertently once every
> six months during a particularly stoned, impromptu three-
> way. The rest of the time they get laid with strangers in a con-
> text that bears the stylistic marks and some of the reality of
> s-and-m.

Both these descriptions are caricatures, but they do catch
one of the features common to a great many gay relationships,
namely a degree of fluidity that allows for considerable variety
and autonomy. What often appears to straight critics as an obses-
sion with sex is more accurately a preoccupation with construct-
ing relationships that can meet our needs for both security and
independence, commitment and variety.

A great deal of the gay writing of the past decade has been
concerned, both explicitly and implicitly, with the construction
of new relationships: just to cite Kate Millett's *Sita,* Michael
Denneny's *Lovers,* Marie-Claire Blais's *Nights in the Under-
ground* (subtitled *An Exploration of Love*), plays like Robert
Patrick's *T-shirts* and Jane Chambers's *Last Summer at Bluefish
Cove* makes the point. Again there is a difference between
female and male writing; much lesbian writing has been concerned with the development of nonpossessive multiple relationships (which underlies Sally Gearhart's fantasies in *The
Wanderground* or Monique Wittig's *Les Guérillères*), while gay
men seem caught between the two myths of finding everlasting
true love and happiness in the same person and constant excite-
ment through sexual adventures. These myths are not as incom-
patible as one might think; much of the tension present in

contemporary male gay writing stems from the attempt to reconcile the traditional image of romantic love and the reality of present-day sexuality, with its demands for constant variety and performance.

The most explicit discussion of the problem is *Faggots,* a Rabelaisian account of contemporary New York fag life that disguises a serious discussion of sexual ethics. Larry Kramer is, in fact, a traditional romantic who believes in monogamous coupling and is upset by its disappearance in the world of fast sex, drugs, and Fire Island—"Our sexual fantasies are ruining us," says one character, speaking (it would seem) for Kramer himself—but his novel poses, nonetheless, very real questions. It is, I suspect, a quite unrealistic novel in its desires, but not necessarily a homophobic one; Kramer just wants the sort of relationship that is less and less possible even outside the rarefied world of Fire Island.

Kramer is, however, fairly exceptional; in practice most gay males accept that fidelity to a relationship is not to be measured in sexual terms. A large-scale study of gay male couples in San Diego concluded that every couple together more than five years had outside sexual contacts as a recognized part of the relationship. As David McWhirter and Andrew Mattison put it: "We never heard the word 'cheating' or 'faithful' applied to outside sex, even though outside relationships caused pain. And many couples reported that sex outside the relationship enhanced or reinvigorated the sexual contact when they were back with their partner.

Just because there *are* no real social sanctions to support gay couples (indeed, it is often easier to remain closeted if one is not in a relationship) and no clear role definitions as to who should do what, it is easier for gay couples to experiment with unusual arrangements, and to maintain relationships that allow more flexibility and freedom than the norm. The absence of gay marriage (except among a very small group who have used gay churches for such purposes) means that it is easier for homosexuals to develop other ways of living than conventional coupledom; there has been considerable discussion, in the new gay writings, of the advantages and disadvantages of a whole range of possible living and sexual arrangements.

In their study of homosexuals in San Francisco Bell and Weinberg did find a number of men in "closed couple" relationships and concluded they were happier than those in "open couple" ones. However, an examination of their definitions reveals that the difference is not a simple one of monogamy versus promiscuity; having defined "closed couples" as those in which the partners "tend to look to each other rather than to outsiders for sexual and interpersonal satisfactions," it is not very difficult to "prove" that people in such relationships are more satisfied with them. For all its protestations of tolerance and understanding, Bell and Weinberg's book is heavily influenced by conventional assumptions about relationships and happiness.

It is my hunch that the illusion of love is more important for homosexual couples than for heterosexual ones, because without it there is much less reason to persist with the relationship, and this becomes truer as the overt gay world grows and there is less fear of never meeting anyone else. At the same time, while homosexuals may well have more illusions than do straights about love, they also have fewer illusions about permanence (I still remember my shock when one of my lovers said to me, early in our affair, "When we finish . . . ," and I recognized the chance of his being right). In a study of lesbian couples Donna Tanner noted that, despite the fact that the majority of women had been involved in at least one previous "paramarriage," several respondents considered their relationship a long-term commitment: they exchanged rings and provided for their partners in case of death through insurance policies and wills. On the other hand, while most of these relationships were monogamous, there was also an acceptance of the possible end of the relationship that differed from the marriage model. "I guess," said one woman, "we are of the mind that we should make it go as long as it goes, and when it stops going we should be reasonable enough to say that it is over and move on."

Both lack of marriage and exclusion from the heterosexual world of conventional families tend to make friendship all the more important for homosexuals; while sociologists in recent years have shown some interest in gay coupling, they have tended to completely miss the significance of friendship among both gay women and gay men. Over the years numbers of people have said to me that they place more importance on their friends than on their lovers, and what many gay lives miss in terms of permanent relationships is more than compensated for by friendship networks, which often become de facto families. (Emily Sisley has described one such network in her story, "The Novel Writers.") Former lovers often are drawn into such networks, so that many gays are surrounded by a rich network of friends (often originally sexual partners) and past and present lovers, which can be far more supportive than are most nuclear families.

I don't want to appear to deny the negative side of gay relationships; it does seem, at least among male homosexuals, that there is often a real fear of commitment and a quite unrealistic level of expectations that dooms many men to never finding a satisfactory relationship. While it is tempting to claim that this reveals something about inherent differences either between gays and straights or between women and men, I suspect it is largely a reflection of social pressures; the low level of self-esteem among many homosexuals hardly helps in establishing the mutual trust and tolerance on which relationships must be based. Nonetheless there is much in the gay experience of relationships that is of more general relevance. It is not just that gay relationships are a threat to the dominant family structures that conservatives are desperately trying to bolster up. (This theme is found in much gay writing; John Reehy sees acceptance of homosexuality as leading to a questioning of "not heterosexuality itself, no, but the stagnant conformity of much of his tribal society.") The attempts of homosexuals to create new forms of relationships can also be seen as part of a more general search to resolve universal problems. Under present conditions no one can be very sure of having solved the problem of how best to order one's personal life.

CHAPTER NINE

Whose Life Is It Anyway?
THE REAL WORLD OF LOVE AND MARRIGE

In the political, moral, and social debate about same-sex marriage, it's all too easy to forget the human dimension. This is not, after all, a debate about whether, for the first time ever, lesbians and gay men are to have long-term relationships. They already do. Same-sex marriage exists in life; it simply doesn't exist in law. What this chapter hopes to do is show a variety of interpretations of that experience—from Dudley Clendinen's account of his fast-changing neighborhood in Baltimore to Ann Landers's all-too-recognizable inability to approve of the sanctifying of the relationship, even if she is tolerant of its existence. An account of an interracial lesbian marriage ceremony is followed by Doug Ireland's sketch of a French lover whom he lost to AIDS and a discriminatory immigration system. Kathy Duggan expresses a surprising need for the emotional and financial closure of divorce. Henry Alford recounts a hilarious tale of setting up an actual wedding between two men in New York

City. Joseph Landau describes how important the institution of marriage may be for the full integration of gay and straight life and the role it might play in blunting the often reductive power of identity culture.

Jack and Bob, Going to the Chapel
DUDLEY CLENDINEN

From The New York Times, *August 7, 1996*

Dudley Clendinen chronicles the changing face of a Baltimore neighborhood.

When I was a boy, the men in my neighborhood had names like Charlie, Wilbur, Jimmy, Homer, T. Paine, Frank, Marvin, Gus, and Sam. They had served in World War II and come back to Tampa, Florida, to settle down. In the morning, they went off to jobs in sales, journalism, banking, law, accounting, dentistry and politics. At night, they came home to women named Mildred, Mary, Bobbie, Nell, Jean, Patti, Cile, Georgie, and Martha. They were married to them. They had to be. It was the South.

The couples lived in single houses. They had children by birth or adoption. The children had dogs. The adults had cocktails. And most of them went to church or temple, belonged to the same clubs, read the same newspapers and magazines, visited back and forth, voted in every election and did not divorce or speak of homosexuals in polite conversation. It was the 1950s.

In the 1990s, some of the offspring of those marriages lead different lives. I live in Baltimore, in the neighborhood of Bolton Hill, not far from where Francis Scott Key wrote the national anthem, where Gertrude Stein, as a medical student, carried on her first affair and where F. Scott Fitzgerald finished *Tender Is the Night*.

Bolton Hill is now a more urban, more eclectic neighborhood. The couples live in brick row houses, two by two. We have fewer children and fewer cocktails.

But we work, we worship, we visit back and forth, we fly the flag and pay our taxes. Most of us vote. Some of us have dogs, and many of us belong to the neighborhood swim and tennis club. There are three categories of club membership: single, family and household—meaning any two adults who live together. It's convenient for couples who aren't legally married—some because they choose not to marry and some because the law won't let them.

The men have names like Ted, Dudley, Jack, Hoult, John, Bob, Mike, David, and Dion. They work at jobs in government, banking, teaching, architecture, medicine and journalism. So do the women. Ted comes home at night to Mary Jo, and Hoult to Nancie, and Bob to Doris, and Dion to Jean.

But Dudley comes home to Stephen, Jack to Bob, John to Peter, Mike to Dean, and David to Joe. There are also Pat and Mary, a doctor and carpenter, in church on Sunday.

The culture is changing. In the house where Fitzgerald sat in a second-floor study, locked in marriage to his mad wife, Zelda, writing the doomed love story of Nicole and Dick, Jimmy now lives in sanity with Will. A block away, in a house where a nonfiction Dick had lived with his wife, Robin, Michael now has a life with Andy. They had a wedding. And Dick got a divorce and now lives with Scott.

It is not as if this were something new. Almost a century ago, Gertrude Stein left 215 East Diddle Street for Paris, where she met, wooed, and secretly wed Alice B. Toklas.

Gertrude and Alice had only each other's blessing. Michael and Andy, when they married on a snowy hill in Ohio, had the blessing of a friendly Roman Catholic priest. David and Bruce were joined by a captain on the deck of a sailing boat in the Aegean Sea.

None of them, of course, had the official blessing of Church or State. Four years ago, on the Fourth of July, two women and their wedding party gathered at the altar of the Memorial Episcopal Church. The slate roof and squat stone tower loom just a block beyond the windows of Scott Fitzgerald's writing room. The women were in gowns, the men in black tie.

The Rev. Bill Rich, assistant rector at Memorial, officiated at the ceremony. Vows were exchanged, the organ thundered and in a hotel downtown that night the couple, their families and friends danced, drank from an open bar, and watched as a parasol of fireworks rose from the harbor and lit the sky in celebration.

It was a short euphoria. The priest could not by Episcopal liturgy or Maryland law pronounce them married. Although the rector of the parish had approved and the vestry and bishop were aware, the event stirred a furor among conservative Episcopalians, who tried to strip the bishop of his office and Bill Rich of his priestly robes.

For almost two hours Bill Rich stood alone at an inquisition, facing a small grim sea of one hundred questioning, accusing fellow priests. The crisis passed, but the bishop ordered a moratorium on blessing the unions of homosexuals.

In truth, the moratorium has not held. Love will out, and quietly, in private settings across the diocese of Maryland, as across the nation, blessings have taken place.

For twenty-six years, beginning with two men in Minneapolis named Jack Baker and Mike McConnell, there has been a public campaign for marriage as a basic right. And more and more not just in marriage but in birth and death as well, churches here and there have been responsive.

Tenderly, with ancient ritual and holy water, the baby of a lesbian couple, faithful Catholics, was baptized here on Bolton Hill, in the white marble sanctuary of Corpus Christi Church. With dignity last year, the Jesuits at St. Ignatius Roman Catholic Church memorialized the life of Don Daniels, with a plain speech by his lover and open emblems of his life as a gay man.

Proudly, in its June bulletin, the Baltimore Hebrew Congregation announced the election of a new assistant rabbi, Peter Kessler, welcoming him—and his male partner, a mechanical engineer—to town.

And regularly, beneath the slender, towering brown stone spire of First and Franklin Street Presbyterian Church, male and lesbian couples are joined in holy union by the Rev. Harry Holfelder. It happens ten or twenty times a year. Mark and Brad had a formal ceremony there before Christmas, with 140 guests, three quarters of them heterosexual.

Why do these couples do it?

Why does anyone? Quietly, for two years, a small committee of laymen and women, priests and doctors, gay and nongay, have been working on Project Blessing. The committee grew from Memorial Church, from the loving spirit of its rector, the Rev. Barney Farnham, and the inspiration of John Payne, a member of Memorial, a doctor at Johns Hopkins, and a trustee of the Episcopal Divinity School in Cambridge, Mass.

Sanctioned by the trustees of the Divinity School, approved by the bishops of ten Episcopal dioceses and more than thirty parishes from California through Indiana to New Jersey, the project would authorize the blessings of gay and lesbian unions in a limited number of churches. But those couples—and all heterosexual couples who ask to be married in those same churches—would have to agree to answer a battery of questions over a period of five years. From all those questions and answers, we may learn something about why it is important to some people, gay or straight, to stand up and have their love and commitment blessed in public, in a holy setting. Judging from the cloud of noise that has blown up around the political issue of same-sex marriage, it is a need that politicians—most of them married, some of them running for president—find incomprehensible. Perhaps they should ask their wives.

"Darling, why do you think it matters to be married?"

And, "Darling, tell me what politician would you trust to judge our love?"

I Earned This Divorce

KATHY DUGGAN

From The New York Times, *July 25, 1996*

There is also the flip side to the right to marry: lesbian and gay relationships need the clarity of legal divorce.

The woman who once stood with me before an altar, promising to share her life with me, is now holding my computer hostage until I give her the VCR. Though the Defense of Marriage Act, passed last week by the House, bars federal recognition of gay marriages, I find myself wishing our marriage was legal for a reason I never anticipated. I want a divorce.

I don't just mean I want to end my marriage. I did that two years ago. I'm single now, having learned how to cook for one and attend weddings alone.

What I want is a forum where I can act out all the anger, frustration, and disappointment of a failed relationship. One where I can hand responsibility for the haggling over our possessions to a professional—a lawyer who can be ruthless on my behalf when I'm likely to just dissolve into tears and say, "No, really, you take the flatware." I want a ritual that takes apart our relationship as deliberately as we put it together.

Mary and I were the perfect couple. Unfortunately, together we made lousy individuals. From the start, people often got us confused. We chalked it up to being the same height and having similar coloring, but the truth is our identities were slowly merging into one.

Oblivious to the consequences of our fused identities, in September 1991 we gathered family and friends at a ceremony in my girlhood church, had a backyard reception and then left for a honeymoon in Provincetown, Massachusetts.

Though we knew we were just as married as any husband and wife, we chose not to use the language of heterosexual marriages. We believed that to use such words as "wedding," "marriage" and "wife" would trivialize that there was no legal or religious recognition.

So we decided on life partner and labeled the relationship a domestic partnership. (I'm still stunned by how many people thought we had opened a small business together.) We struggled over a suitable alternative to the word "wedding." For lack of anything better, we finally just called our ritual exchange of vows "the ceremony."

Taking sacred vows did not help our individuality problems. After two and a half years, I left Mary and found myself in a semantic void. I could call her my ex-lover, but I rarely called her my lover when we were together—the illicit undertones the word carries were the last thing I wanted. "Former life partner" sounds like something Shirley MacLaine would say.

When a relationship that was only marginally recognized comes to an end, it is almost as though it never existed. When filling out forms, I can no more check the box labeled "divorced" than I could have once checked "married." Invisible as we may have been as a couple, Mary and I at least had each other to affirm our relationship.

Some gay men and lesbians have come up with ceremonies of dissolution to mark the radical changes in their lives, but I couldn't imagine planning such an event. For heterosexual couples, the legal process of filing for divorce can serve that function. Oh, sure, Mary and I attended to a few legal matters. But telling coworkers, "Well, we shredded the health-care proxies last night," just doesn't carry the same weight as saying, "Well, I signed the divorce papers last night."

I sometimes jokingly refer to Mary as my first wife. I hope to marry again, and I hope that by the time I do, my partner and I will be able to do it legally. Right now though, I want a divorce.

Ann Can't Give Her Blessing to This Marriage

ANN LANDERS

From the Chicago Tribune, *July 21, 1996*

The pro-gay advice columnist draws the line.

Dear Ann Landers:

Last year, I married the woman of my dreams. She is funny, intelligent, loving, caring, exciting and gentle. Ours is a full and rewarding life together. We have traveled to several states for both business and pleasure. We go to church, get together with friends and relatives, and share the household chores. We have known both good times and bad, and our commitment to one another is stronger now than ever.

So why am I writing to you? Because I hope you will help educate a few million people today. Our marriage, blessed by a minister and approved by many friends and family members, is not legal in the United States. And if Congress has anything to say about it, we may never have a chance to make it legal. You see, Ann, I am also a woman.

My wife and I are hardworking professionals who pay our taxes and vote regularly. We pay our bills on time and are law-abiding citizens. However, we are not accorded all the civil rights that most Americans assume to be their privilege. Because we are not legally married, we have none of the legal rights married couples enjoy, such as gaining immediate access to a loved one in case of an emergency, sharing insurance policies at reduced rates, holding property together, filing joint tax returns, and so on.

We are not seeking "special rights." We simply want the same rights every other American couple has: the right to be free from discrimination in housing and employment, the right to legal protection from harassment and, most importantly, the right to marry whomever we choose and to enjoy the benefits of marriage.

A supportive word from you would give us broader acceptance and might possibly help us with a few legislators. How about it, Ann?

—A Loving Wife

Dear Loving Wife:

I believe same-sex couples should be entitled to the legal rights that married couples enjoy, including the ones you stated: gaining immediate access to a loved one in case of an emergency, sharing insurance policies at reduced rates, owning property together, and filing joint income tax returns. I also believe that same-sex couples should be free from discrimination in housing and employment and should have the right to legal protection against harassment. But, my friend, that is as far as I want to go. I define marriage as a union between a man and a woman.

Before you gay-rights folks land on me with both

feet, I would like to remind you that I have been supportive of your movement for many years, have withstood a great deal of criticism in the process and have risked the wrath of some editors and publishers. I cannot support same-sex marriage, however, because it flies in the face of cultural and traditional family life as we have known it for centuries. And that's where I must draw the line. Sorry.

Love and Marriage
CATHERINE TUERK

From The Flagpole, *the newsletter of Parents, Friends, and Families of Lesbians and Gays of the Metropolitan Washington, D.C., area, October 1996*

The mother of a gay son responds to Ann Landers.

It came to me out of the recesses of my mind as I was walking in the park on a fine Saturday morning. A chant returned to my conscious memory as I watched myself in my mind's eye taking my turn at jumping rope in my Pennsylvania hometown:

> First comes love, then comes marriage.
> Here comes Cathy with a baby carriage.

Perhaps this time-worn rhyme surfaced as a result of a recent Ann Landers column. She was asked by a reader to help others realize that this sequence of desires (love→marriage→baby) is the same among all human couples whether they are homosexual or heterosexual. The reader noted that the desire for marriage naturally follows in a love relationship, and that the wish for a baby carriage is very likely to come next. Thus, the reader told Landers, our society institutionalizes this natural series of events, providing structures that reinforce and support the bonding of adult human beings, and it is only logical that loving homosexual couples would want what heterosexual couples already enjoy.

Ann Landers, however accepting she is of the gay community, noted that she is unable to support the concept of gay marriage because she views marriage as an institution reserved exclusively for people of opposite genders. I understand her position. Gay-accepting and supportive people—myself included—have had at some point a negative visceral response to the idea of same-sex marriage. It seemed to mar the "ideal" of the institution. Then I realized that this concern about leaving marriage "unsullied" has raised its ugly head many times before in our society, such as when we grappled with the idea of interracial marriage. Now we need to redefine marriage as the institutionalized recognition of love and commitment between *any* two people.

Thinking about all this, I am struck by how far we have come within and without the gay community. The older generation of gay people tended to define their feelings as an "identity"—"I am a gay person, whatever that means." That generation, the "Stonewallers," came out in an explosion of sexuality, the area of their lives that epitomized their oppression by, and symbolized their differences from, heterosexuals. Thus, if "Black is Beautiful," then "Gay Sexuality is Good." .

My son once told me that, while the previous gay generation may have been about sex, his generation is about love. His statement was supported by a forty-something gay man whom I met at a Whitman Walker volunteer dinner five years ago. He was raised in a small rural town where his father was a prominent civic leader. From an early age he had felt that something was "wrong" with him. When he reached adolescence, he somehow found the right street corner on which to stand every Saturday night. He waited there, this bewildered young man, with no resources to help him understand his feelings, until someone in a car would pick him up. It was dark and they never spoke, but something sexual always happened, after which he would be dropped off at the same corner. There he would see other people coming and going. Eventually he would return home to live with his fear and shame. One day in a small college town, he found his way to a gay bar. "I looked around," he said, "and saw the faces of gay men. I realized that I found some of them attractive and some unattractive. When I spoke to them I found that I liked some of them and some of them I didn't. That was the first time I realized that I could feel love; up until that moment, I thought that men like me could have sex, but that love could only happen between a man and a woman."

I've told that story many times. It is a poignant reminder of our profound ignorance about the normal personhood of gay people, a state of affairs that still exists today in our society. Several years ago, when I told my neighbor that my son and his boyfriend had split up, she said, "What do you mean 'boyfriend'? Don't you mean the man he has sex with?" I was stunned. This is a well-educated woman who has always been very accepting of our son, but she truly, like most heterosexuals, did not understand.

Some parts of our society—because of gays in the military and other issues—are beginning to realize that gay people feel love for each other just as heterosexual people do. Thanks to Ann Landers and other like-minded public figures, as society gets healthier and less homophobic, our gay children can develop healthy self-esteem and move into relationships that mirror the commitment of heterosexual couples. First comes love, then comes marriage—having one's relationship recognized by society *is* the next logical step.

Remembering Hervé
DOUG IRELAND

From The Nation, *June 24, 1996*

A memoir of a love riven for want of the right to marry.

Hervé was a native Parisian with an infectious sense of humor and a passion for serious literature—his favorite authors were Gombrowicz, Musil, and Genet—who at fifteen had fled the double homophobia of parents who were both working-class Catholic and Communist. When I went to live in France in the eighties, we were introduced by a filmmaker friend—Hervé was twenty-one then—and I was captivated by his intelligence and rebellious spirit. He had a wry attitude toward politics that befitted an addicted reader of *Le Canard Enchaîné,* a visceral compassion for the poorest and most oppressed of any color, an evergreen anger at injustice, and a contempt for bourgeois hypocrisies.

After a year of constant companionship, we decided that our

emotional commitment to each other would be lifelong, and in the ensuing decade we often talked about what it would be like to grow old together, making plans for a cottage in Brittany and, perhaps, for raising a child. Alas, these dreams were cut short when Hervé was diagnosed with H.I.V.

Hervé wanted to see the States before he died, and so I returned to New York to lay the groundwork for his joining me. Not long after, however, George Bush ordered the iniquitous ban on immigration by H.I.V.–positive people, subsequently codified into law by the signature of President Clinton. So Hervé could spend only three months at a time here on a tourist visa. He might have been able to stay illegally and escape detection, but fighting his illness required increasing medical attention.

I was fortunate enough to be working at the time for a newspaper with nondiscriminatory spousal health insurance—*The Village Voice*—but the insurance companies require that one be a legal resident to benefit from such coverage. France's socialized medicine, on the other hand, provided Hervé with first-rate care. So, while he was condemned to visits of a few months until his malady forbade travel, I was cruelly denied the right to be his caregiver. Forbidden by law the loving presence and moral support that are so crucial to fighting AIDS, Hervé lost the will to live; a few weeks from now will mark the second anniversary of his death. I was not able to be at his bedside when the end came.

A heterosexual couple in similar circumstances could have avoided this anguished separation by marrying: Hervé and I would have done so if we could, not because we felt any need to seek the blessings of the state for our relationship but simply to secure legal protection for our right to be together. Our story may be less than common, but the reason that same-sex marriage is such an urgent issue for lesbians and gays—even those of us with radical sexual politics—is that it affords a host of civil guarantees that heterosexual couples take for granted. . . .

My Gay Wedding

HENRY ALFORD

From New York *magazine, June 17, 1996*

An account of setting up a same-sex wedding in New York City. The author is accompanied on his quest by his mother.

On the road to equality, we may encounter pebbles. In my case, it went like this: I was trundling briskly toward the Waldorf Astoria, where, in my capacity as journalist and interested citizen, I was about to claim that my boyfriend and I were getting married soon and that we were interested in holding our ceremony and reception at the hotel. At my side was my sixty-six-year-old Republican mother, a willing accomplice whose presence I hoped would inject my scenario with realism. Several blocks away from the Waldorf, I shared with Mom my long-held opinion that a truly resplendent wedding would include a performance by Cirque du Soleil. Mom said she was unfamiliar with that group; I explained that it is a Franco-Canadian circus troupe that performs without animals. Mom looked slightly concerned. "With 'out' animals?" she asked.

"Without animals," I clarified.

"Oh, I thought you meant with gay animals," she said, relieved. "That sounded very interesting."

Moments later, on meeting our Waldorf contact—a clean-cut, polished corporate fellow in his early thirties named Jim—I asked him whether, when I had called and set up our appointment to inspect the hotel's wedding facilities, I had explained that the ceremony was to celebrate the union of two men. "No, you didn't," he said, somewhat haltingly. An awkward pause. I asked, "Is that okay?" He said it was. Indeed, on our ensuing tour of the hotel, this charming gentleman made every indication that it was. To dispel all doubt, however, I was moved to ask him whether he had ever booked a gay function before; he said he had not but that he had a friend who worked at the Yale Club, where a recent party had celebrated the life partnership of two women.

When we stopped in at the Starlight Roof to marvel over its Art Deco splendor, Mom took one look at the room's twenty-four-foot ceilings and announced, "This would be good for your circus performers." As the words *circus performers* had not yet come up in the conversation with our man from the Waldorf, it was with a certain amount of curiosity and suspicion that he looked to me for an explanation; I sheepishly told him that I planned to have Cirque du Soleil perform during the reception's dinner. The man tried to process this information aloud: "So you're marrying your boyfriend. And then the circus is coming to town." I nodded in a way that I hoped was reassuring; I was suddenly glad that earlier that day Mom had appraised my outfit as "very Potential Big Rentals." The man continued, "Next you're going to tell me that there'll be contortionists."

"No—no contortionists," I wanted to say, "but possibly a kick line of slightly nelly elephants and tigers."

No, my boyfriend and I are not, in fact, about to wed. I am not actually going to broker the Waldorf's introduction to the Danskin crotch panel. But given the likelihood that within the next year or so, lesbian and gay couples in Hawaii will be marrying legally—a prerogative currently denied in all fifty states—I have started my advance work. . . .

Clearly, I am ready for gay marriage. But is the world? Eager to find out, I set out on a series of quests. The first was a search for a site in which I would feel comfortable holding a supposed commitment ceremony honoring my boyfriend and me.

Mom and I headed to the delegates' dining room at the United Nations, shown to us by two personable young women employed by Restaurant Associates, a company that books and plans events at various Manhattan locations. I told these women—as I would tell all of our contacts at sites—that I wanted to have my wedding on a weekend a few months hence; at all locations, our event would be the only one scheduled.

As Mom and I took in the room's handsome East River views, the women reacted enthusiastically to the details of my proposed nuptials. I mentioned plate-spinning; they did not flinch. When our conversation turned to the topic of wedding videotaping, I said that that irritating practice would not be necessary: "One of our guests is a performance artist, sort of a gay Anna Deavere Smith, and he's going to re-enact the wedding Off Broadway." One of the women responded, "He's going to re— he's going to re-enact the wedding Off Broadway?! *Wow!*" Her colleague exclaimed, "We'll want tickets to *that!*" The first added, "That's *adorable.*"

When I asked one of the women whether it would be "okay" if my male friends danced with one another to loud disco music, she assured me it would; she said, "It's your party, and dance how you want to," adding that the U.N. security guards would tell us to turn down the music if its volume became oppressive. When her colleague subsequently took Mom and me across town to look at the lovely Sea Grill at Rockefeller Center, I asked what would happen at that location if my friends, as often occurs at clubs where there is a preponderance of gay men, took their shirts off while dancing. Our Sea Grill contact allowed as how this would not be a problem, particularly as the wedding could be thrown only on a Sunday, when there wouldn't be "many people around."

Having decided, during the course of our visits, that my boyfriend, Jess, and I should travel to our hypothetical ceremony by carriage and dress as Amish farmers, I told our contact at the Equitable Center that the theme of our wedding was "Pennsylvania Dutch–meets–Cirque du Soleil." I asked whether we could decorate either of the function rooms she showed us; she said, "You can't staple or glue anything." When I explained that my decorating plans involved the dramatic display of a large, slightly rusted nineteenth-century farming implement, she said simply, "As long as you don't touch the artwork."

Four locations seemed especially gay-friendly. Although Mom and I did not visit the town house that the National Society of Colonial Dames runs on Seventy-first Street—our party of one hundred was much too large for them, and they prefer not to host weddings—the colonial dame I spoke with said she had no problem with a gay event: "It probably doesn't include children, which is usually one of my objections." Mom and I were greeted warmly in the East Village at Lucky Cheng's, whose jaunty director of operations, Rusty, assured us that although her transvestite wait staff had never "done Amish" before, they had much experience in highly elaborate theme weddings; Mom said of the more elegant, gay-owned Townhouse restaurant on East Fifty-eighth Street, "Not the Waldorf. But a bargain."

The location I felt most comfortable in—indeed, the location I would choose were I actually getting married—was aboard the *Honey Fitz,* a ninety-two-foot-long yacht that has served five presidents, many of whose photographs adorn the yacht's cabin. Mom and I boarded near the World Financial Center; while descending the boat's staircase, Mom announced that she was pretending to be Marion Davies. I told our contact, John, that I was marrying my boyfriend; he earnestly uttered, "Beautiful." When I asked, somewhat disingenuously, whether a gay-themed event would discomfit any of the ship's crew, he said that the ship's captain had grown up on Fire Island and thus had "seen everything." My "Pennsylvania Dutch–meets–Cirque du Soleil" idea seemed as nothing when we learned that the yacht had picked up twenty drag queens in Weehawken for the premiere of the movie *Wigstock*. I was thrilled by the yacht and its pedigree; Mom was more cautious. "Stormy weather is a big possible worry," she said. "And it's hell on the circus performers."

My wedding enjoyed a less-than-enthusiastic response at only two locations. One we did not visit. On a whim, I had called the throbbing nexus of gay New York—the Chelsea Gym—and asked whether I could throw the wedding amid the weightlifting equipment; I was told, "We can't accept that proposal . . . I'm sorry, hon." The other was a place where I once attended a fun bachelor party—New York's oldest steakhouse, the Old Homestead, located on Fourteenth Street at Ninth Avenue. As we sat in the restaurant's dark foyer with our contact—a better-looking Joe Pesci—I asked him whether "the gay aspect" of the wedding made him uncomfortable. He responded, "Can I give you some advice? Don't ask that." I apologized; Mom, clutching her Metropolitan Museum of Art gift bag as if she feared that it might be ripped from her arms by a fast-moving vehicle, asked, "Does that offend you?" He said, "Well, yeah. It's just not an issue. I'd be happy to do your party." But would he be, really? Our subsequent tour of the premises was tense in the extreme; I would not have told him about my little friends in brightly colored leotards even at gunpoint. Mom, once we had departed: "I would say, 'Definitely no.' "

Who would be the officiant at my same-sex wedding? Although I am, at heart, agnostic, and thus would be most inclined to have a civil ceremony, I can imagine a scenario—particularly one in which my wedding was bankrolled by my family—wherein I might be disposed to call upon a person of the cloth. In this second quest, I turned, as I always do in moments of religious doubt, to the Yellow Pages. I called all three of the Episcopal churches listed in the NYNEX community directory for Chelsea, Greenwich Village, and Vicinity. Only St. Peter's in Chelsea was willing to perform the ceremony—I was told that the rector at St. John's on Waverly Place "does not perform unions," because "he would get in a lot of trouble with the mission"; Mother Rockman at the Church of the Ascension on Fifth Avenue said she could not because "there isn't any service outlined by the church for that." Both parties apologized profusely; both parties suggested that I contact either Dignity or Integrity, the organizations for gay and lesbian Catholics and Episcopalians.

To their credit, none of the church people with whom I broached the possibility of my friend's Off Broadway reenactment of the wedding were bothered by the idea; one interfaith minister, when asked, "Would it make you uncomfortable if my friend 'did' you?" responded, "Only if it were unflattering." I also contacted several clergypeople listed in the Manhattan phone directory not under CHURCHES but under WEDDING CHAPELS and WEDDING CLERGY. "First of all, let me say that nothing legal is going on here," the first of these, a Unitarian clergyman, cautioned me rather sternly. He then read me a proviso that he said would have to be read at the ceremony—a statement of the wedding's nonlegality. "I don't want to have some enterprising D.A. who's trying to make a name for himself hear about the wedding, show up, and then decide to prosecute," he told me. I explained that I was thinking about having the ceremony on a boat; the clergyman said he would have to raise his $300 fee "because you're taking me out of circulation." However, it became clear that he would rather not go on a cruise around Manhattan if he didn't have to; his conversation was heavily peppered with the phrase *hop off.*

"What do you mean 'a commitment ceremony'?" an interfaith minister asked me; I explained, "Between two men." I told him that the ceremony was to be on a boat off Manhattan; he said, "To be very truthful, I'm not interested in this. It's too much time for me." However, when I explained that I had budgeted $500 or $600 for the officiant, the minister's spirits rallied. He told me that he had once married a pair of transvestites on a TV talk show. "You know how I did that?" he said. "I did that by not looking at them." I asked him what the significance of his not looking at the couple was; he said he couldn't because he might have burst out laughing. "The way I see it," he told me, "it's in the genes. People have those desires because they were born that way. It's not your fault."

"It's not a fault," I said.

"It's *not* a fault. It's a characteristic of their nature because of their genes. . . . Society frowns, but I don't have to. I accept people for who they are."

"So—you're tolerant?" I tried to anticipate his point. He continues, "Yeah. And I mean, you're not going to be dancing in drag at the wedding." I replied that no, in fact, we might be, particularly as we know many "show people." He said, "That's okay. But not at the ceremony. Once you're at the reception, that's another story. But at the ceremony, it's going to be straight."

"I don't like the word *straight*."

"I'm sorry for *straight*. I meant *serious*."

For our last investigation of the prerequisites of union, I called the St. Moritz hotel and actually booked a honeymoon suite ($295) and an additional room for our best man ($125). When we arrived, it was unclear whether the thirteen minutes it took for our harried clerk to check us in was a result of the fact that I wanted the best man's room to be on the same floor as the honeymoon suite, or of the fact that our best man was our lesbian friend Adrienne. He was unable to give us rooms on the same floor; he did, however, hand me something labeled HONEYMOON DREAM PACKAGE COUPON KIT. Empowered with this booklet of three coupons, I felt like Charlie Bucket in *Charlie and the Chocolate Factory.*

The three of us assembled in the honeymoon suite—a pageant of various hues of green whose provenance Jess pinpointed as "émigré Eva Gabor." Adrienne noted, "A great big bed for having sex in!" Jess, however, remarked that the presence of a television in each of the honeymoon suite's two rooms denoted the management's lack of optimism, Jess called room service to exchange our first coupon for a bottle of champagne and petits fours. The kitchen was out of petits fours—would we take cake? Jess asked for "something savory." Potato chips were offered. We took potato chips. Later we ordered room service. I told our waiter, "We just got married!" He looked first at me, then at Adrienne; I pointed at Jess and said, "No, *we* just got married!" He smiled in a confused manner and threw himself into his duties with a somewhat manic vigor.

Later that night, unable to sleep, I went down to the lobby at 4:10 A.M. and, holding out my second coupon—the one labeled A LOVELY SOUVENIR GIFT FROM THE ST. MORITZ—told the clerk that I was in the honeymoon suite with my new husband. "I don't think the marriage is working out," I said. "My husband is—well, he's ignoring me. Nothing's happening. So I thought maybe a gift would perk me up." The clerk asked somewhat sternly, "What is it that you want, sir?" I told him. "The gift, I'd like to get the gift." He told me I would have to wait till morning. (I did, and received mugs.)

Jess and I awoke five hours later, whereupon we tangled with the epistemological question posed by the third coupon: whether to have "complete breakfast for two in bed" or "breakfast as [*sic*] Rumpelmayer's." The second choice, of course, was the more alluring; and so, imagining ourselves in the tourist-clogged restaurant of a large midtown hotel, we went downstairs, where we ate both as and at Rumpelmayer's. "We just got married," I told our Latin waiter. "Hey, it's a free country!" he said, throwing his arms up in the air in bewilderment. "You do what you want to do!"

I have seen the future, and it is tolerant. Fabulousness will prosper. While traditionalists will always claim that gay marriage is both frivolous and threatening (the former because it blesses unions society has no vested interest in, particularly given the high rate of childlessness among gay couples, and the latter because it thus makes folly of the institution of marriage itself), I would argue that this folly-making is chief among its strengths. To wit: Good-bye, blurry wedding videos shot by your out-of-town cousin with the shakes . . . hello, videography that screams "Dorothy Chandler Pavilion." Good-bye, Pachelbel's Canon and endless selections of *The Prophet* . . . hello, "It's Raining Men" and a sound collage of Thelma Ritter backchat. Good-bye, alcohol-fueled anomie and thirty-seven-year silences over the breakfast table . . . hello, kimonos and sobbing in a foreign language.

To many minds, the gay community and its supporters were not well enough prepared for the 1993 debate about gays in the military. On the issue of legalized marriage, we have more lead time. We must assemble, don berets, and demand that if gay people can't marry, then straight people can't decorate. We must, in short, even the score. Because it's our turn to be deluged with a torrent of Uncle Ben's. It's our turn not to do the catering.

Marriage as Integration

JOSEPH LANDAU

In conjunction with the initial publication of this book in 1997, Joseph Landau, the research assistant for this project, contributed the following article, which explains how the institution of marriage could be central in bringing gays and straights together.

Advocates and opponents of same-sex marriage speak two very different languages, the former employing a discussion about rights, the latter the pursuit of common goods. And in this, the debate reflects the crucial tension that has animated political theory throughout modernity. Yet the case for same-sex marriage cannot be truly made without meeting head-on the arguments of those presumed "traditionalists" who cite a long list of disasters that will be wrought by same-sex marriage. What we need, in short, is an argument for same-sex marriage that can speak in terms of goods, one of which is the social good of cultural integration.

The very fact that lesbian women and gay men want to be a part of the institution of marriage complicates many stereotypes distancing life-long commitment, monogamy, and children from the wants and desires of gay individuals. But the quest for marriage amounts to much more than a radical statement of self-definition; marriage, once broadened to include gays and lesbians, would bring a diverse population together under one common institution. It would provide outlets for living that stretch beyond the segregated world of homogeneous, same-sex communities or "ghettos" (such as the Castro district of San Francisco or Manhattan's Chelsea) and a nongay, "mainstream" or "straight" culture on the other. Today, homosexuality is often culturally severed from non-urban areas, an idea that helps anti-gay marriage advocates plausibly argue that homosexuality is inherently anti-family.

Separated from one another, both gays and straights today enjoy the comforts of a relatively homogeneous style of life. Neither group needs to confront the other directly, for the most part. Yes, places exist where gay men and lesbians coexist harmoniously with their straight counterparts. Many stories from the mainstream press have recently reported an ever-growing number of gay and lesbian parents who raise children in the traditionally straight suburbs. But since the first time that homosexuals were classified exclusively according to sexual orientation, a strict dichotomy between heterosexual and homosexual, or straight and gay, has become rooted in the language of human definition. These identities gained tremendous vigor and have now become associated with a number of defining characteristics. Stereotypes have emerged which both undergird the presumed exclusivity of those identities while all the while invigorating their dominance. A culture of literature, music, and fashion has emerged which has sharpened these supposed differences. The effect of this change has been particularly strong on the young, who often adopt new styles of hair, dress, attitude, speech, and behavior as part of their newfound identity. So from an early age, the cultural distinctions emerge, eclipsing real self-expression, exploration, and risk, stifling genuine human difference. Individuality, once churned through the mill of identity, is reduced to the lowest level of the banal.

Young gays and lesbians are particularly susceptible to the orthodoxy of the gay enclave. They may look back on their childhoods and cringe at the memory of having been ostracized. Ambivalence about the past leads to a wholesale rejection of it, and armed with a new rhetoric of gay/lesbian liberation, they can become downright hostile to what they see as straight society.

Though it may at first be healthy for gay men and lesbians to either adopt new styles of living or choose to live in urban ghettos, without which a thriving gay and lesbian culture could not flourish, it can also be personally limiting. A person is more than his sexuality, and the gay and lesbian subculture cannot sustain a person over an entire lifetime. One cannot live a complete life without being part of the broader culture at the same time.

This is why marriage is so important. It provides an identical institution in which gay and straight love can be expressed. The effects of same-sex marriages will be tremendous: since marriage is so clearly related to where and how people live, it provides a venue through which the boundary between the two communities will be lifted. It slowly allows for lesbians and gay men to move back into the "straight" sector of society with the same self-understanding and self-esteem as their heterosexual peers. There will for the first time be a common language in which to describe both sorts of lives, a language in which concealment and euphemism is no longer embedded. Young men and women coming to terms with their own feelings of homosexuality will have an understanding of the normalcy and legitimacy of homosexual relationships, bringing an end to the shame and silence that is such an unnecessary source of trauma for so many. People will, to coin a phrase, be judged less by the accident of their orientation than by the content of their character. The public debate over homosexuality, now so burdened by the lack of integration between gay and straight members of society, will be transformed by newfound interaction.

Make no mistake: deprived of marriage rights, gays and lesbians will not be able to venture back into mainstream culture. The message sent by a second-class citizenship, undone to a

degree by the private sector's active willingness to extend domestic partnership benefits, is too heavy to surmount. It contributes to the message that identity is more fundamental than
the common sentiment of love, that gay relationships are, at
heart, simply lesser than heterosexual ones, a sentiment that
shrinks, rather than enlarges, the entire human experience.

The M-Word

ANDREW SULLIVAN

From Time, *February 10, 2004*

A personal case for marriage rather than civil unions.

What's in a name?
Perhaps the best answer is a memory.

As a child, I had no idea what homosexuality was. I grew up
in a traditional home—Catholic, conservative, middle class. Life
was relatively simple: education, work, family. I was brought up
to aim high in life, even though my parents hadn't gone to college. But one thing was instilled in me. What matters is not how
far you go in life, how much money you make, how big a name
you make for yourself. What really matters is family, and the love
you have for one another. The most important day of your life
was not graduation from college or your first day at work or a
raise or even your first house. The most important day of your

life was when you got married. It was on that day that all your friends and all your family got together to celebrate the most important thing in life: your happiness, your ability to make a new home, to form a new but connected family, to find love that puts everything else into perspective.

But as I grew older, I found that this was somehow not available to me. I didn't feel the things for girls that my peers did. All the emotions and social rituals and bonding of teenage heterosexual life eluded me. I didn't know why. No one explained it. My emotional bonds to other boys were one-sided; each time I felt myself falling in love, they sensed it, pushed it away. I didn't and couldn't blame them. I got along fine with my buds in a nonemotional context; but something was awry, something not right. I came to know almost instinctively that I would never be a part of my family the way my siblings one day might be. The love I had inside me was unmentionable, anathema—even, in the words of the Church I attended every Sunday, evil. I remember writing in my teenage journal one day: "I'm a professional human being. But what do I do in my private life?"

So, like many gay men of my generation, I retreated. I never discussed my real life. I couldn't date girls and so immersed myself in schoolwork, in the debate team, school plays, anything to give me an excuse not to confront reality. When I looked toward the years ahead, I couldn't see a future. There was just a void. Was I going to be alone my whole life? Would I ever have a "most important day" in my life? It seemed impossible, a negation, an undoing. To be a full part of my family I had to somehow not be me. So like many gay teens, I withdrew, became neurotic, depressed, at times close to suicidal. I shut myself in my room with my books, night after night, while my peers developed the skills needed to form real relationships, and loves. In wounded pride, I even voiced a rejection of family and marriage. It was the only way I could explain my isolation.

It took years for me to realize that I was gay, years later to tell others, and more time yet to form any kind of stable emotional bond with another man. Because my sexuality had emerged in solitude—and without any link to the idea of an actual relationship—it was hard later to reconnect sex to love and self-esteem. It still is. But I persevered, each relationship slowly growing longer than the last, learning in my twenties and thirties what my straight friends found out in their teens. But even then, my parents and friends never asked the question they would have asked automatically if I were straight: so when are you going to get married? When is your relationship going to be public? When will we be able to celebrate it and affirm it and support it? In fact, no one—no one—has yet asked me that question.

When people talk about "gay marriage," they miss the point. This isn't about gay marriage. It's about marriage. It's about family. It's about love. It isn't about religion. It's about civil marriage licenses—available to atheists as well as believers. These family values are not options for a happy and stable life. They are necessities. Putting gay relationships in some other category—civil unions, domestic partnerships, civil partnerships, whatever—may alleviate real human needs, but, by their very euphemism, by their very separateness, they actually build a wall between gay people and their own families. They put back the barrier many of us have spent a lifetime trying to erase.

It's too late for me to undo my own past. But I want above everything else to remember a young kid out there who may even be reading this now. I want to let him know that he doesn't have to choose between himself and his family any more. I want him to know that his love has dignity, that he does indeed have a future as a full and equal part of the human race. Only marriage will do that. Only marriage can bring him home.

CHAPTER TEN

A Federal Marriage Amendment?

THE FUTURE OF THE LEGAL
AND POLITICAL BATTLE

Much of the national debate after the 1996 Defense of Marriage Act was fueled by the notion that a ruling in Hawaii in favor of same-sex marriage rights would mandate legal same-sex marriage across the country. But as Professor Larry Kramer points out in the first article of this chapter, that was never likely to be the case. In controversial marriage recognition cases, states have always been able to invoke what is known as a "public policy" exception to marriages in another state. That means that when one state's marriages offend a deeply held belief or well-grounded public policy of another state, that state need not be obliged to recognize marriages performed in the sister state. In the field of law known as "conflict of laws," it seems clear that this nonrecognition process would regularly occur in the context of the extremely explosive issue of same-sex marriage. The pattern in miscegenation laws, which held in some states and not in others for decades, bears this out, with some exceptions, as Andrew Koppelman details.

But the entire debate exploded again when, first, the Vermont Supreme Court ruled in 1999 that gays and lesbians were entitled to all of the benefits of marriage—giving way to the legislature's enactment of civil unions—and, second, the Massachusetts Supreme Judicial Court ruled in late 2003 that civil marriage was guaranteed under the state constitution and no substitutes could be allowed. Immediately, the opponents of gay civil marriage gave a new push to an amendment to the federal constitution that would prevent any state from enacting civil marriage for homosexuals and also place limits on other benefits that could be given to same-sex couples. We reprint here the wording of the amendment supported by the bulk of the religious right, the speech given by President Bush endorsing it, a piece defending its introduction on political grounds by Stanley Kurtz, and a legal analysis of the amendment's possible consequences by Jacob T. Levy. For good measure, a constitutional amendment to the state constitution of Massachusetts was also introduced to prevent civil marriages being extended to gay couples. The Harvard pastor, Peter J. Gomes, weighs in on its propriety. Finally, historian Nancy F. Cott, in testimony before the Vermont legislature, provides a historical account of the unfolding of marriage throughout modernity and into the present day.

As this book goes to print, governments at the federal, state, and municipal level are considering whether gays and lesbians should be permitted to enter—or should be prohibited altogether from entering—the institution of marriage. As these debates unfold, states will likely create a patchwork of decisions and look to the precedents of both Massachusetts' firm stance on equal marriage, as well as Vermont's "civil union" compromise.

How Other States Can Ignore Hawaii

PROFESSOR LARRY KRAMER

From "How About a Nice Hawaiian Punch?: Same-Sex Marriage, Conflict of Laws, and the Unconstitutional Public Policy Exception." Yale Law Journal, *vol. 106, no. 7 (1997)*

Here, Professor Larry Kramer—not that Larry Kramer, the playwright and AIDS activist, but the one who is one of the most authoritative conflict-of-laws experts in the country—argues that, as a matter of legal precedent, the Full Faith and Credit clause does not mandate same-sex marriage across the country. Kramer also argues, elsewhere in the paper, that the "public policy exception" to the Full Faith and Credit clause, which ensures that a state can refuse to recognize a marriage sanctioned by another state, is, however, nonsensical and, in his view, unconstitutional.

Concern that a decision to legalize same-sex marriages would result in gay couples from the mainland traveling to Hawaii to wed has led conservatives in at least 19 states to seek new state laws denying recognition to such unions. Without specific laws, states would be obliged under the United States Constitution to recognize same-sex marriages performed in another state.

—*The New York Times*, Sunday, July 28, 1996

The newspapers have been filled with stories like this in recent months, reporting how states are scrambling to avoid an obligation they will supposedly be placed under if Hawaii makes same-sex marriages legal. Horrified conservatives feverishly imagine a world where gay and lesbian couples, by marrying in Hawaii, can force their home states to recognize the union fully and for all purposes. Even some legal experts make this assumption, and Congress is actually thinking about jumping in to save states from this lamentable fate with the cynically named "Defense of Marriage Act," which seems well on the way to a promised presidential signature (talk about cynical).

On the one hand, these stories are enough to drive anyone familiar with conflict of laws crazy. As presently interpreted, the Constitution almost never requires states to enforce the marriage laws of other states (though where the Constitution does apply, states obviously cannot avoid it by enacting "specific laws" to the contrary). The brouhaha over Hawaii's anticipated legalization of same-sex marriages is therefore a big dud from a conflict of laws perspective. There simply is no problem: other states do not have to recognize such marriages, and they do not need special laws or federal legislation to make that clear. But more on this below. . . .

Before doing anything else, we need to make sure we understand the basic rules governing choice of law in marriage cases. To fully recapitulate the law in this area would actually take some time—no surprise really, since nothing in conflicts law is ever neat or tidy. There are just too many states making independent decisions and too many different variations of each problem to consider. For present purposes, however, we can work with the following paradigmatic situation: A and B live in State X, which does not recognize their right to marry; they travel to State Y, which does, and immediately after the ceremony (and a brief honeymoon) they return to State X to resume their lives together. How would State X view their marriage?

As a general matter, every state recognizes the validity of a marriage valid where it was celebrated (i.e., where the marriage contract was made). This "place of celebration" rule is not, of course, carved in stone or revealed from heaven. States do not have to adopt it, and nothing in the Constitution precludes them from following a different rule (say, for example, applying the law where the parties are domiciled when they get married). But a variety of considerations—in particular, widely shared policies that favor validating marriages consummated in good faith and enabling partners to know with certainty whether their marriage is valid—have led states to conclude that the best rule is one recognizing marriages legal where celebrated. This has long been the rule in every state of the United States, and it continues to govern pretty much without regard for whether a state adheres to the traditional jurisdiction-selecting rules or opts for one of the fancier modern approaches.

Its general convenience notwithstanding, every state recognizes situations in which it abandons the place of celebration rule. Many states, for example, will recognize a marriage that is invalid in the state where it was celebrated if it is valid where the parties are domiciled. Conversely, some states will refuse to recognize a marriage that is valid where it was celebrated if the partners went there solely to evade restrictions imposed in their domicile. Surprisingly, this entirely reasonable exception is rarely used, and its appearance often depends on how quickly a marriage is challenged and whether the challenger is one of the partners or some other interested party. Even where the rule against deliberate evasion is codified, courts have construed it narrowly and found ways to uphold most marriages.

By far the most common exception to the place of celebration rule is for marriages deemed contrary to the forum's strong public policy—and this again seems to be true regardless of how a state handles its choice-of-law problems. Of course, public policy is not violated every time the forum's law differs from that of the place of celebration—otherwise, the exception would swallow the rule. Rather, as in other contexts where "public policy" is used to avoid a conflicts rule, the exception applies (in Judge Cardozo's well-known formulation) only where another state's law violates "some fundamental principle of justice, some prevalent conception of good morals, some deep-rooted tradition of the common weal." Although invocation of the public policy exception varies somewhat from state to state, a number of common situations are found in marriage law. Typically, states turn to public policy in connection with issues like remarriage after divorce, incest, polygamy, and marriage by minors.

Two refinements should be noted in how public policy is used in marriage cases. First, the exception is not employed as an overly blunt tool, but is selectively refined in application. Rather than repudiate the place of celebration rule in every case that would be incest under forum law, courts in many states recognize that some differences are more matters of degree than of fundamental policy. A state that permits second cousins to marry may be more willing to recognize a law extending the privilege to first cousins than one permitting siblings to do so; a state that permits sixteen-year-olds to marry may apply another state's law permitting fifteen-year-olds to do so, but not one extending the right to nine-year-olds. States may also be more likely to ignore public policy considerations for couples with legitimate expectation interests: there is an obvious difference between a couple that recently married outside the state in order to evade its marriage restrictions and a couple that moved into the state after living together for twenty years in a place that recognized their union.

Second, many courts distinguish between the validity of a marriage and the ability to enjoy its "incidents." There was a time when courts treated marriage as a simple yes-or-no, up-or-down proposition: a marriage was either valid—in which case it was valid for all purposes—or it was not—in which case it was invalid for all purposes. More recently, and with increasing frequency, courts have been willing to draw finer lines, applying the place of celebration rule to the question of validity while saving the public policy exception for particular "incidents" of being married. The right to cohabit, for example, is a usual incident of being married, but not a necessary one. A man married to two wives in India might be able to move to New York without being prosecuted for bigamy, but New York might forbid the three of them from living together. At the same time, the surviving wives might both be permitted to inherit as spouses under the state's law of succession.

Two relevant generalizations can be made about choice of law in marriage cases. First, the place of celebration rule governs the vast majority of cases. Exceptions exist, but these are used with considerable reluctance, even when embodied in statutes. Second, the vast majority of the small subset of cases in which the place of celebration rule is not applied are decided on public policy grounds. Other exceptions exist, but these are seldom invoked and typically appear in conjunction with a public policy objection. (A state may, for example, allow parties to marry elsewhere solely to evade its restrictive law unless they do so in order to get the benefit of a law deemed contrary to the forum's strong public policy.) As same-sex marriages become an issue, then, we can expect reluctant states to turn to the public policy doctrine to protect their interests. . . .

With these principles in mind, we can predict the likely operation of the public policy doctrine in same-sex marriage cases. With or without explicit authorization from state legislatures, courts are relatively free to make an exception to the place of celebration rule for same-sex marriages. They are most likely to do so, moreover, in cases like my initial hypothetical, where a couple travels to Hawaii to get married with no intention of changing domiciles. If applied, the exception will almost certainly lead to a declaration that such marriages are invalid.

It is at least possible that some courts will choose not to classify same-sex marriages as falling within the public policy exception, which may explain why so many states are hurrying to codify the principle. A number of commentators have, in fact, argued valiantly that public policy can and should be narrowly construed in the context of same-sex marriages. These efforts might even succeed in persuading a few courts or legislatures, though I suspect they are as futile as they are well intended. Call me a cynic, but my guess is that same-sex marriages will continue to be, shall we say, frowned upon in most states for at least the foreseeable future. And given the discretion and flexibility inherent in the public policy doctrine, arguments that it is not always applied in similar or even "worse" situations probably will not matter much. The simple fact is that public policy is readily available for use in nullifying same-sex marriages performed in Hawaii, and it is probably naive not to expect most states to use it.

The Miscegenation Precedents

ANDREW KOPPELMAN

"Same-Sex Marriage, Choice of Law, and Public Policy," from Quinnipiac Law Review
vol. 16 (1997)

Law professor Andrew Koppelman points to a couple of fascinating legal precedents that could yet bring state-conferred same-sex marriages to the rest of the country. Those precedents have to do with race.

The closest historical analogue to the radical moral disagreement that will shortly divide the states [on same-sex marriage] is the divide between states that permitted and those that forbade marriage between whites and blacks. Miscegenation prohibitions were in force since the 1660s, but only after the Civil War did they begin to function as the central sanction in the system of white supremacy. At one time or another, forty-one American colonies and states enacted them.

The miscegenation taboo was held in the Southern states with great tenacity; it was close to the psychological core of racism. "Although such marriages were infrequent throughout most of U.S. history, an enormous amount of time and energy was nonetheless spent in trying to prevent them from taking place" (Peggy Pascoe). When they defended the prohibition, Southern courts were at least as passionate in their denunciations as modern opponents of same-sex marriage.

The purity of public morals, the moral and physical development of both races, and the highest advancement of our cherished southern civilization, under which two distinct races are
to work out and accomplish the destiny to which the Almighty
has assigned them on this continent—all require that they
should be kept distinct and separate, and that connections
and alliances so unnatural that God and nature seem to forbid
them, should be prohibited by positive law, and be subject to
no evasion. (*Kinney v. Commonwealth* (1878).)

Yet even in this charged context, the Southern states did not
make a blunderbuss of their own public policy. Their decisions
concerning the validity of interracial marriages were surprisingly
fact-dependent. They did not utterly disregard the interests of
the parties to the forbidden marriages, but weighed them
against the countervailing state interests. Where those state interests were attenuated, Southern courts sometimes upheld
marriages between blacks and whites.

Three classes of choice-of-law problems arose involving interracial marriages. The first were cases in which parties had
traveled out of their home state for the express purpose of evad-
ing that state's prohibition of their marriages, and thereafter immediately returned home. Despite some early authority to the
contrary, Southern courts always invalidated these marriages.
Second were cases in which the parties had not intended to
evade the law, but had contracted a marriage valid where they
lived, and subsequently moved to a state where interracial marriages were prohibited. These were the most difficult cases, and
the Southern courts divided on how to deal with them. Finally,
there were cases in which the parties had never lived within the
state, but in which the marriage was relevant to litigation conducted there. Typically, after the death of one spouse, the other
sought to inherit property that was located within the forum

state. In these cases, the courts invariably recognized the marriages.

The earliest case involving an attempt to evade a prohibition on interracial marriage, *Medway v. Needham,* arose in Massachusetts in 1819. A mulatto man and a white woman, both domiciled in Massachusetts, had gone to Rhode Island, where interracial marriage was legal, in order to evade their home state's prohibition on their marriage. The court upheld the marriage, emphasizing, as modern authorities do, the importance of certainty and uniformity with respect to the existence of a marriage. A contrary rule would involve "extreme inconveniences and cruelty"; the rule it adopted "must be founded on principles of policy, with a view to prevent the disastrous consequences to the issue of such marriages, as well as to avoid the public mischief, which would result from the loose state, in which people so situated would live." The court acknowledged that there would have to be limits to its holding.

> If without any restriction, then it might be that incestuous marriages might be contracted between citizens of a state where they were held unlawful and void, in countries where they were not prohibited; and the parties return to live in defiance of the religion and laws of their own country. But it is not to be inferred from a toleration of marriages which are prohibited merely on account of political expediency, that others, which would tend to outrage principles and feelings of all civilized nations, would be countenanced.

The leading American treatise on conflict of laws defended the result in *Medway,* but it was criticized by others, was never followed in any miscegenation case, and was later overruled by statute. The principal counterargument was that states had a right to govern within their own territories. As a ruling in

Virginia in 1885 put it, "In the very nature of things every sovereign state must have the power to prescribe what incapacities for contracting marriage shall be established as the law of the state among her own citizens, and it follows, therefore, that when the state has once pronounced an incapacity on the part of any of its citizens to enter into the marriage relation with each other, that such capacity attaches itself to the person of the parties, and although it may not be enforceable during the absence of the parties, it at once revives with all its prohibited power upon their return to the place of domicile."

The distinction drawn by *Medway* between moral and political prohibitions was also criticized. Raleigh Minor, law professor at the University of Virginia and author of an important 1901 treatise on the conflict of laws, agreed with the Massachusetts court (many Southern jurists did not) that the miscegenation prohibition did not rely on universal considerations of morality, but he thought that the state's political interest in maintaining the supremacy of the white race could be very strong. "[M]atters of political expediency may become of as tremendous importance as matters of moral expediency. It must be remembered that at the date of this decision (1819) there were (and still are) comparatively few negroes in Massachusetts, and the policy which dictated this statute had ceased to be of great importance." Despite the result in *Medway*, "under precisely similar circumstances it has been held by the courts of the Southern States, where negroes are numerous and marriages between them and the whites are regarded justly as most contrary to public policy and expediency, as well as utterly repugnant to the sentiment of the people, that marriages of this sort will not be sustained in the domicile and forum, though validly contracted by its citizens in another jurisdiction. . . ."

This anti-evasion principle was, however, only applied in

cases where the parties were domiciliaries of the forum at the time of marriage. In cases where they had been domiciled elsewhere at the time of the marriage, and even in one case where they had left the forum before the marriage, intending to reside elsewhere, and after marrying had decided to return to the forum, the marriage was held valid. Even Minor, whose sympathy for Southern racism has already been illustrated, thought that "if the parties remove from the State of their domicile, with the *bona fide* intent to become *domiciled* in another State, and having settled there then marry according to its laws, the marriage, though prohibited by the law of their first domicile, will be deemed valid everywhere, *even in the first domicile,* should they afterwards return thither either temporarily or permanently."

One obvious difficulty with drawing the lines in this way was that a marriage would be valid or not, depending on whether the parties, at the time of the marriage, intended to return to the domicile that prohibited their marriage. The difficulties of determining such intent led Joseph Story to endorse a blanket rule validating all such marriages. It is, he wrote,

> far better to support marriages celebrated in a foreign country as valid, when in conformity with the laws of that country, although the rule may produce some minor inconveniences, than, by introducing distinctions as to the designs and objects and motives of the parties, to shake the general confidence in such marriages, to subject the innocent issue to constant doubts as to their own legitimacy, and to leave the parents themselves to cut adrift from their solemn obligations when they may become discontented with their lot.

The more serious objection was that the Southern states would have to tolerate some interracial cohabitation within their borders after all. There are only two cases in which this result was threatened, and they reach opposing results.

State v. Bell involved a white man and a black woman who married in Mississippi, where they then resided, and later moved to Tennessee, where the husband was arrested and tried. He pleaded the Mississippi marriage as a defense. The state supreme court rejected the defense, complaining that under it

> we might have in Tennessee the father living with his daughter, the son with the mother, the brother with his sister, in lawful wedlock, because they had formed such relations in a state or country where they were not prohibited. The Turk or Mohammedan, with his numerous wives, may establish his harem at the doors of the capitol, and we are without remedy. Yet none of these are more revolting, more to be avoided, or more unnatural than the case before us.

The only other reported case in which a validly married interracial couple changed domiciles and moved to a state that prohibited their marriage is *State v. Ross*. A white citizen of North Carolina, which prohibited interracial marriage, traveled in May 1873 to South Carolina, where she married a black man who lived there. At that time, South Carolina did not prohibit interracial marriage. In August of the same year, they both moved to North Carolina, where they were tried for fornication and adultery. A divided state supreme court held that the South Carolina marriage was a valid defense to the charge.

The court rejected the state's claim that the female defendant had sought to evade the law, because it had not proven that, at the time of the marriage, she had intended to return to North Carolina.

> It is difficult to see how in going to South Carolina to marry a
> negro, without an intent to return with him to this State, she
> could evade or intend to evade the laws of this State. Our laws
> have no extra territorial operation, and do not attempt to pro-
> hibit the marriage in South Carolina of blacks and whites
> domiciled in that State.

The court conceded that interracial marriages were "revolting to
us and to all persons, who, by reason of living in States where the
two races are nearly equal in numbers, have an experience of the
consequences of matrimonial connections between them." This
sentiment was not, however, shared by all Christian nations.
"The general rule is admitted that a marriage between citizens
of a foreign State contracted in that State and valid by its laws is
valid everywhere where the parties might migrate, although not
contracted with the rites required by the law of the country into
which they come and between persons disqualified by such law
from intermarrying." Because of the strong interest in uniformity, marriages not deemed odious to all had to be given extraterritorial recognition by all. Because the civilized world was
not united in rejecting interracial marriages, North Carolina had
a duty to join the rest of civilization in enforcing the common
rule. "The law of nations is a part of the law of North Carolina.
We are under obligations of comity to our sister States."

Two judges dissented, insisting on the forum state's right to
govern itself. "If such a marriage solemnized here between our
own people is declared void, why should comity require the evil
to be imported from another State? Why is not the relation severed the instant they set foot upon our soil?" If this consequence
is inconvenient to some, "individuals who have formed relations
which are obnoxious to our laws can find their comfort in staying
away from us." In coming to North Carolina and asking that

their marriage be recognized, the dissent argued, the defendants were asking for more than North Carolina's own citizens were entitled to.

> It is courteous for neighbors to visit, and it is handsome to allow the visitor family privileges and even give him the favorite seat; but if he bring his pet rattlesnake or his pet bear or spitz dog, famous for hydrophobia, he must leave them outside the door. And if he bring smallpox the door may be shut against him. . . .

The Federal Marriage Amendment
(H.J. Res. 56)

> "Marriage in the United States shall consist only of the union of a man and a woman. Neither this Constitution or the constitution of any State, nor state or federal law, shall be construed to require that marital status or the legal incidents thereof be conferred upon unmarried couples or groups."

The President Speaks

PRESIDENT GEORGE W. BUSH

February 24, 2004

Eight years ago, Congress passed, and President Clinton signed the Defense of Marriage Act, which defined marriage, for purposes of federal law, as the legal union between one man and one woman as husband and wife. The act passed the House of Representatives by a vote of 342 to 67 and the Senate by a vote of 85 to 14. Those Congressional votes and the passage of similar defense of marriage laws in 38 states express an overwhelming consensus in our country for protecting the institution of marriage.

In recent months, however, some activist judges and local officials have made an aggressive attempt to redefine marriage. In Massachusetts, four judges on the highest court have indicated they will order the issuance of marriage licenses to applicants of the same gender in May of this year.

In San Francisco, city officials have issued thousands of marriage licenses to people of the same gender, contrary to the California Family Code. That code, which clearly defines marriage as the union of a man and a woman, was approved overwhelmingly by the voters of California.

A county in New Mexico has also issued marriage licenses to applicants of the same gender. And unless action is taken, we can expect more arbitrary court decisions, more litigation, more defiance of the law by local officials, all of which adds to uncertainty.

After more than two centuries of American jurisprudence and millennia of human experience, a few judges and local authorities are presuming to change the most fundamental institution of civilization. Their actions have created confusion on an issue that requires clarity.

SAME-SEX MARRIAGE: PRO AND CON

On a matter of such importance, the voice of the people must be heard. Activist courts have left the people with one recourse. If we are to prevent the meaning of marriage from being changed forever, our nation must enact a constitutional amendment to protect marriage in America. Decisive and democratic action is needed, because attempts to redefine marriage in a single state or city could have serious consequences throughout the country.

The Constitution says that full faith and credit shall be given in each state to the public acts and records and judicial proceedings of every other state. Those who want to change the meaning of marriage will claim that this provision requires all states and cities to recognize same-sex marriages performed anywhere in America.

Congress attempted to address this problem in the Defense of Marriage Act by declaring that no state must accept another state's definition of marriage.

My administration will vigorously defend this act of Congress. Yet there is no assurance that the Defense of Marriage Act will not itself be struck down by activist courts. In that event, every state would be forced to recognize any relationship that judges in Boston or officials in San Francisco choose to call a marriage.

Furthermore, even if the Defense of Marriage Act is upheld, the law does not protect marriage within any state or city. For all these reasons, the defense of marriage requires a constitutional amendment.

An amendment to the Constitution is never to be undertaken lightly. The amendment process has addressed many serious matters of national concern, and the preservation of marriage rises to this level of national importance.

The union of a man and woman is the most enduring human institution, honored and encouraged in all cultures and by every religious faith. Ages of experience have taught humanity that the commitment of a husband and wife to love and to serve one another promotes the welfare of children and the stability of society. Marriage cannot be severed from its cultural, religious and natural roots without weakening the good influence of society.

Government, by recognizing protecting marriage, serves the interests of all. Today, I call upon the Congress to promptly pass and to send to the states for ratification an amendment to our Constitution defining and protecting marriage as a union of a man and woman as husband and wife. The amendment should fully protect marriage while leaving the state legislatures free to make their own choices in defining legal arrangements other than marriage.

America's a free society which limits the role of government in the lives of our citizens. This commitment of freedom, however, does not require the redefinition of one of our most basic social institutions. Our government should respect every person and protect the institution of marriage.

There is no contradiction between these responsibilities.

We should also conduct this difficult debate in a manner worthy of our country, without bitterness or anger. In all that lies ahead, let us match strong convictions with kindness and good will and decency.

Law Breaker

JACOB T. LEVY

From The New Republic Online, *February 18, 2004*

*A legal scholar examines what he believes are the extremism
and duplicity of the Federal Marriage Amendment.*

Many of the conservative supporters of the Federal Marriage
Amendment (FMA) argue that their efforts are intended to
limit judicial overreach of the sort they perceive in Massachusetts' *Goodridge* decision. They suggest that the FMA bans gay
marriage altogether, but bans civil unions only if they're created
by state or federal judges—suggesting that legislatively created
civil unions would be acceptable. As Ramesh Ponnuru recently
wrote, "[T]he amendment would not bar a state legislature from
enacting civil unions, but only block any future replays of Vermont, in which a court essentially ordered a legislature to enact
them." This is of a piece with a longstanding argument on the
right that social conservative positions can best be presented as
defenses of democratic decision-making against an imperial,
culturally-left judiciary. And it seems to underlie the Bush administration's political strategy of embracing a marriage amendment while fudging on the issue of civil unions.

As written, though, the FMA would make it impossible to
create the type of civil unions FMA boosters like Ponnuru suggest they're open to. More broadly, it's unlikely that any amendment preventing courts from creating civil unions would make it
possible for legislatures to do the same. Worse, not only would
the FMA deny state legislatures the authority proponents claim

it would leave intact; it would also constitute the kind of unprecedented assault on state autonomy conservatives reject in almost every other circumstance.

In their zeal to disguise the anti-gay-marriage cause as a crusade against judicial-supremacy, the framers of the Federal Marriage Amendment came up with the following:

"Marriage in the United States shall consist only of the union of a man and a woman. Neither this Constitution or the constitution of any State, nor state or federal law, shall be construed to require that marital status or the legal incidents thereof be conferred upon unmarried couples or groups."

The second sentence has become the focus of controversy because of the undefined scope of the phrase "legal incidents thereof," which some FMA supporters have said they mean to ban judicially but not legislatively created civil unions. But the text doesn't actually do that.

The reason has to do with the mechanics of how the state would go about "creating" civil unions. In the normal course of things, the legislature would write a civil unions law—let's call it the "Civil Unions Act of 2004"—which the judiciary would then deem to have created a civil union. The problem is that, if you allow the judiciary to deem that the Civil Unions Act of 2004 has created a right to a civil union—in other words, to "construe" the legislation as doing so—you also have to allow the judiciary to construe other sources of law—for example, the equal protection clause of a state constitution—as creating that right as well.

Why is this important? Because the converse is also true. If you try to prevent the judiciary from deeming that something like the equal protection clause creates a civil union—which is what supporters of the FMA hope to do—then you also prevent the judiciary from deeming that the "Civil Unions Act of 2004" creates a civil union. The more moderate proponents of the FMA suggest that they're open to the latter but not the former.

But there's simply no way to allow a judge to find legal justification for civil unions in an act of the legislature while forbidding him to find legal justification for them in the text of the constitution. Doing so would mean prohibiting any judicial interpretation of the more sweeping constitutional clauses, like equal protection, which would be the height of the kind of judicial activism conservatives frequently complain about. The judicial authority to construe one source of law can't be parceled off so neatly from the authority to construe others.

There is another, subtler problem with the FMA's second sentence: It does not merely limit and constrain state laws. It dictates a rule about how state laws and state constitutions will be construed and interpreted by the state's own courts. That is an unprecedented intrusion into the autonomy of the states' legal systems. Instead of limiting state law with federal law, from the outside, it would distort state law from within.

Constraints and limits are the stuff of the federal Constitution and of federal statutes. A state's law prohibiting miscegenation, enacting a poll tax, creating barriers to interstate trade, or creating an internal system of paper money will be overridden by federal courts enforcing the federal Constitution. But the federal courts are interpreting federal law when they do so, not state law. It is an important principle of American federalism that only state courts may do the latter. Even the U.S. Supreme Court defers to state supreme courts as the final interpreters of their own states' constitutions and laws; it only judges compatibility of those laws and constitutions with respect to federal law.

The FMA would be different. It would compel not the conclusion that federal law overrides any state's attempt to create gay marriage or civil unions, but the conclusion that, no matter what the state's legislature, constitutional convention or referendum, or judiciary decided, state law never created gay marriage or civil unions in the first place. For example, if a state's legisla-

ture and voters agreed, by the constitutionally-required super-
majorities, to amend their state constitutions to say that "Civil
marriage in this state shall be available to couples of the same
sex," state judges would be compelled, by their oaths to the federal Constitution and its supremacy clause, to deny that the state
constitution meant what it said. In principle we would never
reach the moment of a federal judge using the federal constitution to override the state law, because the FMA would have
reached within each state's own constitutional processes and dictated the outcome.

Despite this, some conservatives, such as Ponnuru, have argued that the FMA isn't necessarily an assault on federalism.
Federalist principles don't simply demand maximal power and
autonomy for the states, they argue, but rather a balance between states and the center. And, they rightly suggest, some
changes to that balance can be made without altering the fundamental structure.

But meddling for the first time in how states interpret their
own statutes and constitutions isn't a marginal change. It's a
change in the basic status of state constitutions and legal systems. That's because state constitutional provisions can mean
something different from their federal counterparts, even when
they use precisely the same wording. Among other things, state-
level precedent and the different overall constitutional structure
in whose light provisions must be interpreted allow state legal
systems to develop in ways more protective of individual rights
than the federal system. Guarantees of freedom of speech, freedom of association, the right to keep arms, privacy and property
rights, and, yes, equal protection clauses can all be construed
more expansively in a given state than they are at the federal
level—a fact that matters dearly to conservative defenders of
federalism. For those who care about federalism as an institution for protecting freedom—a description most conservatives

would assent to—federal intervention in state constitutional development is a dangerous precedent, imperiling precisely these rights.

The FMA was oddly written in an attempt to meet social conservative aims under cover of shoring up the separation of powers and respecting federalist principles—and while avoiding the appearance of extremism that would be created by banning civil unions altogether. The attempt to do all this simultaneously failed. We're left with an amendment that achieves social conservative aims by subverting both the separation of powers and federalism. In this case, a bad cause seems to have made for bad law.

A Chance and a Choice

PETER J. GOMES

From the Boston Globe, *February 8, 2004*

A Harvard pastor urges a distinction between civil and religious marriage, and urges the Massachusetts legislature to accede to the Massachusetts Supreme Judicial Court's decision to mandate civil marriage licenses to all couples, gay and straight.

When the Pilgrims landed at Plymouth in 1620, among the first things they did for the well-ordering of their new commonwealth was to institute the Dutch custom of civil marriage with which they had become familiar during their long sojourn in the Netherlands.

The Dutch made civil marriage the law of the land in 1590, and the first marriage in New England, that of Edward Winslow to the widow Susannah White, was performed on May 12, 1621, in Plymouth by Governor William Bradford, in exercise of his office as magistrate.

There would be no clergyman in Plymouth until the arrival of The Rev. Ralph Smith in 1629, but even then marriage would continue to be a civil affair, as these first Puritans opposed the English custom of clerical marriage as unscriptural. Not until 1692, when Plymouth Colony was merged into that of Massachusetts Bay, were the clergy authorized by the new province to solemnize marriages. To this day in this Commonwealth the clergy, including those of the archdiocese, solemnize marriage legally as agents of the Commonwealth and by its civil authority. Chapter 207 of the General Laws of Massachusetts tells who may perform such ceremonies. This little bit of social and legal history should prove instructive in the current debate concerning marriage in this Commonwealth, and the controversial ruling thereon by the Supreme Judicial Court in *Goodridge v. Department of Public Health*. The petitioners did not address religious issues, and the court's ruling was not premised on religious grounds: Marriage, its definition, rights, and responsibilities, was understood here as a civil matter, as it has been since 1621.

Thus, while the legitimate interests of religious communities in what some of them regard as the sacrament of marriage are worthy of consideration, those interests must not be confused either with the civil law of the Commonwealth or the civil rights of the citizens under its constitution.

No clergy of any denomination are required to wed anyone of whose union they do not approve: There is no civil right to be married in church or with its blessing. The civil law is just that, and the distinction between it and ecclesiastical law is as important as the necessary distinction between church and state.

Surely, after two years of protracted debate between church law and civil law in the child-abuse scandals we should appreciate the necessity of these distinctions.

It is to the civil rights of the citizens of Massachusetts that the Supreme Judicial Court responded in the *Goodridge* case, and this was no attack on the church, nor on religion. It was recognition that the social custom restricting marriage to heterosexuals, a custom long sanctioned by church and society, was no longer to be regarded as consistent with the rights of citizens under the constitution.

We have seen this before. When the courts eventually invalidated long-established laws sanctioned by church and society that forbade interracial marriage, the so-called "miscegenation" laws that obtained in many parts of this country within living memory, the courts that did this were invariably maligned as interventionist, arbitrary, and usurpatious.

Most now would agree that those laws were wrong, indeed unconstitutional, and that the courts were right in their judgments on behalf of the petitioners.

"Judicial tyranny" is a phrase usually heard from those whose prejudices have not been sustained by a court's decision. Happily, the fundamental rights of citizens in this Commonwealth and republic are in the long run defended against another form of tyranny even more dangerous, the tyranny of the majority.

Legislatures more often than not are subject to the prevailing passions of any majority that can muster sufficient votes; rarely are legislatures in the first instance instruments of social change. It was, after all, legislators who, reflecting the views of those who elected them, kept in place every oppressive law on the books until challenged by aggrieved citizens who sought relief in the courts.

If society waited for majority opinion and legislative action,

African-Americans, for example, would still be enduring the indignities of separate but equal accommodation and the other manifestations of legal, social, and political segregation. If the decision of the Supreme Judicial Court in *Goodridge* is "judicial tyranny," let there be more of it.

In the forthcoming constitutional convention, the legislature will be pressured to develop a politically expedient alternative to the clear and unambiguous meaning of the Supreme Judicial Court's *Goodridge* decision. It will be a stretch of rationality if it can do so. His excellency the governor is as misguided in his efforts to find an agreeable alternative to the court's decision as he is in seeking an error-proof justification for the reintroduction of capital punishment into this commonwealth. Surely, he has other matters with which to concern himself.

These legislative and executive maneuvers are not unlike those of such southern Democrats as Harry Flood Byrd, George Corley Wallace, and Strom Thurmond, who, after *Brown v. Board of Education,* which just fifty years ago mandated the end of segregation in public schools, sought to use every political and legislative means at their considerable disposal to nullify the meaning of the court's unprecedented decision. Is there anyone, save for the most retro-racist, who says now that Byrd, Wallace, and Thurmond were right and Earl Warren and his court wrong?

William Sloane Coffin, former Yale chaplain, civil rights and antiwar activist, in his most recent book defines hell as "truth seen too late." History indicts those who in time of trouble and transition choose the past over the future.

There are always conscientious people of deeply held religious conviction who, alas, on the basis of those convictions find themselves on the wrong side of history, such as those in our own Commonwealth who hanged witches in the seventeenth century and embraced the fugitive slave laws in the nineteenth century; and those who in our own time find the support of custom, reason, and faith in their prejudices against Roman Catholics, Jews, and persons of other colors and ethnicities.

This resistance to extending not special rights but civil rights to homosexuals in marriage is but the most recent instance of this dubious legacy, and is not made any more palatable or respectable today by the support given to it by visible and highly placed clergy across denominational lines, from whom we have a right to expect better.

The way to the future is always paved by extending, not restricting, liberties, especially to those who heretofore have been excluded. The health of a republic may well be determined by its capacity to adapt itself to the extension of its own privileges and responsibilities to those whom it would be easy by custom and conviction to ignore.

John Adams's Massachusetts Constitution, the oldest such document in the world, laid down the rational basis for a civil body politic whose capacious hospitality has successively embraced people and views not contemplated by the founders. The Great and General Court ought not to betray the fundamental principles of our Commonwealth's constitution by promulgating amendments that will, for the first time in our history, restrict rather than extend the rights and liberties of all of our citizens. To do so will do nothing to restore the difficult circumstances of modern marriage.

Divorce will not be halted, abuse will not be eliminated, frivolous heterosexual liaisons such as the recent publicity stunt of Britney Spears will still be lawful, and annulments will still be sought and obtained in the church courts. Nothing will be done to save marriage, and yet in the name of doing so, incalculable, retrogressive, and even punitive damage will be done to those of our fellow citizens who under the civil law crave the legitimization of their loving relationships.

The defense of marriage demands much more than legislative manipulation enshrining the status quo. The defenders of traditional marriage argue that marriage has been a heterosexual affair since "Adam and Eve, not Adam and Steve," and at the same time they argue that this exclusively heterosexual institution is in serious trouble.

Logic would suggest that such troubles as marriage experiences cannot be laid at the door of those who have been, at least until *Goodridge,* rigorously excluded from it.

To extend the civil right of marriage to homosexuals will neither solve nor complicate the problems already inherent in marriage, but what it will do is permit a whole class of persons, our fellow citizens under the law heretofore irrationally deprived of a civil right, both to benefit from and participate in a valuable yet vulnerable institution which in our changing society needs all the help it can get.

The Legislature has a choice, and a chance to do the right thing. In this case, it is to do nothing. That shouldn't be so hard.

An Election Winner

STANLEY KURTZ

From National Review Online, *February 10, 2004*

A conservative writer delights that marriage could become a defining issue in the presidential campaign, hurting the Democrats and helping George W. Bush.

Has the Massachusetts Supreme Judicial Court just spoiled John Kerry's chance to be president? Quite possibly. It's difficult to know exactly how the politics of gay marriage will play out during the campaign. Yet there's every prospect that this issue will weigh heavily against John Kerry and Democratic congressional candidates this fall.

It hasn't quite dawned on many Americans just how big this issue could be. Gay marriage is an awkward and polarizing subject. Neither the public, politicians, nor the media are eager to take it up. Yet there's a dynamic built into this issue that makes it likely to have an explosive impact on the coming campaign.

What will happen after May 17, when Massachusetts begins to issue marriage licenses to same-sex couples? Hundreds, even thousands, of gay couples will pour into Massachusetts, get married, return to their states, and begin to agitate for recognition of their marriages. This huge media event will play out continuously for two months before the Democratic National Convention—in Boston—on July 26. All this will cement the connection in the public mind between gay marriage, Massachusetts liberals, John Kerry, activist judges, and the Democratic party.

But the trouble for Kerry and the Democrats doesn't end

there. The media firestorm over gay marriage is going to continue through the entire campaign (and beyond). This country has never confronted a situation in which the marriages of a substantial body of citizens go unrecognized in large parts of the country. What happens if someone in a same-sex marriage is injured in a non-recognizing state? Will his spouse get hospital visitation rights? What if a marriage dissolves, and property in a non-recognizing state has to be divided? Complications will proliferate, and each new permutation will mean more news stories and more pleas for national recognition.

Although gay-marriage advocates will undoubtedly litigate aggressively to nationalize their Massachusetts victory, it is likely that the politically savvy managers of the gay-marriage movement will try to delay formal legal challenges until after the presidential campaign. They may or may not succeed. Couples could quickly launch challenges of their own to federal and state DOMAs (Defense of Marriage Acts). In any case, there will surely be a continuous stream of news stories about gay marriage, featuring pleas by newly married couples for recognition in their home states.

Meantime, as events in Massachusetts spill over into the country as a whole, a groundswell of support for the Federal Marriage Amendment will place tremendous pressure on candidates at all levels to declare themselves on gay marriage. This will be particularly so if the president endorses a version of the Federal Marriage Amendment, as now seems likely. Constitutional amendments must be approved by a two-thirds vote of Congress and three quarters of the state legislatures. That means every political candidate, from the state level up, will be asked to take a stand.

We're accustomed to politicians handing off polarizing social issues like abortion and affirmative action to the courts. But gay marriage is going to become a live legislative issue right away. We see this most clearly in Massachusetts, where the state legislature meets this week in joint session to consider an amendment to the state's constitution defining marriage as the union of a man and a woman. The same question is likely to be put before a great many other state legislatures.

Despite the fact that three quarters of the states have legislated against gay marriage, in only a few cases (Alaska, Hawaii, Nebraska, Nevada) have states done so through constitutional amendments. But state DOMAs are all vulnerable to constitutional challenges of the Massachusetts type. Every state constitution has a clause guaranteeing citizens equal benefits or rights. So every state supreme court could use *Goodridge* to read a right to gay marriage into its constitution, thus overriding a state-level Defense of Marriage Act. So even many states with junior DOMAs will attempt to amend their constitutions. In fact, a number of states are considering amendments right now.

So the gay-marriage issue is going to be kept alive, not only by dramatic media coverage of married gay couples flooding back from Massachusetts to every non-recognizing state in the union, and not only by a national campaign for the Federal Marriage Amendment, but also by a continuing series of state-level debates over junior DOMAs, state constitutional amendments, and the role of state courts. All this means that the gay-marriage story is going to be pervasive.

The public is not going to like this. Precisely because gay marriage is such an awkward and polarizing subject, we'll see a strong reaction against the Massachusetts liberals and activist judges who've forced this conflict on an unwilling country. And moves to pass constitutional amendments in state after state are going to make the idea of amending the federal constitution seem a lot less strange.

It's a good thing, too. That's because, even if every state besides Massachusetts were to pass a constitutional amendment defining marriage as the union of a man and a woman, gay marriage could still be nationalized by a decision of the United States Supreme Court. And it's a certainty that a challenge to the federal Defense of Marriage Act will work its way up to the U.S. Supreme Court sometime in the next few years.

Given the sweeping nature of the Supreme Court's recent Lawrence ruling on sodomy, and the roles of Justices Kennedy and O'Connor in that decision, national imposition of gay marriage by judicial fiat is very real possibility. There are any number of possible grounds for such a decision. A case based on an equal protection or substantive due process claim is even more likely to nationalize gay marriage than a case based on the Full Faith and Credit clause.

If the Court declines to impose gay marriage on the country as a whole, the confusion will continue. The only way the Court can impose uniformity and stem the conflict is to nationalize gay marriage. Only passage of the Federal Marriage Amendment can impose uniformity in the other direction. So it's going to be a race between the Supreme Court and the amendment process to resolve the issue nationally one way or the other. Until then, our culture war over gay marriage will be at fever pitch.

The White House has given clear signals that the president is going to endorse the Federal Marriage Amendment. The president may not follow through, but it's likely that he will. There is no doubt that presidential backing for the Federal Marriage Amendment—and the enthusiasm of religious conservatives for the enterprise—threatens to turn off socially moderate swing voters. If the president or his supporters conduct this battle in a mean-spirited way, they will harm themselves greatly. Yet the president is keenly aware of this problem, and will likely handle the issue with decency and respect for all.

John Kerry, on the other hand, is greatly endangered by the gay-marriage issue. And the problem goes well beyond the powerful association soon to be set up in the public mind between gay marriage, Massachusetts liberalism, activist judges, the Democratic party, and John Kerry.

For starters, John Kerry was one of only fourteen senators who voted against the federal Defense of Marriage Act in 1996. Although Senator Kerry now claims to be against gay marriage, he is going to have a very tough time explaining that vote. In effect, a vote against DOMA is a vote to nationalize gay marriage. Kerry refused to take even the most minimal steps to prevent four activist Massachusetts judges from imposing gay marriage on the country. That is going to hurt him.

The deeper problem for Kerry is that the gay-marriage issue could turn into a kind of tipping point on public perceptions of his record. Right now, Kerry's hope is to use his war exploits to neutralize Republican attacks on his extraordinarily liberal voting record. But once gay marriage becomes a major focus of the campaign, Kerry's vote against DOMA is going to become a huge problem. In the contest between the image of Kerry the war hero, and the image of a dovish, tax-loving, Massachusetts liberal, Kerry's DOMA vote is going to push attention back onto his votes. Three big issues on which Kerry's votes are well to the left of the country constitute a trend.

Kerry understands that the gay-marriage issue is a serious problem for him. Noam Scheiber reports that Kerry is at least considering supporting an amendment to the Massachusetts state constitution defining marriage as the union of a man and a woman. Of course, endorsing a state marriage amendment would get Kerry into terrible trouble with his Democratic base—and permanently mark him out as an unprincipled flip-flopper. How can a man who condemned DOMA as anti-gay turn around and support a state marriage amendment? And if Kerry does support a Massachusetts marriage amendment, it would be very difficult for him to credibly oppose the Federal Marriage Amendment.

In the end, nothing could be fairer than to link John Kerry to the actions of his state's Supreme Judicial Court. In truth, Kerry is a Massachusetts liberal of exactly the same stripe as the majority justices in *Goodridge*. If John Kerry is elected, gay marriage will surely be nationalized by the end of his term. A Bush defeat would take the wind out of the sails of the campaign for the Federal Marriage Amendment, assure liberal judges that no serious consequences will arise from nationalization, and bring more *Goodridge*-style liberals onto the courts. A Bush victory, on the other hand, would keep the FMA alive, would help signal the courts that they've gone too far, and would stop the proliferation of activist judges on our courts. Whatever else it will be, this election will be a national referendum on gay marriage. That looks like bad news for John Kerry and the Democrats.

The Evolution of Marriage

NANCY F. COTT

From Testimony Before the Vermont House Judiciary Committee, January 17, 2000

On December 20, 1999, the Vermont Supreme Court ruled in Baker v. State *that under its constitution, the state could no longer refuse same-sex couples the benefits created under its marriage laws. The court refused, however, to order the legislature to redraft its marriage statute. Instead, it allowed the legislature to remedy the situation, either by amending its marriage laws or by creating a proxy that would grant gays and lesbians access to the rights and obligations of marriage but without using the "M" word.*

Ultimately, the legislature chose to create a "civil unions" measure that grants gays and lesbians all of the benefits of marriage without formally recognizing those unions as "marriages." Gays and lesbians who enter into civil unions enjoy no federal benefits of marriage and have no assurance that their relationships, which enjoy some protection in Vermont, have any legal significance beyond its borders.

In the months leading up to the enactment of civil unions, the state legislature heard testimony from numerous experts, including Harvard historian Nancy F. Cott, whose informal discussion with the Judiciary Committee is excerpted below.

Prof. Cott: . . . Although most people invest marriage with religious meaning, and there have been religious ceremonies associated with marriage, marriage in the United States has historically been a civil institution as much as a religious one. It has always been authorized by state authorities. . . .

Rep. [Thomas A.] Little: I think we might . . . be interested to know how one got married in, let's say, the Massachusetts Bay Colony in 1630.

Prof. Cott: Well, it was probably similar in Massachusetts and Vermont. The truth is one often didn't bother to get married in Massachusetts. One just lived informally. There was a very famous case about this issue. When the [first] governor of Massachusetts was elected, he had been living with the same woman for twenty years; they had never bothered to get formally married. He just didn't want to be formally married. This wasn't unusual at the time. A lot of people just cohabited in the seventeenth century, without bothering to go to the authorities. . . .

Rep. [Michael R.] Kainen: May I ask a question on that last point, the informal marriages. How were the rights, benefits, and protections dealt with in these relationships?

Prof. Cott: We have to take ourselves back to a time with much less government bureaucracy and far fewer government benefits. The mutual obligations of marriage, the most basic ones, were about economic support. The well-understood economic armature of marriage involved the husband providing for the wife and the wife obeying and working for the husband. Marriage was as contract for mutual economic support, except that the support came in different forms. The husband was considered the independent provider. The wife was like the servant. You can make a parallel between marriage and an apprenticeship contract. The wife contributed her labor to the mutual support bargain and was bound to obey her husband, who had the right to command her labor. He owned not only her literal services but any earnings she made from any third party. He also owned any property she might have owned before the marriage. This was a crucial part of the way marriage was understood under the common law, which ruled England. . . .

A great deal happened in the nineteenth century, the Victorian era. During that time a different sense of respectability and prudishness made formal marriage and the legal apparatus of marriage far more important. After the Civil War, the United States government, as well as state governments, got involved in saying explicitly what kind of marriage ought to be the standard in the United States. For example, the national government carried out a fifty-year campaign to make the Mormons stop practicing polygamy in Utah. . . .

Polygamy is a crucial issue about the history of marriage, one that is very relevant today. One reason people believed that polygamy was impossible is that the most essential characteristic of Christian marriage was the mutual consent of the two parties. Thus informal marriage was counted as marriage by the law, because consent was the only thing needed to make a marriage real for the parties. Cohabitation, sexual consummation, was less important than consent. Even the Catholic Church believed this, at least up until the sixteenth century, although after 1563 the Catholic Church considered consummation and consent equally important. Consent was especially important in America because this was a government based on consent. So the whole foundation of American politics mirrored the marriage contract, and a marriage of two people as the foundation of a household matched very well the notion that America was a government of consent, a government of a whole bunch of people who got together and agreed to live together in one nation. The assumption was that many women could not possibly all consent to marry the same man. . . .

In the mid-nineteenth century, a series of additional laws began to broaden women's rights. . . .

The legal intersection of marriage with racial regulation is another important example of the changing nature of marriage. This wasn't something that ever occurred in Vermont, but it's still an important area of change in this country. Slaves, when there was slaveholding in the United States, could not legally marry. They, of course, formed marital unions, which many slave holders encouraged because they wanted reproduction of slaves, but slaves could not marry legally, because they did not have the power to consent. The master made all the decisions for them. In other words, slaves had no civil rights. . . .

The right to marry is a basic civil right that slaves did not have. This is one of the reasons that after emancipation, slaves flocked to get married legally. They saw it as an expression of having civil rights, of being individuals who in the eyes of the law could consent and therefore could enter legal marriage. . . .

The prohibition on slaves' marrying falls out of the picture once the slaves were emancipated, so that issue was really more about slavery than about race. But even after emancipation, most states still had laws prohibiting marriage between a white person and a person who was defined as a Negro or mulatto. People frequently talk about laws against interracial marriages, but I want to emphasize that these laws were not about marriages between people of different races in general. That is, there was never a law in the United States that prevented a Chinese person from marrying a black person. All the laws were about white people, who white people could or could not marry or who could or could not marry a white person. These laws were clearly about white supremacy, about keeping the white race unmixed as far as possible. These laws were not simply a consequence of or follow-up to slavery. They existed, at some time, in forty-one states [or territories]. . . .

The U.S. Supreme Court did not strike down these laws until 1967, in *Loving v. Virginia.* At that time sixteen states still had these laws. Two decades earlier, in 1948, when a state court first declared such a law unconstitutional, this kind of law existed in thirty states. So these laws were neither a southern phenomenon nor a nineteenth-century phenomenon. . . .

The third area in which there has been great change is the availability of divorce. There was a precedent for divorce in the Puritan belief that marriage was a civil matter. They believed that a marriage contract was a state construction, and if one party was not observing the contractual obligations, the contract ought to be terminated. But divorce really expanded after states recognized that people were breaking up their marriages any-way and the state might as well set the terms of separation to make things more orderly and to have input into how support obligations were carried out. The recent move to no-fault di-vorce means that the couple gets more say about why the mar-riage has broken up, and the state is less involved in that part of the decision making. But the state is still involved in approving the separation terms and making sure that children, especially, will still have some means of support. . . .

Rep. Little: Do you have any observations on what the state of Vermont is now contemplating, assuming for the sake of discus-sion that the legislature is going to proceed to enact something in response to the *Baker* decision, in terms of your work with marriage and social change and social policy?

Prof. Cott: Let me preface this by saying that I'm neither a lawyer nor a futurist. I'm a historian; I'm supposed to look back. But the reason to look back is that the past is a guide for the present, and we can't operate in the present without having a sense of the past.

So, I have two reactions. First, authorizing marriage for same-sex couples would certainly be a large change, since it al-ways seemed self-evident that marriage involved a man and a woman. But then, many of the things that were seen as self-evident about the marital regime in which most Americans oper-ated for 150 years are no longer self-evident. For example, it used to seem self-evident that cohabiting without being mar-ried, or having a child outside of marriage, meant that you would be expelled from respectable society. That is no longer self-evident, and that is a huge change. In 1850, when the law was first giving wives individuality within marriage, people probably viewed that as a huge change, just as great a change as same-sex marriage seems now. What seems in retrospect like the natural evolution of an institution probably didn't feel that way at the time.

So in the long run same-sex marriage may not be as big a change as it seems now. . . . In many ways, same-sex marriage just reiterates many of the traditional values of monogamy. . . .

My second thought is that even though the court decision said that your common benefits law required the legislature give the same rights and privileges to same-sex couples as to hetero-sexual couples, there is nothing that has all the same obligations, rights, and benefits as marriage but marriage. Marriage isn't just the black letter law that creates marriage as a civil and public entity. Marriage is also the whole aura of a status, an aura that exists because marriage has been authorized by governments for hundreds of years. So from a historian's perspective, nothing other than marriage can fully accomplish what the court wanted to do.

Rep. Little: I think the proposal that's being—one of the options we've kicked around here is to essentially replace the institution of marriage with the institution of X and that everybody goes into X instead of marriage and it has the same maybe civil laws significance.

Prof. Cott: But it is not called marriage.

Rep. Little: It does not have a title, and the title, the nomenclature is reserved for a non-secular piece, the religious piece.

Prof. Cott: It seems to me very complicated. I don't usually give policy advice, but it seems to me that system would put Vermont in a very difficult position, both in relation to the other states and to the federal government. In 1996, marriage appeared 1,034 times in federal statutes. There were 1,034 different kinds of benefits, responsibilities, rights, and so forth connected with marriage in the federal code. In a world that wasn't complicated by a close connection to other entities that had the old definition of marriage it might make sense, but it seems to me it's a mine field to try to do that. . . .

Rep. [Cathy] Voyer: This whole thing is a minefield.

Henry Alford is the author of the humor collections *Municipal Bondage* and *Big Kiss*.

Dennis Altman teaches in the politics department at La Trobe University in Melbourne, Australia, and is the author of *Homosexual: Oppression and Liberation* (New York University Press).

Antiga is a writer and workshop creator.

Hannah Arendt, a historian and political philosopher, died in 1975.

Aristophanes was a Greek dramatist who lived from c. 448–c. 388 B.C.

Hadley Arkes is the Ney Professor of Jurisprudence at Amherst College and a contributing editor at *National Review.*

Philip A. Belcastro is the chairman of the department of Physical Education, Health, Recreation and Dance at B.M.C.C.—City University of New York.

William Bennett, a fellow at the Hudson Institute and the Heritage Foundation, is the codirector of Empower America.

Jerry J. Bigner is a professor in the department of Human Development and Family Studies at Colorado State University.

Elizabeth Birch served as the executive director of the Human Rights Campaign from January 1995 to January 2004.

Harry Andrew Blackmun was an associate justice of the U.S. Supreme Court from 1971 to 1994. He died in 1999.

Sonny Bono was the U.S. representative from the 44th district of California when he died in 1998.

About the Contributors

Frederick W. Bozett, a professor in the Graduate Program in the College of Nursing at the University of Oklahoma, died in 1990.

David Brooks is an op-ed columnist at *The New York Times*.

Frank Browning is the author of *A Queer Geography: Journeys Toward a Sexual Self* (Crown).

Tammy Bruce is a Fox News Channel contributor and the author of *The Death of Right and Wrong* (Prima).

George W. Bush is the 43rd president of the United States.

Robert Byrd is a U.S. senator from West Virginia.

Dudley Clendinen is a freelance writer living in Baltimore, Maryland, and a former national correspondent for *The New York Times*.

Nancy F. Cott is Jonathan Trumbull Professor of American History at Harvard University and Pforzheimer Foundation Director of the Schlesinger Library on the History of Women in America at the Radcliffe Institute for Advanced Study. She is the author of *Public Vows: A History of Marriage and the Nation* (Harvard).

William Orville Douglas was an associate justice of the U.S. Supreme Court from 1939 to 1975. He died in 1980.

Kathy Duggan is a freelance writer living in New York City.

Mary C. Dunlap is a writer and director of the Office of Citizen Complaints in San Francisco, California.

Jean Bethke Elshtain is the Laura Spelman Rockefeller Professor of Social and Political Ethics at the University of Chicago.

Paula Ettelbrick is director of the Family Policy Program at the National Gay and Lesbian Task Force Policy Institute.

David K. Flaks, Psy.D., is a psychologist licensed in Pennsylvania and New Jersey.

About the Contributors

Paula Fomby was an intern at *Mother Jones* in 1991.

Barney Frank is the U.S. representative from the 4th district of Massachusetts.

Maggie Gallagher is the editor of MarriageDebate.com and the co-author of *The Case for Marriage* (Broadway).

Peter J. Gomes is the Plummer Professor of Christian Morals and Pusey Minister in the Memorial Church at Harvard University. He is an American Baptist minister.

E. J. Graff is the author of *What is Marriage For?* (Beacon).

Melville J. Herskovits was a professor of anthropology at Northwestern University from 1927 to 1963. He died in 1963.

Ralph Hexter is a professor of Classics at the University of California at Berkeley.

Bret Hinsch is an associate professor at the National Chung Cheng University, Taiwan.

Henry Hyde is the U.S. representative from the 6th district of Illinois.

Bob Inglis is the U.S. representative from the 4th district of South Carolina.

Doug Ireland is a contributor to *The Nation* and a former *Village Voice* contributor.

Jeffrey John is a parish priest and theology lecturer in London.

Rabbi Yoel H. Kahn was rabbi of Congregation Sha'ar Zahav in San Francisco from 1985 to 1996, and is now director of the Jewish Community Center of San Francisco's Taube Center for Jewish Life.

Anthony McLeod Kennedy is an associate justice of the U.S. Supreme Court.

John F. Kerry is a U.S. senator from Massachusetts.

About the Contributors

Andrew Koppelman is a professor of law and political science at Northwestern University School of Law.

Larry Kramer is Russell D. Niles Professor of Law at New York University School of Law.

Charles Krauthammer is a syndicated columnist.

Stanley Kurtz is a contributing editor at *National Review Online* and a fellow at the Hoover Institution.

Joseph Landau is an attorney in New York City. He is a former assistant managing editor of *The New Republic*.

Ann Landers was a syndicated columnist. She died in 2002.

Jacob T. Levy is Assistant Professor of Political Science at the College at the University of Chicago, and the author of *The Multiculturalism of Fear* (Oxford).

John Lewis is the U.S. representative from the 5th district of Georgia.

James McGough is an epidemiologist specializing in AIDS research with the Seattle–King County Department of Public Health. He lives in Seattle, Washington.

Michel de Montaigne was a French essayist who lived from 1533 to 1592.

Sandra Day O'Connor is an associate justice of the U.S. Supreme Court.

Camille Paglia is a professor of humanities at the University of the Arts in Philadelphia.

Charlotte Patterson is a developmental psychologist at the University of Virginia.

Plato, a disciple of Socrates, was an Athenian philosopher who lived from c. 427 to 347 B.C.

About the Contributors

Richard A. Posner is a judge on the 7th U.S. Circuit Court of Appeals in Chicago and the author of *A Guide to America's Sex Laws* (University of Chicago).

Lewis Franklin Powell, Jr., was an associate justice of the U.S. Supreme Court from 1972 to 1987. He died in 1998.

Dennis Prager is a lecturer, writer, and nationally syndicated radio talk show host in Los Angeles, California.

Jonathan Rauch is a columnist for *The Atlantic Monthly* and *National Journal,* and the author of *Gay Marriage: Why It Is Good for Gays, Good for Straights, and Good for America* (Times Books).

William Safire is a *New York Times* columnist.

Antonin Scalia is an associate justice of the U.S. Supreme Court.

Amy E. Schwartz is a member of the *Washington Post* editorial page staff.

Jay Alan Sekulow is the chief counsel for the American Center for Law and Justice.

Brent D. Shaw is a professor of classical studies at the University of Pennsylvania.

William S. Skylstad is the bishop of the Spokane, Washington, diocese.

John Shelby Spong, the retired Episcopal bishop of Newark, is the author of *Living in Sin?* (Harper San Francisco).

Andrew Sullivan is a senior editor at *The New Republic* and the author of *Virtually Normal: An Argument About Homosexuality* (Vintage).

Cass Sunstein is a professor of jurisprudence at the University of Chicago Law School.

Catherine Tuerk is the president of the D.C. Metropolitan Chapter of PFLAG.

About the Contributors

Earl Warren was the chief justice of the U.S. Supreme Court from 1953 to 1969. He died in 1974.

Byron Raymond White was an associate justice of the U.S. Supreme Court from 1962 to 1993. He died in 2002.

Walter L. Williams is a professor of anthropology at the University of Southern California.

James Q. Wilson is James A. Collins Professor of Management and Public Policy Emeritus at UCLA.

Evan Wolfson was for twelve years Marriage Project Director of Lambda Legal Defense and Education Fund. He is the author of *Why Marriage Matters* (Simon & Schuster).

ACKNOWLEDGMENTS

"The Speech of Aristophanes" from the *Symposium* by Plato, translated by Alexander Nehamas and Paul Woodruff (Indianapolis: Hackett Publishing Company, Inc., 1989). Reprinted by permission.

"A Groom of One's Own?" by Brent D. Shaw (*The New Republic*, July 18 and 24, 1994), copyright © 1994 by The New Republic, Inc. Reprinted by permission of *The New Republic*.

"Same-Sex Unions in Pre-Modern Europe: A Response" by Ralph Hexter (*The New Republic*, October 3, 1994), copyright © 1994 by The New Republic, Inc. Reprinted by permission of *The New Republic*.

"A Strange Brotherhood" by Michel de Montaigne, March 18, 1581, journal entry from *Travel Journal* in *The Complete Works of Montaigne*, translated by Donald Frame (Stanford University Press). Reprinted by permission of Stanford University Press.

"Deviant Marriage Patterns in Chinese Society" by James McGough from *Normal and Abnormal Behavior in Chinese Culture*, edited by Arthur Kleinman and Tsung-Yi Lin (Kluwer Academic Publishers, 1981, pp. 171–201). Reprinted by permission of Kluwer Academic Publishers, Dordrecht, The Netherlands.

"Husbands, Boys, Servants" by Bret Hinsch from *Passions of the Cut Sleeve: The Male Homosexual Tradition in China* by Bret Hinsch, copyright © 1990 by The Regents of the University of California. Reprinted by permission of the Regents of the University of California and the University of California Press.

Acknowledgments

"A Note on 'Woman Marriage' in Dahomey" by Melville J. Herskovits (*Africa*, the Journal of the International African Institute, Vol. 10, 1937). Reprinted by permission of the International African Institute, London.

"A Normal Man" by Walter L. Williams from *The Spirit and the Flesh* by Walter L. Williams, copyright © 1986, 1992 by Walter L. Williams. Reprinted by permission of Beacon Press, Boston, and Georges Borchardt, Inc., on behalf of the author.

"The Precedents Abroad" by the Editors, from "Inching Down the Aisle" (*Harvard Law Review*, Vol. 116, no. 7), copyright © 2003 by the Harvard Law Review Association. Reprinted by permission.

Material from *The King James Bible*. Reprinted by permission of HarperCollins Publishers, London.

"Statement on Same-Sex Marriage" by Rev. Joseph L. Charron and Rev. William S. Skylstad (National Conference of Catholic Bishops), copyright © 1996 by the United States Catholic Conference. All rights reserved. Reprinted by permission of the Office for Publishing and Promotion Services, United States Catholic Conference, Washington, D.C.

"Marriage's True Ends" by the Editors (*Commonweal*, May 17, 1996), copyright © 1996 by Commonweal Foundation. Reprinted by permission of *Commonweal*.

"Against Gay Marriage" by Jean Bethke Elshtain (*Commonweal*, October 22, 1991), copyright © 1991 by Commonweal Foundation. Reprinted by permission of *Commonweal*.

"Homosexuality, the Bible, and Us—A Jewish Perspective" by Dennis Prager (*Ultimate Issues*, Vol. 6, No. 2). Reprinted by permission of *Ultimate Issues*, 10573 West Pico Blvd., #167, Los Angeles.

Acknowledgments

"Blessing Gay and Lesbian Commitments" by John Shelby Spong from *Living in Sin? A Bishop Rethinks Sexuality* by John Shelby Spong, copyright © 1989 by the Rt. Rev. John Shelby Spong. Reprinted by permission of HarperCollins Publishers, Inc.

"The Kedusha of Homosexual Relationships" by Rabbi Yoel H. Kahn from the *CCAR Yearbook XCIV* (New York: Central Conference of American Rabbis, 1989), copyright © 1989 by Yoel H. Kahn. Reprinted by permission of the author.

"Creation and Natural Law" by Jeffrey John from *Permanent, Faithful, Stable: Christian Same-Sex Partnerships* by Jeffrey John, copyright © 1993 by Jeffrey John. Reprinted by permission of the author, Affirming Catholicism, St. Giles Church, London.

"What You Do" by Andrew Sullivan (*The New Republic*, March 3, 1996), copyright © 1996 by The New Republic, Inc. Reprinted by permission of *The New Republic*.

"Since When Is Marriage a Path to Liberation?" by Paula Ettelbrick (*OUT/LOOK National Gay and Lesbian Quarterly*, No. 6, Fall 1989). Reprinted by permission of the author.

"Choosing" by Mary C. Dunlap from "The Lesbian and Gay Marriage Debate: A Microcosm of Our Hopes and Troubles in the Nineties" (*Law and Sexuality: A Review of Lesbian and Gay Legal Issues*, Vol. I, No. 63, 1991). Reprinted by permission of *Law and Sexuality*.

"Why Marry?" by Frank Browning (*The New York Times*, Op-Ed, April 17, 1996), copyright © 1996 by The New York Times Co. Reprinted by permission of *The New York Times*.

"Retying the Knot" by E. J. Graff (*The Nation*, June 24, 1996), copyright © 1996 by The Nation Company, L.P. Reprinted by permission of *The Nation*.

Acknowledgments

Acknowledgments

Presidents and Fellows of Harvard College. Reprinted by permission of Harvard University Press, Cambridge, Massachusetts.

"Same-Sex Marriage Nears" by William Safire (*The New York Times*, April 29, 1995), copyright © 1995 by The New York Times Co. Reprinted by permission of *The New York Times*.

"Gay Marriages and the Affirmation of an Ideal" by Amy E. Schwartz (*The Washington Post*, June 3, 1996), copyright © 1996 by *The Washington Post*. Reprinted by permission of The Washington Post Writers Group.

"The Power of Marriage" by David Brooks (*The New York Times*, November 22, 2003), copyright © 2003 by The New York Times Co. Reprinted by permission of *The New York Times*.

"Respecting Marriage and Equal Rights" by Tammy Bruce (*Front-Page Magazine*, February 24, 2004). Reprinted by permission of *FrontPage Magazine*.

"Defending Marriage" by Jay Alan Sekulow (written testimony provided to the House Judiciary Committee from the American Center for Law and Justice, May 15, 1996). Reprinted by permission.

"Children of Lesbian and Gay Parents: Summary of Research Findings" by Charlotte Patterson from *Lesbian and Gay Parenting: A Resource for Psychologists*, copyright © 1995 by the American Psychological Association. Reprinted by permission of the American Psychological Association.

"Lesbians Choosing Motherhood: A Comparative Study of Lesbian and Heterosexual Parents and Their Children" by David K. Flaks et al. from *Developmental Psychology*, Vol. 31, copyright © 1995 by the American Psychological Association. Reprinted by permission of the American Psychological Association.

Acknowledgments

"A Review of Data Based Studies Addressing the Effects of Homosexual Parenting on Children's Sexual and Social Functioning" by Philip A. Belcastro et al. (*Journal of Divorce and Remarriage,* Vol. 20, 1/2, 1993). Reprinted by permission of The Haworth Press, Inc.

"Coming Out to My Children" by Antiga from *Politics of the Heart,* edited by Sandra Pollack and Jeanne Vaughn, copyright © 1987 by Sandra Pollack and Jeanne Vaughn. Reprinted by permission of Firebrand Books, Ithaca, New York.

"Parenting by Gay Fathers" by Jerry J. Bigner and Frederick W. Bozett from *Homosexuality and Family Relations,* edited by Frederick W. Bozett and Marvin B. Sussman (1990). Reprinted by permission of The Haworth Press, Inc.

"Why I'm Glad I Grew Up in a Gay Family" by Paula Fomby (*Mother Jones,* August 16, 1996), copyright © 1996 by Foundation for National Progress. Reprinted by permission of *Mother Jones.*

"What Marriage Is For" by Maggie Gallagher (*The Weekly Standard,* August 4–11, 2003). Reprinted by permission of *The Weekly Standard.*

"Leave Marriage Alone" by William Bennett (*Newsweek,* June 3, 1996), copyright © 1996 by Newsweek, Inc. All rights reserved. Reprinted by permission of *Newsweek.*

"Three's a Crowd" by Andrew Sullivan (*The New Republic,* June 17, 1996), copyright © 1996 by The New Republic, Inc. Reprinted by permission of *The New Republic.*

"When John and Jim Say 'I Do'" by Charles Krauthammer (*Time,* July 22, 1996), copyright © 1996 by Time Inc. Reprinted by permission of Time Life Syndication.

Acknowledgments

"Marrying Somebody" by Jonathan Rauch, copyright © by Jonathan Rauch. Reprinted by permission of the author.

"Sexual Freedom and the End of Romance" by Dennis Altman from *The Homosexualization of America* by Dennis Altman (1982). Reprinted by permission of Curtis Brown (Aust.) Pty. Ltd.

"Jack and Bob, Going to the Chapel" by Dudley Clendinen (*The New York Times,* Op-Ed, August 7, 1996), copyright © 1996 by The New York Times Co. Reprinted by permission of *The New York Times.*

"I Earned This Divorce" by Kathy Duggan (*The New York Times,* Op-Ed, July 25, 1996), copyright © 1996 by The New York Times Co. Reprinted by permission of *The New York Times.*

"Ann Can't Give Her Blessing to This Marriage" by Ann Landers (*The Chicago Tribune,* July 21, 1996). Reprinted by permission of Ann Landers and Creators Syndicate.

"Love and Marriage" by Catherine Tuerk (*Flagpole,* the newsletter of Parents, Families and Friends of Lesbians and Gays of the Metropolitan Washington, D.C., Area, October 1996). Reprinted by permission of the author.

"Remembering Hervé" by Doug Ireland (*The Nation,* June 24, 1996), copyright © 1996 by The Nation Company, L.P. Reprinted by permission of *The Nation.*

"My Gay Wedding" by Henry Alford (*New York Magazine,* June 17, 1996), copyright © 1996 by New York Magazine. Distributed by the Los Angeles Times Syndicate. Reprinted by permission.

"Marriage as Integration" by Joseph Landau, copyright © by Joseph Landau. Reprinted by permission of the author.

"The M-Word" by Andrew Sullivan (*Time,* February 10, 2004), copyright © 2004 by Time Inc. Reprinted by permission.

Acknowledgments

"How Other States Can Ignore Hawaii" (originally titled "Same-Sex Marriage, Conflict of Laws, and the Unconstitutional Public Policy Exception") by Larry Kramer (*The Yale Law Journal,* Vol. 106, no. 7). Reprinted by permission of the author and The Yale Law Journal Company and Fred B. Rothman & Company.

"The Miscegenation Precedents" by Andrew Koppelman, from "Same-Sex Marriage and the Conflict of Laws" (*Quinnipiac Law Review,* Vol. 16), copyright © 1997 by Andrew Koppelman. Reprinted by permission of the author and the *Quinnipiac Law Review.*

"Law Breaker" by Jacob T. Levy (The New Republic Online, February 18, 2004), copyright © 2004 by The New Republic, Inc. Reprinted by permission of *The New Republic*.

"A Chance and a Choice" by Peter J. Gomes (*The Boston Globe*, February 8, 2004), copyright © 2004 by Peter J. Gomes. Reprinted by permission of the author.

"An Election Winner" by Stanley Kurtz (*National Review Online,* February 10, 2004). Reprinted by permission of *National Review Online* / Distributed by United Feature Syndicate, Inc.

"The Evolution of Marriage" by Nancy F. Cott, from testimony before the Vermont House Judiciary Committee, January 17, 2000. Reprinted by permission.

ALSO BY ANDREW SULLIVAN

LOVE UNDETECTABLE

Notes on Friendship, Sex, and Survival

When former *New Republic* editor Andrew Sullivan publicly revealed his HIV positive status in 1996, he intended "to be among the first generation that survives this disease." In this book of essays, he reflects on his faith in God, and expresses his bittersweet joy upon learning about new AIDS treatments, which he believes led to the virus's recent transformation from plague to chronic illness. He revisits Freud to seek out the origins of homosexuality and reviews the works of Aristotle, St. Augustine, and W. H. Auden to define friendship for a contemporary, post-plague world. Sullivan's last essay extols the virtues of friendship, elevating platonic love over romantic love, as he memorializes his best friend who died of AIDS.

Social Science/Gay Studies/0-679-77315-0

VIRTUALLY NORMAL

An Argument About Homosexuality

No subject has divided contemporary America more bitterly than homosexuality. Addressing the full range of the debate in this pathbreaking book, Sullivan assesses the prevailing public positions on homosexuality—from prohibitionist to liberationist and from conservative to liberal. In their place, he calls for a politics of homosexuality that would guarantee the rights of gays and lesbians without imposing tolerance. At once deeply personal and impeccably reasoned, written with elegance and wit, *Virtually Normal* will challenge readers of every persuasion; no book is more likely to transform our sexual politics in the coming decades.

Current Affairs/Gay Studies/0-679-74614-5

VINTAGE BOOKS
Available at your local bookstore, or call toll-free to order:
1-800-793-2665 (credit cards only).